COMPETITIVE ELECTIONS AND THE AMERICAN VOTER

AMERICAN GOVERNANCE:
POLITICS, POLICY, AND PUBLIC LAW

Series Editors:
Richard Valelly, Pamela Brandwein,
Marie Gottschalk, Christopher Howard

A complete list of books in the series
is available from the publisher.

COMPETITIVE ELECTIONS AND THE AMERICAN VOTER

Keena Lipsitz

PENN

UNIVERSITY OF PENNSYLVANIA PRESS

PHILADELPHIA

Published by
University of Pennsylvania Press
Philadelphia, Pennsylvania 19104-4112
www.upenn.edu/pennpress

Printed in the United States of America on acid-free paper
10 9 8 7 6 5 4 3 2 1

Library of Congress Cataloging-in-Publication Data
ISBN 978-0-8122-4334-5

For Grigo

CONTENTS

ILLUSTRATIONS

TABLES

Figures

CHAPTER 1

Introduction

Americans love to hate political campaigns. Voters find them tiresome, politicians find them draining, and scholars find them shallow. As a consequence, the list of campaign reform proposals grows longer with each election cycle. For example, the Alliance for Better Campaigns wants broadcasters to provide free air time to candidates for political advertisements and debates while the Institute for Global Ethics wants candidates to sign codes of conduct in which they promise to adhere to ethical campaign practices. In addition, a handful of organizations have cropped up recently, largely due to the largesse of the Pew Charitable Trusts, to train candidates and young people who want to become political consultants how to run fair and ethical campaigns. Finally, a group of scholars have developed a set of reforms to increase public deliberation during elections, including a "deliberative poll" (Fishkin 1995) and a national Day of Deliberation (Ackerman and Fishkin 2004). In short, a vast amount of money and effort has been expended in recent years to figure out ways of providing voters with better campaign information.

Although the intentions of these groups are laudable, recent research suggests that these efforts have had little effect on campaigns. For example, scholars have discovered that "ad watches" on news programs, which are designed to critique campaign advertisements and reveal what is misleading or deceptive about them, have the perverse effect of reinforcing the advertisement's content rather than countering it (McKinnon and Kaid 1999). In addition, a recent study of reforms designed to improve campaign discourse, such as voluntary codes of conduct and pledges to avoid negativity, describe their results as "disappointing" (Maisel et al. 2007, 2). Few candidates and consultants are willing to sign such pledges, and if in the off chance they do, they are more than willing to break them when the need arises. Thus, the main problem with the current campaign reform movement appears to be that a great deal of energy and resources is being wasted on reforms that do nothing to improve campaigns for voters.

This situation suggests that the United States campaign reform movement is in need of a major course correction and the goal of this book is to help it identify a new path. It argues that if reformers are truly seeking to improve campaigns for voters, their best course of action is to pursue reforms that will make elections more competitive. This conclusion is likely to make many uncomfortable because competitive elections are often associated with more negative campaigns, and it is not a stretch to say that negativity is the arch-nemesis of today's campaign reform movement. Many view campaign negativity not only as an irritation but as a scourge that afflicts the body politic each election cycle and must be eradicated. Yet, this book argues that negativity is a hobgoblin that prevents reformers from seeing the benefits of competitive elections. The fact is such contests generate information environments with characteristics that are highly desirable from the perspective of democratic theory. In other words, competitive elections expose voters not only to more information, but to better information.

To be fair, this study will argue that too much competitiveness, what one might refer to as "hypercompetitiveness," can generate campaign information environments that are less helpful for voters because they find it difficult to process the deluge of information inundating them (as is sometimes the case in Senate and presidential elections). In Chapter 6, the analysis also shows that some hypercompetitive campaigns, such as those conducted by presidential candidates in battleground states, can lead to feelings of ambivalence, that is, having both positive and negative feelings about the candidates, which depress voter willingness to participate despite the campaigns' relentless mobilization efforts. Such hypercompetitive elections are becoming rarer and rarer in American politics, however, especially in congressional elections, and the discovery that they may not be as helpful for voters should not blind us to the fact that uncompetitive elections enervate and demobilize the electorate.

The close nature of recent presidential elections might lead one to believe that electoral competition is alive and well in this country but the "vanishing marginals" in congressional and statewide races tell a different story (Mayhew 1974). Many political observers recognize that as the marginals vanish, so too does the ability to hold representatives accountable, but they may not fully appreciate that the information, which is necessary in a democracy if voters are to make informed decisions about their representatives, disappears as well. Electoral challenges force incumbents to tell voters what they have done for them and offer their opponents a platform for disputing those claims. This information is rarely available at any other time during a candidate's term in office. Even if this information is available at other times, most voters are only interested in hearing it when it directly bears on a decision they need to make, that is, right before an election. Research also suggests that most of these voters do not actively seek out such information, but rather passively absorb it. They might pay attention to it if doing so does not require any effort on their part—for example, if it happens to cross their path in the form of a television or radio advertisement—but they are unwilling to expend valuable time and energy informing themselves. If this is the case, then the quality of campaign information environments is crucial and the only reforms that give candidates, consultants, and journalists the incentive to create such information environments are those that enhance electoral competitiveness.[1]

Democracy and Political Campaigns

To understand why competitive elections are so beneficial for voters, one must first understand what kinds of information voters need from the standpoint of democratic theory. Gaining this vantage point, however, is difficult for two reasons. The first is suggested by Robert Dahl, "There is no democratic theory—there are only democratic theories" (Dahl 1956, 1). In other words, democratic theory comes in many shapes and sizes and there is by no means a consensus about which form is preferable. Consequently, my analysis in Chapter 2 draws on three schools of democratic thought, including "competitive," "egalitarian" and "deliberative" accounts of how democracy should function. If one were to attach the names of particular theorists to these schools, they might include Joseph Schumpeter, Robert Dahl, and James Fishkin, respectively.

Second, democratic theorists have historically paid little attention to campaigning, preferring to dwell more on governance rather than on the means by which candidates are elected to office. This lack of interest stems in part from the fact that the arena of governing offers enough food for thought, but also from the belief that campaigns are just plain unruly and wild. Alexis de Tocqueville provides an example of this attitude toward campaigns when he describes the nineteenth-century electioneering he observed while traveling in the United States: "At this time factions redouble their ardor; then every forced passion that imagination can create in a happy and peaceful country spreads excitement in broad daylight. . . . The whole nation gets into a feverish state" (1969, 135).

Tocqueville's description is more positive than James Madison's, who suggests that the best way to deal with the "vicious arts" by which elections are won is to create a large republic so "unworthy candidates" have less of a chance to attract a majority of voters (Hamilton et al. 1961, 82). For these two theorists, then, campaigns are battles or "fevers" that the democratic machinery must periodically withstand so it can function. This combative conception of the political campaign persists today among both practitioners and scholars, as evidenced by the titles of books on the subject. For example, Mary Matalin and James Carville (1994) call their book about the 1992 presidential election *All's Fair: Love, War, and Running for President*, while Ed Rollins (1997) calls the autobiographical account of his life in politics as a GOP consultant *Bare Knuckles and Back Rooms.* Many scholars take the same view of campaigns, as evidenced by titles such as *The Battle for Congress* (Thurber 2001), *Campaign Warriors* (Thurber and Nelson 2000), and *Air Wars* (West 2005).

The problem with conceiving of political campaigns as battles, however, is that it makes the notion of considering them in light of democratic theory seem at best naive and at worst irrelevant. In fact, it is possible that some opt for the war metaphor precisely because it suggests that "anything goes," that any action in a campaign is justified. What else could Matalin and Carville mean by the title *All's Fair*? Yet, just as Michael Walzer (1977) makes the case that morality has a place on the real battlefield, democratic theory can and should have a bearing on political campaigns. For this to happen, however, we need to learn to think differently about them.

What Is a Political Campaign?

When we think about political campaigns, the first thing that comes to mind is the paid media candidates use to persuade the public. A campaign is a much more dynamic process, however—one that looks different depending upon one's position in it. From the perspective of the candidate, the purpose of the campaign is to persuade and mobilize more voters than the opponent to ensure victory on Election Day. Yet from the perspective of citizens, the purpose of a campaign is to educate them about their electoral choices and help them make an informed decision.[2] A voter experiences the campaign as multiple information streams emanating from different sources: the few seconds that the local news station devotes to covering the campaign; the handful of articles that appear in the paper every morning; the colorful pieces of mail in the mailbox that extol the virtues of one candidate while denying those of the other; the occasional phone call from a campaign volunteer; the state-issued voter pamphlet; the conversations with coworkers over the water cooler; and if he or she lucky, the visit from a neighborhood canvasser. If the election is at the state or federal level, it is likely that the voter will see an occasional ad and some additional news coverage on the national networks.[3]

All the campaign features and news coverage combine to create a particular voter's campaign "information environment." By information environment, I mean all the various forms of information voters have access to about the candidates and parties during a campaign. Citizens may or may not take advantage of this environment; in fact, their willingness and ability to do so will hinge on a number of factors, such as their interest in politics, education, and the amount of attention they pay to various media forms, among others. As I will discuss in the next chapter, a *quality*—or what I will also call a "rich"—campaign information environment has several important features, including a high volume of information from a range of sources and an equal opportunity to hear from candidates who engage one another's substantive arguments.

As Figure 1.1 demonstrates, the quality of an information environment is shaped by three factors: election law, media attention, and candidate strategies and resources. *Election laws* can directly affect both the amount and content of information voters receive during a campaign by regulating the amount of money candidates can raise and spend, and constraining the way they campaign. For example, individual contribution limits, which are designed to minimize corruption or the appearance of corruption in politics, reduce the amount of money that candidates can spend and, as a consequence, limit how much candidates can communicate with voters. Another example is the Bipartisan Campaign Reform Act's (BCRA) "Stand by Your Ad" provision, which requires candidates to appear in their advertisements and clearly state that they approve them. It was intentionally designed to change the way candidates campaign by giving them an incentive to clean up their advertising.[4] Figure 1.1 also shows that election law has an indirect effect on campaign information environments. For example, the fact that most states allocate electoral votes using a winner-take-all system gives candidates an incentive to ignore states in which they are a sure winner or a sure loser and focus all their energy on courting voters in a handful of battleground states (Shaw 1999; Bartels 1985). This ensures that the information environments for voters in safe states will be poorer than the ones in battleground states.

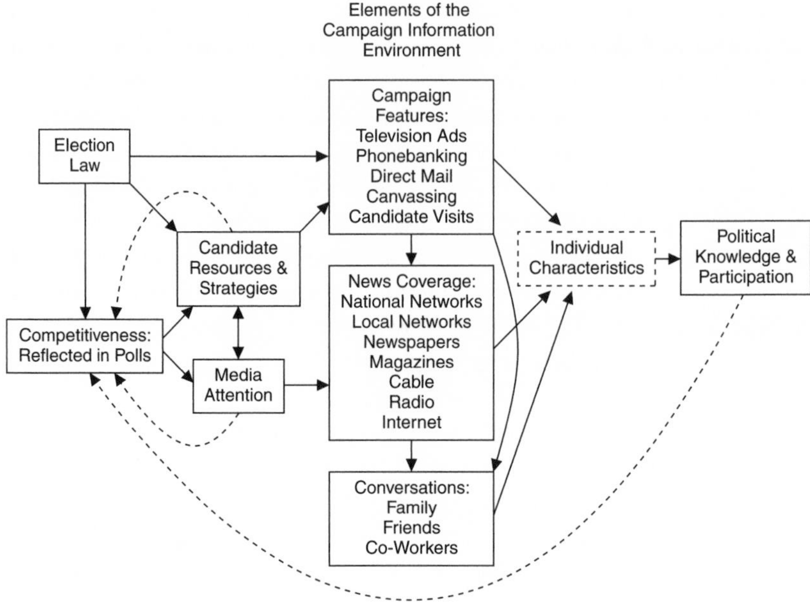

Figure 1.1. Dynamics of a campaign.

The *media* also affect voters' information environments by deciding whether to cover a campaign and, if so, how much time they should spend reporting on it. In a presidential election, the decision of any single media organization regarding news coverage is likely to have less impact on the information environments of voters than in down-ticket races where citizens have fewer alternative information sources. For instance, individuals who were not satiated by the coverage the major networks devoted to covering the party conventions in 2008 could turn to PBS, C-SPAN, or the Internet to see more of the proceedings. Individuals who are interested in a mayoral or congressional race, however, do not have as many options if the local news station decides not to cover the race. The media also affect the quality of voters' information environments by how they cover campaigns. For example, if they choose to report on the campaign as a "horse race" instead of covering the issue positions of the candidates, they lower the quality of the campaign information environment (Joslyn 1984; Patterson 1980).

Third, as Figure 1.1 suggests, a *candidate's resources and strategy* affect voter information environments by determining the mix of campaign features to which they will be exposed (e.g., television versus radio ads or direct mail versus phone calls), the quantity of information they will receive, and the content of that information. For example, a candidate in a down-ticket race may decide to forgo television ads because of their cost and to focus on radio ads, which may reach fewer voters. Candidates may also choose to include more or less substantive information in their communications or to engage one another's arguments or not, all of which influences the quality of the information environment.

Voter information environments are indirectly affected by a whole host of factors that work through media attention and candidate strategy. According to Kahn and Kenney (1999), news coverage of a political campaign is determined by four factors: (1) the behavior and experience of the candidates; (2) the characteristics of the media organization; (3) the presence or absence of competing news events; and (4) the uncertainty of the election outcome (105). Candidates with more money and experience attract more news coverage because they can afford expensive media relations operations and because their involvement in various political activities makes them more newsworthy from the standpoint of the media. As a result, incumbents often receive more news coverage than their challengers. News coverage is also dependent on the political bias of the media organization and the resources it has for covering campaigns. In addition, political campaigns must compete with other events—including other campaigns—for finite media coverage. The competitiveness of an election, as reflected in early polls, is the most important driver of how much news coverage a campaign receives. In their study of newspaper coverage, Kahn and Kenney found that a one-point increase in the closeness of a Senate race was associated with seven more paragraphs of news coverage during the campaign (111). They also found that the competitiveness of a race was the strongest predictor of a campaign article receiving front-page placement (113) and a weaker, but still significant, predictor of an article having increased issue content (118).

When developing their campaign strategies, candidates must answer two crucial questions: how much money will they spend and how will they spend it. The number one predictor of how much money candidates will spend is the closeness of the race.[5] The less certain an electoral outcome is, the more candidates—especially incumbents—will spend. The closeness of a race can also affect the tone and content of candidate communications. For instance, candidates in competitive races are more likely to criticize their opponents. Research has also found that they are more likely to talk about issues and take clear positions on them (Kahn and Kenney 1999). As a result, the competitiveness of an election drives both candidate and media strategy.

What determines the competitiveness of an election, however?[6] First, a candidate's characteristics, including whether she is an incumbent and how much money she can raise, interact with other factors, such as the composition of the district or state in which she is seeking office, to determine how competitive an election will be. Second, external events also play a role by setting the agenda of the campaign or making an issue especially salient in the minds of voters. For instance, a poorly performing economy will weaken an incumbent's advantage—even if the incumbent had little control over economic performance—because voters will want to punish whoever is an office. This will improve the chances of the challenger and, thereby, increase the competitiveness of the race. Third, the political and demographic characteristics of a jurisdiction will also affect the competitiveness of an election by determining whether one of the major parties has an advantage. For instance, a Republican running in a congressional district with a large proportion of African Americans will have a difficult time because that community traditionally favors Democratic candidates.[7] States such as Ohio, in contrast, have consistently been battleground states in presidential elections because of their particular demographic mix. The economy of Ohio, for instance, is based on heavy industries, which have made the trade unions strong and provided the Democrats with a solid base. Yet the culture of Ohio is conservative, as evidenced by the fact that the state legislature has voted to ban gay marriage and allow concealed weapons. The state is also divided between industrial cities in the north, which lean Democrat, and the southern part of the state, which is more rural and leans Republican. Such demographic factors make states like Ohio highly competitive while relatively homogeneous states such as Wyoming are traditionally safe for one party.

What if the electoral votes of a state were split between the candidates depending upon the proportion of votes each one received in the state, instead of all the electoral votes going to the candidate with the most votes, as is currently the case?[8] What if there was no Electoral College at all and the president was elected by a direct popular vote? The point is that electoral law interacts with the social and demographic characteristics of an area to create competitive and uncompetitive jurisdictions. Perhaps this is most clear at the congressional level where state legislators draw district lines using census data, which enables them literally to shape the demographic composition of every district.

As this discussion has demonstrated, political campaigns are dynamic processes that produce a variety of information environments for voters. For example, in their study of the 1992 presidential campaign, Marion Just and her colleagues found that Los Angeles, Boston, Winston-Salem, and Moorhead, Minnesota, had very distinct information environments that were shaped by a combination of candidate strategy and media coverage. Boston, for example, was "news rich" because it was home to two award-winning local television news programs, but "ad-poor" since it was located in a non-battleground state (1996: 38–39). Winston-Salem, on the other hand, was ad-rich because both candidates were heavily targeting the state, and news-poor because the local affiliate made a decision not to use stories fed by the network and to rely on ones it produced locally (95).

The final piece of the campaign puzzle is the voter, whose ability to absorb what is provided by a particular information environment depends on factors such as his or her interest in the campaign, attention to the media, and political sophistication. The opinions of voters are then fed back into the campaign cycle through countless polls, creating a loop that ends only on Election Day.[9]

Even though the campaign process is complex, one thing stands out: if we care about the richness of voter information environments, then we must also care about electoral competitiveness because it provides candidates and the media with incentives to reach out to citizens and provide them with more information. The analysis that follows will show that competitive elections also provide candidates with the incentive to provide voters with *better* information, that is, information that has features which are highly desirable from the standpoint of democratic theory.

A Closer Look at Election Law and Campaign Information Environments

With all the factors and actors described in Figure 1.1, one might be inclined to side with theorists such as de Tocqueville and Madison, who believe little can be done about the nature of campaigns. Yet I argue that the nature of campaigns is largely determined by the electoral laws and regulations that shape candidate behavior: the laws that determine the boundaries of jurisdictions, how candidates enter the race (e.g., ballot access laws), how candidates fund their efforts, what candidates can and cannot say to voters, and the rules by which the winner is determined. Many of these laws are constitutionally constrained in the United States, but others can be reformed in ways that encourage candidates to provide better information to voters. There are generally two obstacles to adopting such reforms, however: lack of willpower and lack of imagination. I address the lack of willpower in the Epilogue, but it seems more appropriate to approach the lack of imagination here as a prelude to the discussion and as a means of opening the reader's eyes to the full range of regulatory possibilities that exist. There is no better way to illustrate this than to briefly consider the campaign experiences of citizens in other democracies.

The most comprehensive comparative study of campaigns to date, *Global Political Campaigning* (Plasser and Plasser 2002), finds that political campaigns differ significantly throughout the world, creating a whole range of campaign information environments for citizens. For example, Japanese campaigns are among the most restricted. Although political parties may purchase an unlimited amount of television spots, they can mention only programmatic and policy positions and must steer clear of the name or record of individual candidates (208). Candidates may make joint appearances in front of community organizations, but debating is prohibited by law because it is seen as "incompatible with Japanese cultural traditions of avoidance of direct confrontation" (138). Newspaper advertisements and direct mail are restricted in frequency and size, while certain activities, such as door-to-door canvassing, are prohibited altogether. On the other end of the spectrum is the United States, which has what some have called the least regulated campaign system in the world (Buchanan 2001: 366). Although the U.S. system has many unique institutional features, such as direct primaries and term limits that affect party and candidate campaign strategy, candidates' access to media is largely limited only by their access to funds.[10] This is due in large part to this country's First Amendment tradition, which makes it difficult to regulate political speech.

There are a whole host of other regulations that directly and indirectly affect campaign information environments and differ from country to country. For example, in terms of campaign finance regulation among established democracies, only the United States, the United Kingdom, India, and Switzerland do not provide public funding to parliamentary or congressional candidates. In addition, many countries restrict candidate spending levels, albeit with varying levels of enforcement. Other regulations more directly affect the campaign information environment for voters. For example, many countries limit the period of official election campaigns. Although such restrictions are frequently circumvented by pre-campaign activities, they affect the information environment by limiting candidate access to free air time and public funding, as well as their ability to purchase television spots (Plasser and Plasser 2002: 155). Moreover, of the 67 countries studied, Plasser and Plasser found that all of them offered candidates some form of free air time on television, except for the United States, Ecuador, Honduras, Switzerland, Belarus, Singapore, and South Africa. Finally, many countries prohibit publication of public opinion polls for a certain period of time before an election. The duration of the prohibition ranges from none at all (United States, Germany, Netherlands, Australia, among others) to the entire duration of the campaign (Lithuania and Singapore), but more frequently 2–15 days. Such regulations are designed to limit the effect of polls on voting and discourage "horse race" journalism (156).[11]

As this brief discussion demonstrates, the U.S. approach to regulating political campaigns is somewhat extreme in its "hands-off" nature. As David Butler and Austin Ranney have observed, "Few Americans appreciate how unique their system [is]" (1992: 4). If more did, and if they had a better understanding of how their system might be reformed in ways that encouraged candidates to provide higher quality information, there might be more willpower for reform. This book is devoted to understanding what good campaign information is and what kinds of reform might encourage candidates to provide such information to Americans.

Structure of the Argument

Before proceeding to the organization of the book, I want to be clear about the scope of this project. As Robert Dahl pointed out, elections are composed of three stages: the pre-voting period, the voting period, and the post-voting period (1956: 67). The primary focus of my analysis will be the pre-voting period, and the voting period insofar as it affects the dynamics of the pre-voting period. I confine the parameters of this analysis in this manner for several reasons. First, this narrower focus forces us to take political campaigns seriously and confront them on their own terms. Most of the time, our attention to campaigns stems from a concern about how the manner they are conducted, particularly the way they are financed, affects decisions by elected officials in the post-voting period. Although corruption (or the appearance of it) is no small matter, I believe the information environments in which citizens make their voting decisions are equally important. To focus properly on this aspect of the democratic process, then, we need to concentrate our efforts on understanding the dynamics of campaigns. The consequence of this focus, however, is that the arguments in the following pages will attend to how certain reforms bear on the pre-voting period, and leave their effects on the post-voting period to others. For example, two recent studies have argued that competitive elections are at odds with representation. One study argues that competitive elections undermine satisfaction with Congress and its members (Brunell 2008), while another claims that competitive elections produce less representative outcomes (Buchler 2005). These arguments pertain to the post-voting period which I do not address in this book. The potential costs of competitive elections, which they identify, must be weighed against the benefits identified by this study.

To determine whether competitive elections are indeed beneficial for democracy, we need to understand what kinds of information voters need to make informed voting decisions. Thus, in Chapter 2, I develop standards for judging campaign information environments by considering what three political values—competition, equality, and deliberation—require of those environments. I argue that each goal demands something unique from the campaign process. Those who value electoral competitiveness, which promotes accountability, should be concerned about the alarming number of uncontested elections in the United States. Not only are voters in such jurisdictions deprived of their sovereignty because they do not get to choose their representative, but the representative has no incentive to communicate with them. Incumbents have an incentive to communicate only when challenged. In this way political competitiveness also ensures that incumbents are held accountable. Those who value equality should be concerned about the candidates having an equal opportunity to communicate with voters and ensuring that no candidate has a monopoly on the information environment. Finally, those concerned with deliberation should worry about the content of political communication. The discussion in this chapter helps identify the characteristics of a quality campaign information environment, which are then operationalized in subsequent chapters.

The theoretical discussion in Chapter 2 suggests that reformers should be concerned with five aspects of the campaign information environment: (1) the amount of political information that is available to voters; (2) the diversity of that information; (3) the amount of candidate dialogue occurring, that is, the extent to which they are discussing the same issues in the campaign rather than "talking past" one another; (4) the extent to which citizens are hearing equally from the candidates; and (5) and how deceptive the candidates are being. To assess whether competitive elections enhance these aspects of campaign information environments, in Chapter 3 I turn to an analysis of political advertising in House, Senate, and state-level presidential campaigns. In Chapter 3, the analysis shows that electoral competitiveness improves campaigns along virtually all the dimensions desired from a normative standpoint. In the case of House and Senate elections, even modest improvements in competitiveness can create substantially richer campaign information environments for voters.

Many studies would be content to stop at the point where they have found that competitiveness generates the kinds of information that are beneficial from the standpoint of normative theory. Yet, we must confirm that the information generated by competitive contests has the effect on voters that we expect it to have. In other words, we must confirm that information volume, equality, diversity, and dialogue—as well as negativity—affect voter knowledge and engagement in the manner expected. Thus, I begin Chapters 4, 5, and 6 I by examining the relationship between electoral competitiveness and voter knowledge or engagement, and then turn to an analysis of whether and how the kinds of information generated by competitive elections account for this relationship. In House contests, the analysis reveals that even low levels of electoral competitiveness contribute to voter learning, with information volume and equality mattering most. In Senate campaigns, only voters who are exposed to moderately or highly competitive contests know more about the candidates. The analysis also shows that these elevated knowledge levels can be attributed to the higher quality information generated by such contests rather than to the large volume of information they generate. In particular, information equality, negativity, and dialogue all appear to help voters learn in Senate campaigns.

Chapter 5 shows that electoral competitiveness matters much less for political knowledge in state-level presidential contests than in congressional ones. The residents of battleground states are slightly more knowledgeable than the rest of the country, but the difference is small compared with how much knowledge increases generally across the nation over the course of the campaign season. This smaller difference is due to the fact that voters have access to information about presidential candidates no matter where they live, whereas the same is not true for congressional elections. The analysis also shows that the high level of campaign dialogue that occurs in battleground states actually appears to confuse some voters.

In Chapter 6, I turn to the question of engagement and analyze the degree to which competitive elections affect political participation. To do this, I use county-level turnout data as well as survey data to analyze the effect of competitiveness on non-voting forms of participation. The analysis reveals that the relationship between electoral competitiveness and participation is different in House, Senate, and state-level presidential campaigns. What is surprising is that in House and Senate elections participation is often highest when elections are only moderately competitive. The elevated levels of participation disappear as the race becomes highly competitive. With respect to the informational mechanisms underlying these patterns, this chapter reveals that the volume of ads in a campaign has diminishing—or even negative—returns for participation. In addition, the negative television ads generated by competitive contests tend to spur participation, while the high level of dialogue they contain tends to depress it. This is very likely because candidate dialogue is associated with voter ambivalence, which studies have found undermines the participatory impulses of citizens. The diminishing returns of advertising combined with the high level of dialogue that occurs in competitive races are part of the reason that participation declines in hypercompetitive contests.

I turn to the issue of how to enhance electoral competitiveness in Chapter 7. This chapter examines the promise of existing proposals to help challengers in congressional elections, and proposes several new reforms, such as including designated media markets as a relevant "community of interest" when redistricting. The chapter also discusses how eliminating the Electoral College would change candidate incentives and voter information environments during presidential elections. Finally, the chapter turns to a discussion of who is most likely to advocate reforms to boost electoral competition and the likelihood that such reforms will be adopted.

Four important themes emerge from the analysis in this book. First, the analysis reveals that competitive elections are not an unmitigated good. Extremely high levels of competitiveness can generate an information environment that is confusing for some voters. We will see that the volume of advertising generated by high visibility elections yields diminishing if not negative returns for candidates in terms of voter participation. We will also see that the high level of dialogue or issue convergence that occurs in closely contested races confuses some people and occasionally depresses participation, presumably because it creates feelings of ambivalence in citizens. Despite these findings, the overall argument holds: improving electoral competitiveness in American elections is the only sure-fire way to improve campaign information environments for voters. The analysis will show that even moderately competitive elections often generate information environments that are just as beneficial—if not more so—for citizens than those that are highly competitive. This is an important fact that scholars have ignored but is crucially important for reformers to understand because it suggests that the road that lies ahead of them is not as steep as is often assumed.

Second, the effect of electoral competitiveness on voter knowledge and engagement is usually indirect rather than direct. Voters in competitive jurisdictions learn not because they are motivated to seek out more information but because they passively absorb information from the rich information environments generated by the close contests. Likewise, they are more likely to participate not because they know their chances of being the deciding vote in an election are higher than they would normally be, but because they are more likely to be mobilized on Election Day. This may be bad news for those who have hypothesized and hoped competitive elections might lead to a more excited and engaged citizenry (e.g., Macedo et al. 2005), but the flip side of this finding is that it confirms just how important campaigns are for the health of a democracy. Voters need political campaigns to inform them and encourage them to get involved.

Third, because this study is not content simply to show that electoral competitiveness enhances voter knowledge but seeks to understand what aspects of the campaign information account for this relationship, it begins to answer an obvious but heretofore largely ignored question in the literature: is it the quantity or quality of campaign information that matters more for voter knowledge? This study can only offer a partial answer because it focuses on television advertising, and a voter's campaign information environment includes other information sources, as I have discussed. Still, it does show that the answer to this question seems to hinge partly on whether the campaign has low or high visibility. House races, for instance, are typically low-visibility affairs. In such cases, the quality of campaign information seems to matter much less than information volume for voter knowledge. Under such circumstances, a burst of information, irrespective of its quality, is likely to yield big gains for voters in familiarizing them with the candidates and raising their dismally low knowledge levels. In high-visibility elections, however, voters are already familiar with the candidates and may even know something substantive about their issue positions. In such elections, the quality of information in terms of its tone, whether the information is provided by a diverse range of sources or engages the opponent's claims, plays a much bigger role in improving voter knowledge than a high volume of information. Some scholars have argued that political ads are the equivalent of "multivitamins" for voters (Freedman et al. 2004), but I would argue that this is mainly the case in high-visibility elections where people are already familiar with the candidates and media coverage is high. In down-ticket races where voters know little about the candidates and media coverage is poor, ads are more than just vitamin supplements; they are the calories a starving electorate needs. In such cases, it matters less if the ads are of high quality or "healthy" because voter knowledge is so poor that any information helps.

Finally, because this study is the first to examine House, Senate, and state-level presidential campaigns together, it is the first that allows us to compare campaign information effects across campaigns for these different offices. Specifically, this comparison reveals the importance of focusing our attention on House and other information-poor elections not only in terms of promoting reforms to enhance competitive elections but also when looking for campaign information effects. The strongest effects of electoral competitiveness, in terms of both how it shapes the overall campaign information environment and how that information affects voter knowledge, are felt in House elections. Moreover, the bulk of the research on the effects of campaign information focuses on presidential and Senate elections, but this study suggests that by focusing on these types of elections researchers have been missing the campaigns in which campaign information matters most.

CHAPTER 2

Democratic Theory and the Campaign Information Environment

Popular criticisms of campaigns tend to focus on their negativity and, perhaps less often, on the way they are financed, which has led reformers to concentrate on these issues. Yet, plunging headlong into reform without developing a comprehensive and systematic critique of campaigns is putting the cart before the horse. In other words, it is necessary to identify the values or goals one believes campaigns should uphold and the kind of information environment that is required to promote these values *before* one begins to make claims about specific campaign funding schemes and the way candidates should campaign. This chapter explores one way of conducting such a critique by considering what a campaign would look like if certain political values or goals representing different strains of contemporary democratic thought were applied to the campaign process. Specifically, I focus on what political competition, political equality, and deliberation require of the information that candidates and their supporters provide to voters. The reliance on normative political thought for developing standards to evaluate political campaigns distinguishes this study from others that have used insightful but less systematic methods (Bartels and Vavreck 2000; Just et al. 1996; Jamieson 1992; Kelley 1960).

The following discussion focuses specifically on campaign information because the primary purpose of a political campaign from the standpoint of democratic theory is to inform voters about their choice on Election Day. Even "minimalist" conceptions of democracy recognize that voters must have information about the candidates to make a legitimate voting decision. Thus, this chapter asks what a campaign information environment would look like if competition, political equality, or deliberation were emphasized. Ideally, we would want campaigns to function in a way that advanced all these goals, but by focusing on them individually, we can assess whether any tensions exist among them, and perhaps more important, where they prescriptively overlap. This is especially important for identifying what kind of campaign and election reforms deserve the most attention from scholars and political reformers. To this end, I will argue that it is useful to consider the goals of political competition, political equality, and deliberation as concentric circles with the requirement of political contestation at the center. This suggests that deliberation demands equality and that both of these goals require political contestation at a minimum.

The following discussion will focus explicitly on what these values and goals demand of information in political campaigns or the pre-voting period when voters are formulating their electoral decisions (Dahl 1956: 67). This means I will not elaborate on the implications of these goals for post-electoral information requirements. I will also minimize my discussion of how they might be applied to our voting methods and procedures, broaching the subject only when such matters might have a significant effect on the kinds of information provided to voters in the pre-voting period.

Political Competition

When political scientists write about competition, they often invoke an economic understanding of the concept. Joseph Schumpeter (1947) was one of the first political scientists to elaborate the parallel between voters and consumers. For him, competition in the political realm translated into the idea of "free competition for a free vote." At a basic level, this meant that citizens—like consumers—should be able to choose which group of political elites runs the government, and political elites should have the opportunity to sell themselves to voters.

In this way, political competition ensures two key features of democracy: choice or sovereignty, and accountability. For democracy to function, voters must have a choice in an election between at least two parties or candidates. Otherwise, they have no real role to play in an election. Democracy also requires that there be a link between representatives and citizens, which ensures that the former represent the latter. Political competition provides that link by giving citizens the opportunity to pass judgment on their representatives and opt for others if they believe those in power are not doing a good job. Thus, political competition is not an end in itself, but rather a means of achieving other more substantive goals related to democracy.

From the standpoint of voters, contestation is necessary to ensure not only choice, but also that candidates have an incentive to communicate with them. Usually candidates who are unopposed are popular incumbents or belong to a party that is heavily favored by the district or state. An unopposed incumbent has absolutely no reason to defend her record or tell voters what she plans to do in her next term. Ideally, a challenger not only points out the weak points of the incumbent's performance but also describes an alternative future to voters—one in which different policies will be advocated and different choices made. At least theoretically, as the incumbent and challenger thrust and parry, a voter's electoral choice should become clearer. Some find the exchanges that are an inevitable consequence of contestation distasteful, but when there is no contestation in an election there is only silence, which is not conducive to a healthy and vibrant democracy. This may seem obvious, but the point underscores that political contestation serves as the basis of a substantive campaign information environment by providing candidates with an incentive to communicate with voters.

As political competition increases,[1] that is, as the number of candidates increases, one might expect the richness of the campaign information environment to increase as well, since a greater number of candidates would diversify the information available to citizens in the campaign, which may in turn help them refine their position on the candidates and issues confronting them.[2] If this is the case, then enhancing political competition beyond the minimal level of contestation may prove beneficial to voters. There are likely to be diminishing returns to enhanced competition, however. As the candidates and parties proliferate, it may be more difficult for voters to absorb the information communicated to them and keep the various candidates and their positions straight. Such a problem is very unlikely to occur in the U.S. two-party system, however.

Aside from the issue of third party competition, our discussion of political competition leaves one important question unanswered. Does contestation in a primary substitute for the lack of contestation in a general election? In other words, is a contested primary enough to guarantee accountability in a democracy? After all, the Progressive reformers, who advocated direct primaries, based their support on the fact that they would introduce contested elections into one-party jurisdictions (Ansolabehere et al. 2006, 76). Many political scientists also believe that primaries ensure that incumbents are held accountable because they must compete without the benefit of party support for a victory that is by no means guaranteed. For example, Anthony King compares the situation of American incumbents to that of incumbents in other countries who are simply renominated by their party: "so long as he or she is reasonably conscientious and does not gratuitously offend local or regional party opinion, [he or she] has no real need to worry about re-nomination" (1997: 36). In contrast, "the possibility of not being re-nominated as the result of a primary election . . . is ever present" for American politicians (36). Presumably, then, incumbents in a contested primary still have the incentive that contestation provides to communicate with voters. This argument, however, overlooks the simple fact that most primaries are closed, which means that only registered members of the party can vote in them. Thus, the candidates in most primaries only have an incentive to communicate with members of their party. Unless independent voters or supporters of the out-party are disingenuous and register as a member of the party they do not support, they are effectively shut out of the electoral process and have no say in those who govern them. Holding an open primary would remedy this situation, but the parties have fought and will continue to fight them on the grounds that they undermine their associational rights.

Even if all primaries were opened to all voters, research has found that the state of competition in U.S. primaries is anything but healthy. Examining data from primary elections for statewide offices, as well as the House and Senate, for 1900–2004, Stephen Ansolabehere and his colleagues find that throughout this period "the modal primary is uncontested," and that competitiveness in contested races has declined precipitously during that time period. Whereas approximately 40 percent of primaries were won by less than 60 percent in 1930, only 20 percent were in 2004. Thus, the pervasiveness of closed primaries and general lack of contestation and competitiveness in them mean one cannot depend on primary competition to compensate for uncontested or uncompetitive general elections.

Finally, for a political contest to involve "free competition for a free vote," as Schumpeter would have it, the rules of the game must be applied equally to all candidates.[3] In his book, *Just Elections*, Dennis Thompson contends that fairness demands candidates have "comparable opportunities to raise resources, unbiased rules for conducting primaries and elections, and impartial procedures for resolving disputes" (2002: 6). The United States electoral process arguably violates these basic fairness requirements in a number of ways. For instance, Thompson points to the unfairness of our campaign finance system, which allows wealthy candidates to spend as much as their pocketbooks allow while their poorer rivals must raise money from supporters in limited amounts (7). Third party supporters might contend that rules designed by the two major parties to make it more difficult for third parties to compete in elections violate basic rules of fairness. Others would argue that the methods used to determine district boundaries are unfair because they allow the party that controls state government to draw the lines in a manner that protects both partisan and incumbent interests.

Irrespective of whether one believes such rules are unfair, such laws translate into distorted campaign information environments for voters. For example, the fact that self-financed candidates can spend as much of their own money as they please means that voters will hear more from them than from their poorly financed opponents. Some would argue that laws that diminish third party participation in elections and campaigns impoverish political discourse, restricting the breadth of ideas to which voters are exposed. Finally, drawing district boundaries to diminish competitiveness means that voters will be exposed to less information, and quite possibly a more restricted range of viewpoints.[4] This suggests that when one begins to demand fair political competition, that is, that everyone play according to the same rules, one moves a step closer to the goal of political equality.

Political Equality

Many scholars who are concerned about political equality embrace the notion of "equal political influence," which requires that no citizen have more power over the political process than other citizens.[5] Often this means ensuring that wealth does not translate into more control over the political process, or conversely that poverty does not severely diminish one's political power. The principle of one person-one vote is a natural extension of the belief in the intrinsic equality of citizens, but as many scholars have pointed out, if one acts to preserve equality at the voting stage, one has waited too long; inequalities can manifest themselves at the agenda-setting stage and during the deliberative period preceding the vote, that is, the campaign. Consequently, many scholars concerned with preserving equal political influence call for campaign finance reform to prevent well-heeled candidates from using the advantage of wealth to defeat poorly financed opponents.[6] Obviously, the funding of campaigns is an enormously important issue, but we often lose sight of the fact that money in American campaigns affects voters only *indirectly*. That is to say, it is used to purchase the media through which candidates communicate. It is the political communication itself that *directly* affects voters. Consequently, I will focus this discussion on the type of information needed in a campaign to preserve equal political influence.

In *A Preface to Democratic Theory*, Robert A. Dahl argues that the preservation of equal political influence and voter autonomy require that voters possess identical information about the choices confronting them on Election Day. Dahl explains that meeting this condition allows us to say that voter choice has not been, "manipulated by controls over information possessed by any one individual or group" (1956: 70). The question is what he means by "identical information." Does he mean that information must be identical in amount, content, or something else? Dahl's concern about certain candidates or parties developing a monopoly on information provision suggests that inequality in terms of the quantity—not content—of information makes him most uneasy. In other words, Dahl's call for "identical information" would require that all candidates for a given office be able to disseminate a similar amount of information to voters. Clearly, no candidate for office ever possesses a total monopoly on the information communicated in a campaign, but Dahl reminds us that he is looking for "conditions against which real world achievement can actually be measured" (70). This suggests he might very well be concerned about situations in which one or even two candidates are able to communicate with voters significantly more than other candidates.

Ronald Dworkin (2000) reaches a conclusion that is similar to Dahl's but rests on a slightly different theoretical foundation. Whereas Dahl is concerned about manipulation of voters—and therefore voter autonomy—Dworkin asks readers to consider what the terms of fair political engagement are in a situation where every citizen, including candidates for office and elected officials, is regarded as an "equal partner in a cooperative political enterprise." In other words, he claims that citizens are equals not only as judges but as participants in the political process. This means we should be just as concerned about the equality of candidates for office and elected politicians as we are about the equality of voters. Dworkin argues that this understanding of equality demands that all citizens—including elected officials, candidates for office, and organized groups—have a fair and equal opportunity to publish, broadcast, or otherwise command attention for their views, which implies that candidates for office should be able to disseminate similar amounts of information to voters.[7]

What is implicit in Dahl's argument about monopolies on information provision is made explicit in Dworkin's conception of equality.[8] If one candidate controls the flow of political communication, she will be able to manipulate the opinions of voters; as a consequence, her viewpoint will carry more weight than those of other candidates—not to mention the viewpoints of average citizens. Obviously, such an outcome undermines equal political influence. Overall, the important lesson is that political equality demands that candidate campaign communication be as equal as possible.

Deliberation

Like the value of political equality, the value of deliberation has roots that run deep within the western democratic tradition. For example, in his eulogy of Athens, Pericles called the period of discussion preceding a political decision in a democracy "an indispensable preliminary to any wise action at all." Democratic theorists of varied persuasions have long propounded the salutary effects of lively discussion and debate among citizens. In recent years, however, many scholars have begun to examine the value of deliberation more closely by asking what kind of content it should have. To be sure, theorists who study deliberation offer a variety of answers to this question, but at a basic level they all agree that democratic decision-making requires that citizens who deliberate must provide justifications for the positions they take; if a citizen has no such opportunity, as is often the case in modern mass democracies, they should be prepared to offer such justifications should the opportunity arise (Freeman 2000: 377).

Deliberative democrats offer several reasons for why their conception of democracy is superior to others. First, they claim it is simply a fairer version of democracy. In a democracy where all citizens are politically equal and bound to disagree, deliberative democrats argue that each citizen should be able to explain why he or she believes the power of the state should be exercised in a particular way, especially when it is very likely that other people will disagree. In this way, this strain of democracy is an alternative to "aggregative" democracy in which "might makes right" or a majority is able to decide the government's course of action without justifying its position to the minority. Other deliberative democrats argue that deliberation should lead to more agreement among citizens, which may enable us to work through some of the more intractable moral dilemmas that confront our society, such as abortion. Despite the popularity of deliberation, however, there is considerable disagreement about what should count as a legitimate reason or justification for taking a position. Some democratic theorists argue that legitimate "public reasons" should be based upon certain democratic values,[9] while others argue that deliberation would suffer if people were constrained in such a manner.[10]

Aside from the debate concerning what constitutes a "legitimate" reason, which I return to below, the main problem for deliberativists is that citizens often have no incentive to deliberate or to inform themselves in a manner allowing them to develop solid reasons for holding the opinions that they do. There are direct and indirect ways of overcoming this dilemma in the context of a campaign. First, one can confront voter apathy and ignorance head-on by creating institutions, such as Bruce Ackerman and James Fishkin's "Deliberation Day," to increase deliberation among the electorate (2002, 2005).[11] A less direct method of promoting deliberation is to advocate better news coverage to increase political interest and knowledge among voters, which may encourage them to seek out and engage in deliberative opportunities. Such is the goal of the public journalism movement (Fallows 1996). Another indirect method is to design the rules and regulations governing campaigns and their financing in a way that they create incentives for candidates to impart better information to voters.

Perhaps the best way to describe what deliberation requires is an "information-rich" campaign environment, which has several key elements. First, citizens need to be exposed to diverse information from a variety of sources. This information should not only be conveyed to them through different types of media but represent a variety of viewpoints. If the aim is for citizens to develop more considered judgments and to be able to offer reasons for holding their views, they need to know their full range of options so they can develop a sense of why they hold one particular view over others. Part of this process involves exposing citizens to viewpoints they disagree with. Scholars have found that, if left to their own devices, people—especially those who hold a majority opinion—will generally avoid discussing political issues with those they disagree with (Huckfeldt and Sprague 1988).[12] The tendency to avoid disagreeable viewpoints may lead to polarization of the electorate as citizens adopt more extreme positions (Sunstein 1994). From the vantage point of deliberativists, this means that citizens should be exposed to information that is both diverse and, at times, disagreeable.

Second, deliberative scholars should also be concerned about the amount of information voters receive because research has found it can seriously affect an individual's ability to offer reasons for her vote choice. For example, Just et al. found that people living in cities with rich information environments, such as Boston and Los Angeles, were able to offer "the widest range of considerations about the candidates," whereas citizens in Winston-Salem, North Carolina, where the political information environment was the poorest of the four cities studied, offered the fewest reasons for preferring one candidate over another (Just et al. 1996: 235). This leads Just et al. to conclude that

> the ability and willingness of people to talk about the campaigns and candidates is closely linked to the richness of the political information environment, as measured simply by the amount of news and ads in the locale. Given citizens' haphazard and often inadvertent ways of encountering information, the more information available, the greater the chance it will get through. (235–37)

Third, deliberation requires political communication to have a particular content, which the goals of political competition and political equality do not. In *Democracy and Disagreement*, Gutmann and Thompson outline standards for deliberating, which they call "principles of accommodation." Fundamentally, these standards require deliberators to maintain a "favorable attitude toward" and seek to "constructively interact with" one another (1996: 79). This means they must remain open to the possibility of changing or modifying their positions and generally avoid moral dogmatism of any kind. It also requires the candidates to engage in a dialogue about the issues that are important to voters and to refrain from talking past one another.

Gutmann and Thompson offer another principle of communicating that is relevant in a campaign context: publicity. Publicity requires that candidates offer reasons for the positions they take. It is not enough for a candidate to simply say, "I stand for X" and then leave it up to voters to make a choice based on whether they agree with that position. According to Gutmann and Thompson, by offering reasons, politicians sustain the legitimacy of the system and contribute to the "broadening of moral and political perspectives" (100). Moreover, providing reasons helps clarify the nature of disagreements and may encourage people to change or modify their positions. Merely stating one's position provides no such impetus for change.

Many deliberativists, including Gutmann and Thompson, limit the types of reasons people offer when they deliberate to those that are mutually acceptable by all participants. In practice, this means that reasons based on a worldview that others do not share—especially a religious worldview—cannot be offered. Obviously, this is the most controversial part of such theories. Sidestepping the issue of whether such claims should be excluded from public debate, I want to focus on the practicality of such constraints, particularly in the context of a campaign. It is simply unrealistic to demand that candidates constrain the justifications for the positions they hold in such a manner. It is enough of a challenge to get them to offer any justifications at all. James Fishkin is one deliberativist who has tackled the issue of how to increase deliberation in the context of a campaign. Partly as a consequence, his requirements for deliberation are much less stringent than Gutmann and Thompson's. Fishkin starts with Jürgen Habermas's description of an "ideal speech situation," in which the resolution of any question is determined by "the force of better argument," and argues that the best we can hope for is some "incomplete" version of this. He explains,

> When arguments offered by some participants go unanswered by others, when information that would be required to understand the force of the claim is absent, or when some citizens are unwilling or unable to weigh some of the arguments in the debate, then the process is *less deliberative* than [an ideal speech situation]. In practical contexts, a great deal of incompleteness must be tolerated. (1995: 40)

Fishkin then focuses on the importance of engaging the arguments offered by others, that is, dialogue, and providing reasons—*any reasons*—to back up claims.

The goal of deliberation, then, requires that voters be exposed to a rich information environment that conveys a variety of viewpoints, including some that are disagreeable. Moreover, candidates must communicate their positions clearly and civilly, making sure to provide reasons for the positions they hold. They must also engage one another's arguments, participating in a dialogue that will allow voters to compare and contrast their views.

The Concentricity of Political Competition, Political Equality, and Deliberation

When one reflects upon what the three political values discussed above require of the campaign information environment, one sees that each one forces us to examine a different part of the campaign process. Enhancing political competition requires us to focus on how electoral law and campaign finance regulation structure the political market. Concerns about equality turn our attention to the campaign information environment and oblige us to consider whether candidates have an equal chance to make their cases to voters. Deliberation forces us to balance the need to give candidates an equal opportunity to communicate their opinions with the need to maintain a rich information environment, which entails both a diversity of viewpoints and a high volume of information.

The discussion above also suggests that competition, political equality, and deliberation are interdependent in many ways. For example, we saw that it is not enough to promote competition in the political arena if it is not fair competition. Fairness demands that the rules and regulations structuring political competition apply equally to all parties and candidates. In addition, the fact that when we talk about the value of free speech we often invoke the concept of a "marketplace of ideas" suggests that deliberation thrives on competition in a certain sense. Moreover, most theorists who write about deliberation claim that it can only take place between political equals; others go farther, arguing that personal resources should not affect the ability of citizens to deliberate, which suggests that the deliberative ideal might require economic equality as well (Cohen 1998: 194).

Although the goals of political competition, political equality, and deliberation do overlap, they do not overlap completely. Many measures that advance deliberative goals, such as holding a national day of deliberation, would have no effect on the level of political competition in an election. Similarly, reforms that ensure candidates can communicate with voters on an equal basis will not necessarily affect the level of political competition either. This suggests that it might be useful to consider the relationship of these goals to one another as having a concentric nature.

Viewing the goals of political competition, political equality, and deliberation in a concentric manner is useful when considering where to focus campaign reform efforts because it underscores that reforms enhancing the more basic goal of political competition may have a multiplier effect, meaning they should enhance political equality and deliberation in the campaign. Although it by no means guarantees perfect equality or enlightened deliberation, a contested election makes it more likely that candidates will attract the resources necessary to communicate with voters and, as a consequence, that voters will hear more equal amounts of information from candidates. It also increases the odds that voters will be exposed to candidate dialogue and a greater diversity of viewpoints during the campaign.

There are essentially two ways to enhance political competition in our two-party system. The first involves making it easier for candidates, especially

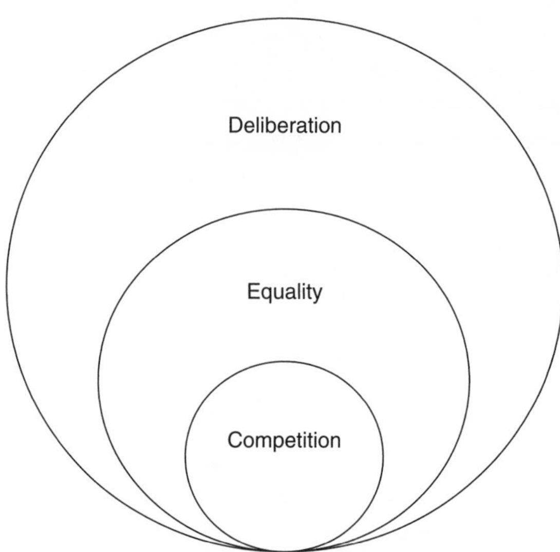

Figure 2.1. Concentric nature of political competition, political equality, and deliberation.

those from third parties, to compete in elections; the second requires adopting reforms that enhance electoral competitiveness, that is, put candidates on more equal footing, thereby ensuring closer electoral contests. The first method primarily involves removing the maze of laws and regulations that make it difficult for minor party candidates to compete in elections. Several authors have already written excellent analyses of how to boost political competition in this manner, so I will refer the reader to these works.[13] Enhancing electoral competitiveness, at least at first glance, appears to advance political competition, political equality, and deliberation at the same time. First, it ensures that a race is contested. Even a modestly competitive race has, by definition, at least two candidates. Once two candidates have entered a race, electoral competitiveness gives them an incentive to provide more information to voters. There is also reason to believe that candidates who begin an election on a more level playing field will be able to communicate more nearly equal amounts of information to voters, thereby enhancing the goal of political equality. Candidates who face stiffer competition may also be more inclined to engage one another in dialogue and offer reasons for holding the opinions they do, not to mention that closer contests may attract the attention of a diverse range of interest groups, exposing voters to a wider range of appeals. In the next section, I consider what the existing literature has to say about the benefits of electoral competitiveness. As we will see, the extant literature leaves many questions unanswered, especially if one is trying to understand whether competitive elections create an information environment that advances all the political values discussed above.

What We Know

Numerous studies have found that competitive elections generate richer campaign information environments for voters in terms of the volume of information provided to them. Studies of House elections have found that "hard fought" congressional races generate more news coverage (Goldenberg and Traugott 1984) and television advertising (Goldstein and Freedman 2002). Researchers have found that the same is true of news coverage in Senate elections (Kahn and Kenney 1999; Westlye 1991), as well as television advertising in them (Goldstein and Freedman 2002). In presidential elections, it has long been recognized that electoral competitiveness at the state level shapes the behavior of presidential candidates, encouraging them to allocate their resources to states that could potentially swing toward either party (Huang and Shaw 2009; Shaw 1999, 2006; Bartels 1985; Lake 1979; Colantoni et al. 1975). In terms of the specific features of the information environments generated by competitiveness at the state-level, many studies have found that residents of swing states are exposed to more television (Shaw 1999, 2006; Johnston et al. 2004; Goldstein and Freedman 2002; Just et al. 1996; Bartels 1985) and radio (Bartels 1985) advertising. Research has also found that candidates are more likely to travel to competitive states (Charnock et al. 2009; Doherty 2007; Shaw 1999; Kelley 1961, 1966) where their visit is likely to generate local news coverage (Barrett and Peake 2007). In terms of the other features of the campaign information environment that were identified in Chapter 1, there is little research on how competitiveness affects direct mail, phone-banking, and canvassing, although it is probably safe to assume that competitiveness drives them as well. Thus, one might say that there is something of a consensus in the literature that voters receive more information when elections are competitive than when they are not. The question, however, is whether the information provided has characteristics that promote the democratic values discussed or whether citizens are simply being inundated by useless or—at worst—harmful information.

Less attention has been given to how competitiveness affects the substantive content of campaign information. Conventional wisdom has it that closely contested races generate more negative information. Strangely, however, few studies have examined this question directly because researchers have been far more interested—perhaps understandably—in exploring the effects of negativity than identifying its root causes. One study has found that advertising in competitive House races is substantially more negative than in noncompetitive races (Goldstein and Freedman 2002), and a handful of others have shown that this is true of Senate races as well (Goldstein and Freedman 2002; Kahn and Kenney 1999; Hale et al. 1996). The one study that has compared the proportion of attack advertising in competitive House and Senate races has found that competitiveness has a much stronger relationship with negativity in the former than in the latter. When comparing the proportion of ads featuring attacks in competitive and noncompetitive races, Kenneth Goldstein and Paul Freedman found that nearly half (45 percent) of the ads in competitive House races featured attacks, while only 21 percent of the ads in noncompetitive races did. In Senate campaigns, those numbers were 31 and 20 percent, respectively (10). The one study (Geer 2006) that has examined how electoral competitiveness affects negativity in presidential elections has examined its effect at the national level, that is, how the closeness of a race nationally affects the general tone of advertising and finds no relationship. Geer speculates that the reason is that

> presidential elections are always "competitive" by the standards employed by congressional scholars....There is, in short, not as much variance as we see in races for the House of Representatives or the Senate. Even in the most lopsided presidential contests, there is a degree of competition that is still absent in most congressional races. (Geer 2006: 40)

Perhaps a similar logic explains why competitiveness is a stronger predictor of negativity in House than in Senate races. Senate races are usually more competitive than House races. Thus, one might argue, to use Geer's language, that even the most lopsided Senate race has a degree of competition that is absent in most House races. In terms of how the competitiveness of state-level presidential elections affects advertising negativity, no study to this author's knowledge has examined the question.

The other feature of the campaign information environment that has been investigated with respect to the relationship between its negativity and electoral competitiveness is news coverage. In their study of Senate campaigns, Kahn and Kenney found that newspapers were more likely to criticize candidates and use negative traits to describe them when "campaign intensity" was high (1999).

Recently, scholars have turned their attention to exploring electoral competitiveness' effect on another measure of advertising content: dialogue, a term that has been used interchangeably in the literature with "issue convergence." This concept captures the extent to which candidates are talking about the same topics during the campaign. Despite Anthony Downs's median voter theory, which leads one to expect the range of issues discussed by candidates to converge as they try to appeal to the median voter, many studies have argued that candidates tend to emphasize the issues on which their party is perceived to be more competent (Petrocik et al. 2003; Simon 2002; Spiliotes and Vavreck 2002; Petrocik 1980, 1996; Powell and Whitten 1993). One might argue that certain important issues, such as the economy or government performance, are not "owned" by any party and candidates will converge on them as a result (Kaplan et al. 2006; Petrocik 1996; Budge and Farlie 1983). Yet in her study of presidential campaigns from 1952 to 2000, Lynn Vavreck (2009) carefully and convincingly demonstrates that in virtually every election one candidate's party has an advantage on the issue of the economy, and will emphasize it as a result, while the other candidate must scramble to convince the electorate that another issue is more important. Thus, dialogue is unlikely. Few of these studies explicitly examine the relationship between electoral competitiveness and dialogue, however. Those that have given the issue attention offer conflicting results. One study of dialogue in Senate campaigns, which coded candidate statements in newspaper accounts, found little evidence of it (Simon 2002) while another that examined television advertising in 1998 House and Senate races similarly found no relationship (Sides 2006). Yet two studies, one of Senate television advertising and another of presidential candidate statements in newspapers, found a strong relationship between competitiveness and dialogue (Kaplan et al. 2006; Sigelman and Buell 2004). No studies have examined how state-level competitiveness in presidential elections affects it, however. Clearly this area of study warrants further investigation.

What We Don't Know

Based on the extant literature, we are fairly confident that competitive elections encourage candidates to provide more information to voters and that this information tends to be more negative. We also have a conflicting set of findings regarding the effect of competitiveness on dialogue. In terms of the known unknowns, it is less clear how electoral competitiveness is related to information equality and diversity. In competitive races, it is natural to expect a wide range of voices to speak because they are responding to the same incentives that candidates are. In other words, because interest groups and parties also have finite resources, they will spend those resources as efficiently as possible, which means they will target elections where their efforts have the greatest potential to affect the outcome of a race, that is, close elections. This means that competitive elections should generate information environments with a wider range of voices. In terms of the equality of information about candidates, we know that candidate spending differences are much smaller in competitive elections, which suggests that the volume of information should be more balanced as well.

Although some of these hypotheses, such as the relationship between advertising diversity and equality, seem straightforward enough, it is unclear what the relationship between competition and each of these information characteristics looks like. A goal of this book is to understand just how competitive an election needs to be to give political elites enough of an incentive to provide voters with better information. As I discuss in more detail in the next chapter, studies that examine the effects of electoral competitiveness typically use one of two types of measures: a linear measure, such as the margin of victory in a previous election, or a dichotomous measure, which classifies a race as "hot" or "cold." The linear measure assumes that each unit increase in the measure of competitiveness yields the same increase in whatever variable is being explained, which is a strong assumption. For example, a 5 percent reduction in the margin, from, say, 10 percentage points to 5 percentage points, is likely to yield a bigger change in the information environment than a reduction in the margin from 25 to 20 points. Using a dichotomous measure assumes that no races are "lukewarm." Yet, not only are there plenty of lukewarm races out there, but we need to know whether they generate information environments that are substantially better than cold races or substantially worse than competitive contests. These are important questions for reformers because the answers to these questions will indicate the difficulty of the task that lies ahead for them. As I discuss in Chapter 7, our electoral laws would have to be drastically reformed to make a significant number of Senate and House races highly competitive. Yet there are a host of more modest reforms that might increase the number of marginally competitive elections. Thus it is important to understand exactly what the relationships between electoral competitiveness and dialogue, information diversity, and information equality look like.

Though there is still much to be learned about the relationship between electoral competitiveness and the quality of voter information environments, there is a considerable amount of research documenting the poor health of electoral competitiveness in this country. In the following section, I briefly review this research to underscore one of the chief reasons for why it is so important to understand the precise nature of the relationship between electoral competitiveness and the quality of voter information environments: if the health of electoral competitiveness is poor and perhaps even declining in the United States and it drives the quality of campaign information environments for voters, then the electorate, which many already consider to be poorly informed, will only become more so.

The State of Electoral Competitiveness

If one were to judge the state of electoral competitiveness in the United States by the claims of newspaper editorials, one would think competitive elections had completely disappeared from the American landscape. The Greensboro, North Carolina, *News & Record* claims that in state legislative elections, "it's futile for a candidate of the opposing party to challenge an incumbent, whether Democrat or Republican."[14] The *Christian Science Monitor* bemoans "the lack of truly competitive elections" across the nation,[15] which leads to "political entrenchment." Many scholars agree. "It is somewhat scandalous that there are no competitive elections anymore, " says Samuel Issacharoff (2002), a legal scholar at New York University. But exactly how bad is the state of competitiveness in American elections? We often hear about the lack of competitiveness in House elections, but the state of competitiveness in presidential elections appears to be quite healthy. What about Senate and gubernatorial elections? If electoral competitiveness turns out to be key to generating the types of information environments that a healthy democracy demands, is there really cause for concern? This section provides a brief overview of how electoral competitiveness is currently faring in the United States. Although the next four chapters focus on federal elections, in this section I also discuss what is known about the state of electoral competitiveness in state and local elections. I mention them because they are too often overlooked. Moreover, if electoral competitiveness is decreasing at the state and local levels, then the analysis in the chapters that follow might be relevant for understanding what is happening with voters in these types of elections as well.[16] In the following section, I draw for the most part on the research of other scholars who have examined trends in electoral competitiveness. In the few instances where the literature is silent, I draw on available data to describe those trends myself. As a result, different measures of competitiveness are used for each type of election discussed. Unfortunately, this was unavoidable.

State-Level Presidential Elections

Given how close recent presidential elections have been in this country, one might think that electoral competitiveness is thriving here. Due to the nature of our electoral system and the peculiarities of the Electoral College, however, to fully understand the health of electoral competitiveness in presidential contests, one must understand what is happening at the state level. This is because there are actually 51 different presidential elections in the United States (this includes the District of Columbia, which has three electoral votes). Scholars who study how presidential candidates allocate their resources have shown that candidates focus their resources on states in which the outcome of the election is uncertain and devote significantly less to those where one candidate is likely to win (Huang and Shaw 2009; Shaw 1999, 2006). Since candidates tend to focus their resources on "battleground" states, we should be concerned if the pool of such states is shrinking because such a trend would suggest that fewer voters are actually experiencing the full brunt of a presidential contest. The very fact that recent national elections have been close, however, may mean that the battleground state pool has been expanding, since a close national contest might encourage candidates to compete in more states (Shaw 2006: 69).

The evidence on this score is decidedly mixed. Prior to the election in 2008, there was evidence that candidates were targeting their resources more narrowly, suggesting that electoral competitiveness in state-level presidential elections was shrinking. Daron Shaw writes that "the Gore and Kerry campaigns both had extraordinarily focused targeting plans. Not only were they more focused than Bush's, they were undoubtedly more focused than either of Clinton's" (69). Shaw believes that the focused targeting of Al Gore and

John Kerry's campaigns may be a "troubling" sign of declining competitiveness in state-level presidential contests, but he hastens to note that this leaner targeting was the result of both candidates being down in the polls for much of the campaign and having fewer resources than George Bush.

If there was any concern about declining competitiveness in presidential contests after 2004, the 2008 campaigns should have alleviated it. In part because he was so flush with funds, Barack Obama was able to campaign in states that had not experienced a presidential campaign for some time, such as North Carolina, Indiana, and Virginia. Early in the campaign, he even dedicated resources to states such as Georgia and North Dakota. Whereas Obama's strategy has been described as more "offensive," John McCain's was more defensive (Huang and Shaw 2009). Not only was his list of battleground states shorter than Bush's in 2004, but he was faithful to his Electoral College plan. This means he allocated his resources more efficiently, concentrating them to a greater extent on battleground states. Although his campaign was less ambitious than either of the George W. Bush campaigns, it was also not as narrowly focused as the Gore and Kerry campaigns (288). Thus, the 2008 election should put concerns about declining competitiveness in state-level presidential contests to rest for the time being, but there is no guarantee that future candidates will have the kinds of resources that allowed Obama to campaign in as many states as he did.

It should be noted, however, that voters in chronic safe states such as California, New York, and Texas might argue that just because competitiveness is not declining in state-level presidential elections does not mean that it could not be improved.

Senate Elections

U.S. senators have always been among the most vulnerable elected officials in the United States. As Gary Jacobson explains, this is due to the fact that states are large jurisdictions and tend to be diverse both economically and socially, which contributes to them having a more politically balanced electorate (Jacobson 2006: 49). The greater likelihood of winning Senate elections, as well as the need to raise substantial amounts of funding, also means that these races attract higher quality candidates from both sides of the aisle, which in turn contributes even further to their competitive nature. That said, there are indications that the competitiveness of Senate elections is declining. For example, the percentage of senators winning their election by less than 60 percent stayed fairly constant at just under 65 percent between 1952 and 1980, but slowly began to decline after that, with a brief recovery in the mid-1990s.[17] In 2004, just 47 percent of Senate races were won with less than 60 percent of the vote. Strong partisan tides typically create more competitive races across the country, yet the tide in favor of the Democrats in 2006 and 2008 did not yield a higher percentage of close Senate races (49 and 46 percent respectively).[18] The Republican tidal wave of 2010, however, put a high number of Senate races in play. Although 60 percent of the races were won with less than 60 percent of the vote, it is surprising that the percent of competitive races was not even higher given the general tenor of the election. In addition, recall that it was once quite common for approximately 65 percent of the Senate campaigns in any given election year to be competitive, which suggests that the effect of partisan tides on electoral competitiveness is still considerably more muted than it once was. It remains to be seen whether 2010 heralded a return to elevated levels of electoral competitiveness in Senate elections or was simply a brief uptick in an otherwise slow decline.

Gubernatorial Elections

Although one might think that the trends in electoral competitiveness for gubernatorial elections would mirror those for Senate races because they involve similar constituencies, this does not appear to be the case. Since no study has examined trends in the competitiveness of gubernatorial elections, I examined them myself using available data. The only easily accessible measure of competitiveness available for elections prior to 1990 is the average election margin, so I calculated the average margin for each two-year period from 1978 (the earliest available year) to 2010.[19] From 1978 to 1994, the margins stayed fairly constant with an average of approximately 16 percent. The margins in the 1996 and 1998 election cycles increased to 23 and 20 percent, respectively, but the next three election cycles—2000, 2002, and 2004—exhibited exceptionally high electoral competitiveness, with average margins of approximately 10 percent in each cycle. In 2008, the average election margin soared to an all time high of 29 percent, but it returned to 14 percent in the next election cycle. Thus, the only thing that can be said with certainty is that electoral competitiveness in gubernatorial elections was moderate and fairly constant from 1978 to 1995, but since then has been characterized by a high degree of volatility with no clear trend in either direction.

House Elections

The most noticeable decline in electoral competitiveness has occurred in House elections. Numerous scholars have documented this decline, although the reasons for it are the source of much debate. Gary Jacobson (2006) examined various measures of electoral competitiveness, including seat turnover, election margins, and the number of races for which there was no major party competition, from the 1940s to 2004, and found that there was considerable fluctuation in all these measures during this time period. He did find, however, that low turnover elections have become more common and that narrow vote margins are becoming scarcer. In the last two decades, margins in House races have declined dramatically. The proportion of House seats won with less than 60 percent of the vote declined by half, from just under 40 percent in 1992 to approximately 20 percent in 2004 and 2006. The swing toward the Democrats in 2008 increased the percentage of competitive House seats to 30 percent and the swing toward the Republicans in 2010 ensured that the percentage of competitive House seats remained moderately elevated (33 percent). It is unlikely, however, that this is the beginning of a new upward trend in electoral competitiveness, since we are likely to see levels return to those of 2004 and 2006 in the absence of such extraordinarily large partisan tides.

State Legislative Elections

Declining electoral competitiveness in state legislative elections has been a major concern for scholars for some time. A study of such elections from 1950 to 1986 found that "marginal legislative seats are vanishing in some U.S. state legislatures, just as they have been vanishing in the U.S. Congress" and that this was especially true of elections in the lower houses of state legislatures (Weber et al. 1991: 45). A more recent study examined trends in competitiveness from 1992 to 2002 to assess whether this downward trend had continued (Niemi et al. 2006). They concluded that if the scholars of the previous study "were disturbed by what they observed fifteen years ago . . . they would be even more concerned now" (65–66). The measure used by the earlier study was the median percent of competitive contests in the lower houses of the 20 state legislatures for which they had data. Across the states examined, Weber et al. found that the median percent of competitive races was 46 percent. Using a similar method, Niemi et al. found this number had declined to 25 percent for 1992–2002.[20] They underscore that there is considerable variation in the levels of electoral competitiveness across states, but that it is fair to characterize state legislative elections as having "relatively little overall competition" (72).

Municipal Elections

Few studies examine trends in electoral competition at the local level, although municipal elections are generally recognized as being mostly noncompetitive. For example, a study of mayoral races in 38 large cities from 1979 to 2003 found that the median electoral margin was 22 percent (Caren 2007: 37). The same author, however, also found that the margin of victory did not significantly increase during that 25-year period (42). Although there is too little research to draw any definitive conclusions, the story appears to be that competitiveness is not waning in local elections, but it is certainly not thriving.

This brief review of trends in electoral competitiveness suggests its health in national presidential elections masks deterioration in many down-ticket contests, especially Senate, House, and state legislative elections. While there are no clear trends in the competitiveness of gubernatorial elections, the competitiveness of local elections is chronically low. If political competition proves to enhance campaign information environments in ways that promote democratic decision-making, then its current state is worrisome indeed.

Campaign Information Environments, Democracy, and Electoral Competitiveness

Democracy requires more than periodic elections. It requires that voters have access to certain types of information during the campaign. Ideally, voters would have an equal opportunity to hear from at least two candidates and a range of their supporters. In addition, each side would engage the arguments of the other, offering reasons for holding their positions and endeavoring to persuade voters that their arguments are superior. Of course, political campaigns often fall far short of such normative ideals, but such ideals must be developed to offer a yardstick against which actual campaigns can be judged. Such normative ideals also offer a point on the horizon that can guide reformers. Once the direction has been determined, the question is how to move forward. There is ample research suggesting that competitive elections generate richer information environments for voters in the sense that they encourage candidates to generate *more* information, but there is much less research that addresses the question of whether competitive elections generate *better* information for voters, that is, information that accords with the normative values described in this chapter. The analyses in the following chapters examine not only whether competitive elections generate better information, but whether this information has the salutary effect on voters that we expect it to have.

CHAPTER 3

Electoral Competitiveness and the Campaign Information Environment

Chapter 2 suggested that adopting reforms that enhance electoral competitiveness might be the most promising way of improving campaign information environments for voters. Although there is certainly an abundance of literature suggesting that competitive campaigns generate *more* information, as we saw, there is much less evidence that competitive campaigns improve the quality and equality of campaign information. In this chapter, I analyze data from 2000, 2002, and 2004 Senate and House elections, as well as the 2000 and 2004 presidential elections, to determine how electoral competitiveness is related to these aspects of a campaign information environment. In addition, I address a question that the extant literature does not speak to: how competitive does an election have to be to produce a better information environment for voters? Providing an answer to this query is particularly important for reformers and policy-makers who advocate enhancing electoral competitiveness. If one can demonstrate that modest levels of competitiveness encourage candidates to provide significantly better information to voters, they have one more argument in their arsenal to persuade others that the adoption of measures to improve electoral competitiveness is prudent. The following analysis finds that this is indeed the case with respect to congressional races: an election does not have to be a toss-up to encourage candidates to give voters better information. In fact, modestly or moderately competitive contests provide candidates and their supporters with incentives to do so. The story of electoral competitiveness at the state level in presidential elections is different, however. Only states that are highly competitive attract the attention of presidential candidates and encourage them to provide voters with better information.

Electoral Competitiveness and Campaign Information Environment Quality

Given the dearth of studies on the link between competitiveness and information quality, we do not know the answers to some very basic questions. Do the relationships tend to be linear or are there diminishing returns to competitiveness? In other words, do its benefits plateau at a certain point? Another question is whether this relationship is similar in different types of races. For example, is electoral competitiveness related to campaign dialogue in the same way across House, Senate, and state-level presidential races, or are there reasons to expect that the nature of the relationships might vary?

As mentioned in the previous chapter, the relationship between electoral competitiveness and virtually any dependent variable of interest—whether it is the amount of candidate advertising, voter turnout, or candidate spending—is typically assumed to be linear. This is evidenced by the fact that the measure of electoral competitiveness included in most explanatory models of such dependent variables is usually continuous, such as the margin of victory in the election under investigation or the margin in recent polls. If a continuous measure is not used, then it is typically collapsed into a dichotomous measure, suggesting that the relationship between competitiveness and the variable of interest is of a threshold nature. For example, House races are often classified as being competitive or not according to the margin of victory. Traditionally, if the two-party margin is expected to be (or was) 10 points or less, then the race is classified as competitive. If the margin is expected to be higher, then the race is considered "safe" or uncompetitive. Perhaps such decisions are justified if one is simply using electoral competitiveness as a control variable that captures a general sense of the campaign's dynamics, but if one is trying to understand how electoral competitiveness shapes candidate behavior and voter information environments, then the nature of those relationships should be part of the investigation.

One might ask whether there is reason to believe that candidates facing less competitive contests might have an incentive to generate helpful information for voters. There is. First, incumbents know that the best guarantee of victory is ensuring that serious challengers do not run in the first place (Jacobson 1997: 43). This requires raising a sizable war chest early on and demonstrating that one is not afraid to use it to avoid slipping in the polls. The most obvious way to send a signal to an opponent that one is prepared to fight is to advertise, which is one way of providing information to voters. Second, incumbents also think about future challenges and know that to appear weak or vulnerable in one election might attract primary or general election challengers in the next one. An election that is closer than predicted, even if the incumbent still wins by a wide margin, might send undesirable signals. As one incumbent congressman explains, "It is important for me to keep the young state representatives and city councilmen away. If they have the feeling that I'm invincible, they won't try. That reputation is very intangible. [But] your vote margin is part of it."[1]

Thus, incumbents have been described as "running scared" (King 1997) and likely to "exaggerate electoral threats and overreact to them" (Jacobson 1997: 77). This means, as Gary Jacobson explains, that "we find members who conduct full-scale campaigns even though the opposition is nowhere to be seen" (77). Jacobson is not exaggerating. Even unopposed candidates can raise and spend large sums with the goal of scaring off future competition. For example, Representative Larry Combest (R-Tex.) spent $390,000 on his 2002 reelection campaign—one of the most expensive that year—despite being unopposed. This suggests that moderate or even modest levels of competitiveness might provoke incumbents, encouraging them to reach out to voters and, perhaps, to provide them with more substantive information that engages their opponents' arguments.

Challengers in congressional races typically raise and spend much less than their opponents. For example, the average House incumbent raises approximately four times more than the average House challenger, and the typical Senate incumbent raises approximately 60 percent more than the average Senate challenger. Even so, challengers in Senate races are usually able to raise several million dollars—more than a dollar per eligible voter—for their campaigns, which still translates into a substantial amount of political communication. Moreover, challengers are not only more likely to spend all the money they raise, but they are more likely to spend it on campaign communications (Herrnson 2004: 83). This means that even uncompetitive challengers are using whatever means are at their disposal—if not on television advertising, then on newspaper advertising, direct mail, and canvassing—to reach out to voters. Finally, candidates competing in open seat races usually raise slightly more than incumbents, and because of the less predictable nature of such contests are likely to come out of the gates fighting irrespective of what their chances really are. All this suggests that even minor threats might elicit a strong reaction from candidates, especially incumbents, encouraging them to behave as if the election were much closer than it actually is.

Aside from congressional elections, I also analyze the behavior of presidential candidates. Instead of examining the effects of electoral competitiveness at the national level, however, I assess how the electoral competitiveness of states in a given election affects the way candidates campaign. I argue that presidential candidates are likely to respond to electoral competitiveness in a very different manner than congressional candidates. Even though *Cook's Political Report* and other election rating sources might use the same categories to classify states in presidential and other types of elections ("safe," "leans," "toss-up," etc.), presidential elections are fundamentally different from other elections. The most obvious difference is that they involve 51 separate contests featuring the same major party candidates, who know that expending resources in one place means they will have fewer resources to expend in others. In contrast, there might be 37 different Senate contests going on, as there were in 2010, but each one features two unique candidates who have the luxury of devoting whatever resources they might have to that single state. What this means is that presidential contests might treat a "safe" or "leans" state very differently from Senate candidates in races that have been classified in a similar manner.[2] Whereas Senate candidates might spend a considerable amount of money in a safe race for the reasons discussed above, presidential candidates are likely to ignore such states entirely. This means that voters in safe states or those that are only modestly competitive might receive very little information from candidates and their supporters.

As the discussion suggests, congressional candidates in less competitive contests might have incentives to provide more information to voters. The following analysis will determine if this is the case, as well as if modest levels of competitiveness also encourage them to provide voters with better information. Presidential candidates should respond differently to electoral competitiveness, however. The incentives created by the Electoral College and the unit rule means they will ignore states that are not highly competitive.

Data and Methods

To assess the impact of competitiveness on campaign information environments, I used Senate, House, and presidential political advertising data collected by the Campaign Media Analysis Group (CMAG). CMAG tracked ad airings in the 75 largest media markets in 2000 and the 100 largest media markets in 2002 and 2004.[3] It then generously shared its data with the Wisconsin Advertising Project (WAP). WAP, under the guidance of its director

Kenneth Goldstein, codes the advertising data and shares it with researchers for a nominal fee.[4] The unit of analysis in the CMAG dataset is the ad airing, as opposed to the ad itself. If one simply examined the content of a single ad as many studies have done (Petrocik et al. 2003; Kahn and Kenney 1999), one might get a very skewed idea of what a voter's campaign environment looks like because we have no sense of how often that ad was aired or where it was aired (Prior 2001). The CMAG data provide this information.

Despite the strengths of the CMAG data, using them to analyze congressional ad airings poses a problem that researchers seldom acknowledge. Because CMAG monitors only 75 to 100 of the largest media markets in the country and media market boundaries are not congruent with congressional districts, it is possible that the CMAG monitoring area only partly covers a congressional district. This raises a problem. If the CMAG dataset has no ad airings for a congressional race, but monitors a media market that only serves a small portion of that district, we might mistakenly conclude that no ads were aired in the race when in fact the candidates and their supporters might have done all their advertising in a neighboring media market that serves more of the district but is not monitored by CMAG. To address this issue, I used GIS to determine what portion of a given media market's population lies in each congressional district by aggregating from tract-level data. By doing this, I was able to identify which congressional districts are completely monitored by CMAG, which are partly monitored, and which lie totally outside the CMAG monitoring areas. Districts that fell completely outside of CMAG monitoring areas were not included in the following analysis. To determine whether a partly covered district should be included in the analysis, I examined districts that fell completely within the CMAG monitoring area but were served by at least two media markets. I found that candidates and their supporters usually air at least a handful of ads in a media market if it serves more than 40 percent of the district's population. Based on this, I concluded that I could fairly code districts that had more than 40 percent of their population living in CMAG-monitored media markets, but had no ads in the dataset, as having no ads overall. If a congressional district had less than 40 percent of its population residing in CMAG-monitored media markets, I did not include it in my analysis regardless of whether the CMAG dataset indicated there was advertising in the district or not.

One might ask whether political ads are the best measure of how rich a campaign information environment is. After all, as I discussed in the Introduction, a voter's information environment includes the news broadcasts of local, network, and cable television stations. It also includes the articles voters read in newspapers and magazines as well as what they hear on the radio about the races in their area. Aside from these more obvious purveyors of information, an individual's information environment also consists of the information conveyed by family, friends, and coworkers in conversation. Although television ads are clearly just one element of a voter's information environment, I would argue they are a central component of it. Television advertisements have become an increasingly important element of political campaigns for both candidates and interest groups. Even candidates in House elections spend the bulk of their money budgeted to communications on television advertising. For example, a candidate in a typical House campaign spends 22 percent of her budget on television ads, 12 percent on radio ads, 8 percent on direct mail, 8 percent on campaign literature, and less than 5 percent on other forms of communication (Herrnson 2004: 83). The average Senate campaign spends approximately a third of its budget on television ads (85), while presidential candidates devote a whopping 75 percent of their budget to advertising on television. Although the bulk of television advertising is sponsored by candidates and parties during campaigns, interest groups rely more heavily on it with each campaign cycle. Clearly television advertising has become the most important means of communication for politicians and their supporters during campaigns, which makes them a key source of campaign information for voters.

Although candidates and their supporters might rely heavily on ads, there is mixed evidence that television advertising is representative of a citizen's overall information environment. It is probably most representative in terms of the volume of information that voters are receiving. As mentioned in the previous chapter, news reporters and news editors are more likely to cover a campaign when it is competitive (Kahn and Kenney 1999). Because candidates and their supporters are more likely to air political ads when a race is closely contested, it is likely that the amount of news coverage is highly correlated with the amount of political advertising in a race. Studies examining the ability of candidates to shape media discourse, however, suggest that the content of television advertising in terms of the issues and themes it discusses may not represent the content of voters' general campaign information environment particularly well. Although a handful of earlier studies found a high level of congruence between candidate messages and the themes discussed in newspaper coverage in presidential elections (Dalton et al. 1998; Just et al. 1996), more recent studies have found mixed or little evidence of convergence (Hayes 2010; Farnsworth and Lichter 2007; Petrocik et al. 2003). Studies of television advertising and news agenda convergence in Senate races are slightly more positive, however. A study of 2002 Senate races found that it varies considerably across states with it being quite high in some and low in others (Ridout and Mellen 2007). Another study of 2000 Senate races found substantial evidence of Senate candidates being able to influence the agenda of local television stations, although their influence hinged on the type of issue that the Senate candidate was discussing.

Instead of focusing on whether the media cover the same issues as those discussed in candidate ads, two studies have examined how often the ads themselves are covered. One study that examined ten 2004 Senate races found substantial discussion of advertising in campaign-related articles in local daily newspapers. In the ten races studied, the percentage of articles mentioning ads ranged from 6 to 28 percent; of these, 66 percent discussed the ads in depth. The authors conclude that "press coverage of political advertising is considerable. Moreover, candidate advertising is often the primary focus of newspaper articles; coverage of advertising is not an afterthought" (Ridout and Smith 2008: 605). A 2006 study of ad coverage in five gubernatorial and four Senate races found it to be "extensive," although generally of low quality (Fowler and Ridout 2009).

Thus, even though television ads may be a central component of an individual's campaign information environment and a very reasonable object of study for the purposes of this book, it must be acknowledged that there is no guarantee that they are representative of the kinds of information voters are getting. The level of advertising may be generally indicative of the volume of information voters are receiving, and there is a chance that the issues and themes discussed in ads will be reflected in other forms of communication that voters are exposed to during campaigns. The ads themselves may even receive media attention. Yet the bottom line is that this study is fundamentally about television advertising in political campaigns, and one should be wary of generalizing the claims made here to other forms of campaign information. The analyses in the following chapters take steps to ensure they are isolating the effects of television advertising from those of other forms of campaign information.[5]

Political competitiveness has been measured in a variety of ways in the extant literature. Researchers have used measures such as the margin of victory in the previous two elections (Johnston et al. 2004; Shaw 1999), the number of ads aired in the state (Wolak 2006; Benoit et al. 2004), and CNN rankings (Bergan et al. 2005). The problem with the first measure is that past margins of victory may not be a good predictor of how close an election is in the current year.[6] The second measure is also problematic; competitiveness determines, in large part, how many ads will be aired, but by using ad airings to capture the former, one is in a sense confusing the cause and the effect. Moreover, other factors do affect how a candidate allocates his resources. For example, in terms of political advertising, previous research has shown that the cost of advertising in a state is a powerful predictor of where candidates choose to spend their dollars (Shaw 1999). Thus, one should use a measure of state competitiveness that is independent of the candidate practices it drives.

Moreover, to avoid the issue of endogeneity, one must use a measure of competitiveness that reflects candidate strategies early in the campaign; otherwise, it is unclear if the competitiveness of the race is driving the activity of political actors or if the activity of political actors is making the race tighter. As a result, I use the *Cook Political Report* ranking of House, Senate, and state-level presidential contests issued in August, just prior to the start of the general election campaign. This measure, which distinguishes among districts and states that are safe, lean heavily toward a candidate, likely to favor a candidate, or are considered a toss-up, avoids both the issue of endogeneity and the problems associated with using measures of campaign practices.

In the following analysis, I examine the effect of a race's competitiveness on five dependent variables that measure different aspects of a voter's campaign information environment: (1) the total number of ads aired during the campaign; (2) the diversity of the information as determined by the number of unique advertising sponsors in the race; (3) the ratio of the incumbent or favored candidate's ad airings to the challenger's; (4) the amount of dialogue in the advertising; and (5) the proportion of the total ads aired that attack a candidate. To create the first measure, I counted the total number of ads aired between Labor Day and Election Day. For the diversity measure, I counted all the individuals and organizations sponsoring ads in the campaign as identified by CMAG. In the number of total sponsors, I included candidates and party organizations, but I did not allow for more than one party committee to be represented in the total number. Thus, if the Republican National Committee and the Republican party committee at the state level sponsored ads, I added only one sponsor to the total number of ad sponsors in the campaign. This is because it is unlikely that the two party committees speak with distinct voices.[7]

The equality or balance of information measure reflects the ratio of ad airings in favor of one candidate to the number of ad airings in favor of the other. Specifically, I created this measure by dividing the number of ad airings supporting the candidate with the fewest number of ad airings (usually the challenger) by the number of ad airings supporting the candidate with the greatest number (usually the incumbent). This method yields a continuous measure ranging from zero to one, with "0" indicating that only one candidate was supported in the advertising and "1" indicating that they were equally represented. If a race did not feature any ads, it was excluded from the analysis.

To create the dialogue measure, I started with Kaplan et al.'s measure (2006), which involves determining the percentage of time that political actors devote to speaking about a particular issue in a campaign (Sigelman and Buell 2004). Working with the CMAG data, Kaplan and his colleagues interpret this as the percentage of the candidates' total ad airings that mention a particular issue. Because I was interested in capturing the total amount of dialogue in all the campaign advertising, as opposed to the amount in just candidate advertising, I modified their approach. First, I determined the percentage of total attention that sponsors (candidates, party committees, and interest groups) favoring the Republican candidate and sponsors favoring the Democratic candidate spent talking about a given issue in their campaign advertising and then summed the absolute differences across all the issues. This number was divided by 2 and then subtracted from 1 to yield a dialogue measure ranging from zero to one. Interpreting this measure is straightforward; if a race received a dialogue measure of .40, it means that there is a 40 percent overlap in the issue emphases of Republican and Democratic advertising sponsors. I took the additional step of coding cases in which there was no advertising or only one side advertising as "0," since there was no candidate dialogue occurring in such situations.

Instead of measuring the absolute number of attack ads in a campaign, I measured the proportion of ads in which a candidate or one of his or her supporters attacked an opponent. Most studies that examine the effect of negative advertising simply use a measure of negative advertising volume, either the total number of advertisements or the natural log of that number. Yet, when average Americans or political observers talk about a campaign's negativity, they usually mean that it is more negative than positive. In other words, they consider the level of negativity in relation to how many positive things are being said. Moreover, a 2009 study by Daniel Stevens found that negative advertising has both a *volume* and a *proportion* effect and that the latter is potentially more damaging. Numerous studies using volume measures of negativity have found that it is beneficial to democracy because it boosts turnout and knowledge. Yet Stevens finds that the proportional effects of negativity are not so helpful or benign. If this is the case, then we want to capture the more harmful side of negativity, which requires using the proportional measure. To create this measure, I used the Wisconsin Advertising Project coding of each ad as intended primarily to promote a candidate, contrast the two candidates, or attack a candidate. For each race, I divided the total number of attack ad airings by the total number of ads aired overall to create the dependent variable, which ranges from 0 to 1. If there was no advertising in a race, it was excluded from the analysis of negativity.

In the analyses that follow, I use a variety of methods to analyze the effect of competitiveness on my dependent variables of interest. In the models that examine what accounts for the number of ad airings and unique advertising sponsors in an election, I use a negative binomial regression model because the dependent variable involves count data. Because the measures of information equality and dialogue range from 0 to 1, I use a generalized linear model with a logit link (for a binomial distribution) and robust standard errors for my analysis of each measure. This approach is recommended by Papke and Wooldridge (1996) for modeling proportional data (measures with a range of 0 to 1) because, in contrast to ordinary least squares models, such an approach produces predicted values that fall between zero and one.

All the following analyses control for standard demographic characteristics of the state, congressional districts, and media markets I analyze. Specifically, I control for population (in the case of Senate races and presidential media markets), median age, percentage of the population with a bachelor's degree, percentage of the population that is white, and median income. I also control for the average cost of an ad airing in the particular congressional race or, in the case of presidential campaigns, a given media market. In congressional races, the models include a dummy variable for whether the race is open. I do not control for factors such as candidate spending in the election, because such measures are in fact *intervening* variables. The competitiveness of an election as reflected in polls and previous electoral margins drives how much money the candidates spend in a campaign. As a result, including such variables in the models risks masking the effect of electoral competitiveness, and wrongly concluding that it does not matter. Finally, for clarity of presentation, the following discussion presents predicted probabilities based on fully specified regression models that can be found in Appendix Tables A.1–A.3.

Findings

In the following analysis I examine how electoral competitiveness affects not only the quantity of information that voters receive in House, Senate, and state-level presidential campaigns but the quality of that information as well. The analysis shows that although the relationship between electoral competitiveness and the quantity of information that voters receive in congressional races is largely linear, that is, it increases steadily as competitiveness increases, the relationship between competitiveness and the quality of that information is of a different nature. In this case, there appear to be diminishing returns to competitiveness. The relationship between electoral competitiveness and both the quantity and quality of the information environment in the media markets of presidential battleground states is altogether different and might be best described as having a "threshold" nature. Both the quantity and quality of information is poor in safe states and those that are likely to favor a candidate, but media markets in moderately and highly competitive states exhibit elevated levels of both.

Volume of Information

One component of a rich campaign information environment is an abundance of information. As Marion Just and her colleagues say, "Given citizens' haphazard and often inadvertent ways of encountering information, the more information available, the greater the chance it will get through" (1996: 235–37). It is widely recognized that competitive elections generate more information, and there is little reason to believe that this analysis will find anything different. Although the relationship between electoral competitiveness and the amount of information voters receive is typically assumed to be either linear or of a threshold nature, I hypothesized that in congressional elections it might reflect the fact that incumbents are "running scared" and prone to overreacting to the slightest threat. If this is true, then we should see a significant jump in the quantity of information provided by incumbents and their supporters to voters between safe districts or states and those that are moderately competitive. By contrast, we should see large quantities of advertising only in media markets belonging to states that are highly competitive in a presidential election.

Figure 3.1 contains graphs for the predicted number of ad airings in House, Senate, and presidential campaign media markets.[8] For congressional races, I have presented the predicted number of ads aired in favor of

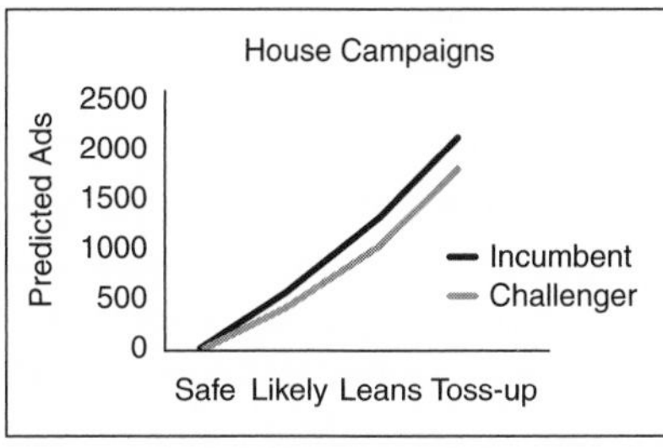

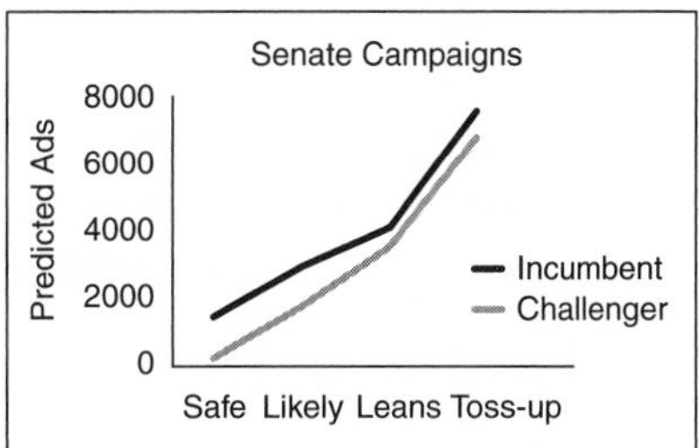

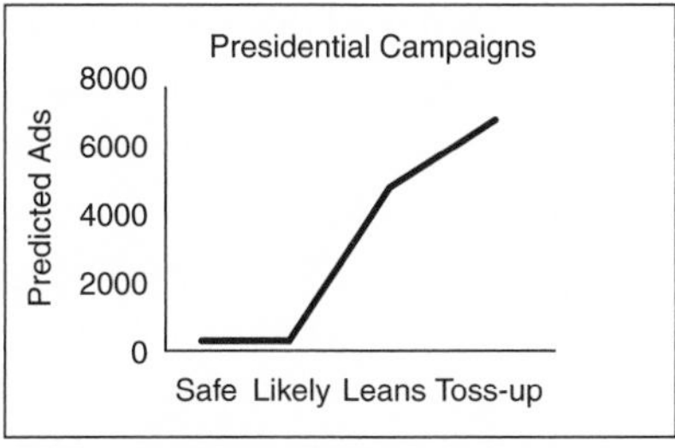

Figure 3.1. Effect of competitiveness on advertising volume in House, Senate, and state-level presidential campaigns. Goldstein et al. 2002; Goldstein and Rivlin 2005, 2007. House and Senate campaign data from 2000, 2002, and 2004; presidential campaign data from 2000 and 2004. Full models can be found in Models 1–6 of Table A.1.

incumbents and challengers separately. The first graph depicts the relationship between electoral competitiveness and the quantity of information in House races. Overall, one might describe this relationship as being nearly linear for both incumbents and challengers. As one might predict if incumbents were running scared, electoral competitiveness does have a slightly stronger relationship with the volume of incumbent advertising than with the volume of challenger advertising. As competitiveness increases across the four levels of competitiveness, the predicted number of incumbent ad airings is 34, 602, 1,272, and 2,086 respectively. Those numbers for the predicted number of challenger ad airings are 9, 446, 966, and 1,781. Thus, the scale of the graph masks some significant differences in how competitiveness affects incumbent and challenger ads, especially as the level of competitiveness increases from safe to modestly competitive. While incumbent ad airings are 18 times higher, challenger ad airings are 51 times higher. After that, the ad airings increase at a similar rate for incumbents and challengers, although the rate is always slightly higher for the latter. Between modestly and moderately competitive elections, the predicted number of ad airings increases by 211 percent for incumbents and 216 percent for challengers. As competitiveness increases between the two highest levels, the number increases by 164 percent and 184 percent respectively.[9]

The level of competitiveness in Senate races affects the volume of information aired by challengers and their supporters more dramatically than the volume of information that favors the incumbent. As the second graph in Figure 3.1 reveals, the discrepancy between incumbent and challenger races is quite high in races that are expected to be safe. The predicted number of ad airings for incumbents is 1,462, while it is just 212 for challengers. Thus, in safe races, the number of ads favoring incumbents is expected to be 7 times higher than for challengers. As the level of competitiveness increases, the predicted number of ads increases by 200 percent for incumbents and 838 percent for challengers, thereby resulting in rapidly declining inequality ratios between candidates. The smallest increase for both candidates occurs between modestly and moderately competitive races with the expected number of ad airings favoring an incumbent increasing by 142 percent to 4133 and those favoring a challenger increasing by 200 percent to 3556. As the level of competitiveness increases between moderately and highly competitive, there is another surge in the predicted number of ad airings. Incumbent ad airings increase by 185 percent to 7,656 airings; those in favor of the challenger increase by 192 percent to 6,833 airings.

The House data, then, reveal evidence of incumbents overreacting to threats, since electoral competitiveness has a considerably stronger effect on the volume of information they provide than on the number of ads supporting challengers, at least initially as competitiveness increases from safe to moderately competitive. There is no evidence of incumbents overreacting in Senate races. Instead, competitiveness initially has a stronger effect on challenger advertising. As a result, the considerable advertising advantage enjoyed by Senate incumbents in safe and "leans" races disappears in moderately and highly competitive contests.

State-level presidential contests are quite different. The predicted number of ad airings in media markets serving safe states and those that are likely to favor one candidate is less than 300, but the number soars to over 7,000 in media markets serving states that lean toward a candidate, and over 10,000 in battleground states. Thus, battleground state media markets are saturated with ads, while those in less competitive markets are virtually ignored. Usually, the only reason that a safe state media market receives any ads is that it crosses a state border and reaches voters in a neighboring competitive state.

Although the relationship between electoral competitiveness and the quantity of information might be described as linear in congressional elections, there appears to be more of a threshold effect in presidential elections. Unless a media market serves a state that is closely contested, the candidates and their supporters ignore it.

Information Diversity

Aside from elections being free and fair, democratic theorists argue that voters should have the opportunity to hear from a wide variety of interests about the pros and cons of each candidate in an election. At the very least, the candidates themselves should have ample opportunity to present themselves to voters and explain why they are better for the job than their opponent, which means that we would like to see at least two advertising sponsors in a campaign. The first graph in Figure 3.2 shows that this is not the case for safe House contests, nor is it the case in media markets belonging to safe states during presidential campaigns where the predicted number of sponsors is less than one (see third graph). This means that many residents of safe districts, or states that are safe in presidential contests, do not see ads for a single candidate, let alone hear from a variety of voices. Safe Senate elections appear to be different, however, as the second graph in Figure 3.2 indicates. In such cases, residents are typically exposed to ads from at least two sponsors, who are usually the candidates themselves.

The main focus of this research, however, is how electoral competitiveness affects the number of sponsors trying to communicate with voters. The graphs in Figure 3.2 reveal that, while competitiveness is generally associated with greater diversity, this relationship is slightly different in House, Senate, and presidential contests. In House elections, the most significant jumps in the number of ad sponsors occur between safe and modestly competitive races, where the predicted number of sponsors increases from less than one to two sponsors, and between modestly and moderately competitive contests, where the number of sponsors is expected to more than double to nearly five sponsors. The difference in the predicted number of sponsors between moderately competitive contests and those that are toss-ups is marginally significant ($p < .10$) but the increase from five to six sponsors is not as substantively impressive. In addition to the national and state party committees, some of the most frequent advertising sponsors in campaigns from 2000 to 2004 were the Chamber of Commerce, Business Roundtable, and American Federation of Labor. The group that sponsored by far the most advertisements in the

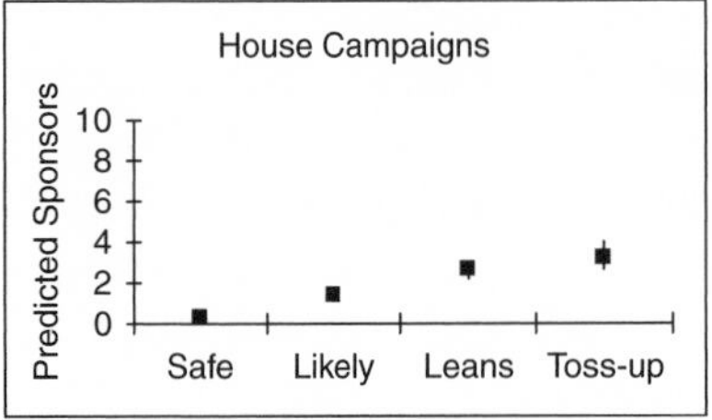

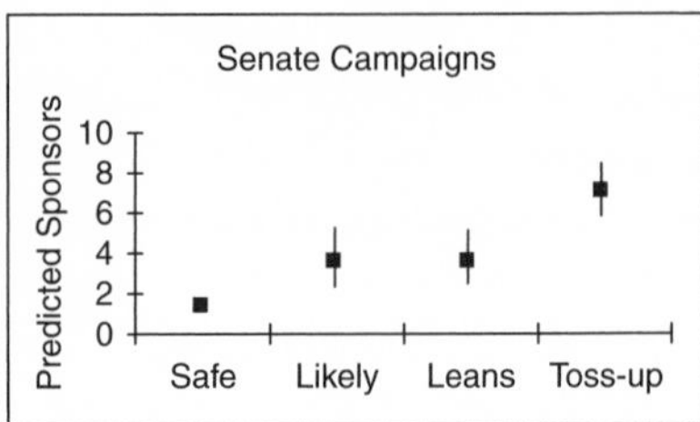

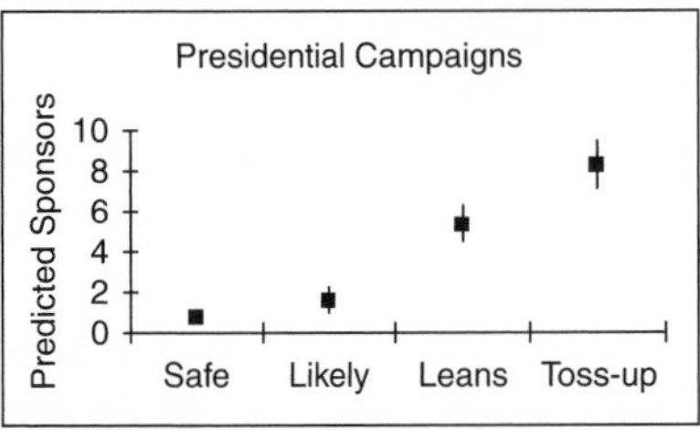

Figure 3.2. Effect of competitiveness on information diversity in House, Senate, and state-level presidential campaigns. Goldstein et al. 2002, Goldstein and Rivlin 2005, 2007. House and Senate campaign data from 2000, 2002, and 2004; presidential campaign data from 2000 and 2004. Vertical lines indicate upper and lower bounds of 95 percent confidence intervals. Full models can be found in Models 1–3 of Table A.2.

2000 and 2002 elections, however, was a 527 committee that called itself Citizens for Better Medicare (CBM), which was funded primarily by the pharmaceutical industry to fight adding a drug benefit to Medicare. Although one might argue that the pharmaceutical industry has a right to air its views as much as other groups, CBM was criticized for claiming to be a grassroots organization and using an innocuous name to hide the real identity of its backers.[10] Thus, even though competitive elections might draw more sponsors, there is no guarantee that the sponsors will present their views in a candid and truthful fashion. Still, these findings do suggest that modest increases in district competitiveness can result in substantially more information diversity in a campaign.

Whereas the analysis suggests that there may be diminishing returns to competitiveness in House races with respect to diversity because the difference in the number of groups sponsoring ads in moderately and high competitive contests is quite small, the situation is different in Senate contests. As the second graph in Figure 3.2 indicates, the number of predicted sponsors increases initially from 2 to 4 sponsors ($p < .001$) but then levels out between modestly and moderately competitive contests.[11] Residents who live in a state with a toss-up race, however, are exposed to a significantly wider variety of voices than at any other level of competitiveness with the expected number of advertising sponsors hovering around 10. This is nearly double the predicted number of sponsors in races that lean toward a candidate ($p < .01$). Despite the fact that the most significant boost in the diversity of voices occurs at higher levels of competitiveness, the analysis reveals—just as in the case of House elections—that even modest increases in competitiveness do improve voters' campaign information environment.

The same cannot be said for presidential contests, however. The difference in the predicted number of sponsors advertising at the media market level does not increase significantly between those in safe and those in modestly competitive states. One sees the biggest increase between media markets in modestly competitive states and those that are moderately competitive; the predicted number of sponsors more than doubles from just under two to just under five ($p < .001$). Media markets in toss-up states are predicted to get an additional boost in the diversity of advertising sponsors with approximately seven expected to purchase ads.

Even though the shape of the relationship between competitiveness and the number of voices trying to persuade voters is slightly different in House, Senate, and presidential campaigns, the one commonality is that the relationship is nonlinear in each case. The analysis also reveals that there are significant improvements in sponsor diversity in House and Senate elections that are just modestly competitive.

Equality of Communication

Democratic theorists who promote the political value of equality emphasize the importance of candidates having equal opportunity to make their case to voters (Dahl 1956; Dworkin 2000). Moreover, for a vote choice to be truly free, the citizen must be aware and informed about all the options. Scholars such as Robert Dahl contend that if a candidate sways voters simply because he has a monopoly or near-monopoly on the information environment, then the election is neither free nor fair (1956: 70). Thus, one way to gauge the quality of a voter's information environment is to determine the extent to which she is exposed to equal amounts of information from the candidates. A voter's information environment includes not only candidate-generated information but information provided by interest groups and parties as well. Thus, in the analysis that follows, I use a measure that compares all Republican advertising, irrespective of sponsor, to all Democratic advertising. As discussed earlier, I believe this is a much better measure of information equality than one that simply focuses on candidate-generated communications.

The mean equality ratio for both House and Senate races was .58. Another way to think about this relationship is that, among the House and Senate races examined, there were typically 1.7 times more ads aired about one candidate (usually the incumbent) than about the other candidate (usually the challenger). The mean equality ratio for presidential advertising at the media market level was slightly lower at .53.[12] To determine how competitiveness is related to the equality ratio, I regressed the measure of information equality on the same independent variables that I used in the analysis of sponsors above.

The graphs in Figure 3.3 show that the relationship between competitiveness and a campaign's equality ratio is nonlinear across all types of races.[13] In the case of House and Senate campaigns, there appear to be diminishing returns to competitiveness with the difference in the predicted equality ratio between moderately competitive and toss-up races being statistically insignificant. In House contests, the first graph in Figure 3.3 shows that the biggest

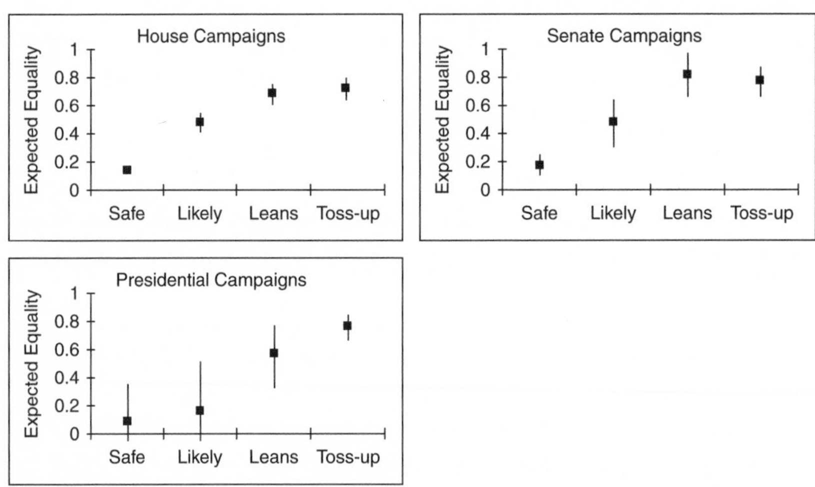

Figure 3.3. Effect of competitiveness on equality of information in House, Senate, and state-level presidential campaigns. Goldstein et al. 2002; Goldstein and Rivlin 2005, 2007. House and Senate campaign data from 2000, 2002, and 2004; presidential campaign data from 2000 and 2004. Vertical lines indicate upper and lower bounds of 95 percent confidence intervals. Full models can be found in Models 4–6 of Table A.2.

increase in the equality ratio occurs between safe districts and those that are modestly competitive, with the predicted equality ratio tripling from .12 to .43 ($p < .001$). In Senate contests, the equality ratio doubles from .18 to .41 between safe and modestly competitive contests, and doubles again to .80 as competitiveness increases from modest to moderate ($p < .05$). These findings are not surprising given the impact that modest competitiveness has on challenger advertising we saw in the section on information volume.

At the media market level in the 2000 and 2004 presidential races, we see that there is no difference in the predicted equality ratio of markets that belong to safe states and those that serve states that are likely to favor one party. If residents are seeing any advertisements in such states, those ads heavily favor one party. The largest jump in equality occurs between media markets in modestly and moderately competitive states with the expected equality ratio increasing from .16 to .55 ($p < .001$). Toss up races receive an additional though smaller boost with the equality ratio increasing to .76 ($p < .05$). This pattern is similar to the one between competitiveness and the diversity of advertising sponsors. Modest competitiveness in a state does not appear to significantly improve the information environment of voters, but moderate competitiveness does.

Candidate Dialogue

In the previous chapter, we learned that research, which has examined how electoral competitiveness affects dialogue, has yielded conflicting results. In this section, I find that the relationship is positive but nonlinear.

As the graphs in Figure 3.4 show, the relationship between competitiveness and candidate dialogue in House and Senate races is virtually identical. In both cases, the most significant increase in dialogue occurs between safe contests and those that are likely to favor a party. In the case of House contests, the predicted level of dialogue increases from just .05 to .21 ($p < .001$) while it jumps from .11 to .34 in Senate contests ($p < .001$) as competitiveness increases between the two levels. House races that are moderately competitive receive an additional boost as the expected level of dialogue increases to .33, while the same increase in competitiveness yields a marginally significant ($p < .10$, one-tailed) increase for Senate races from .34 to .44. In both cases, the predicted level of dialogue is not expected to be any higher in toss-up contests.

The pattern in presidential contests is by now familiar. Just as in the previous sections concerning the diversity of advertising sponsors and the equality

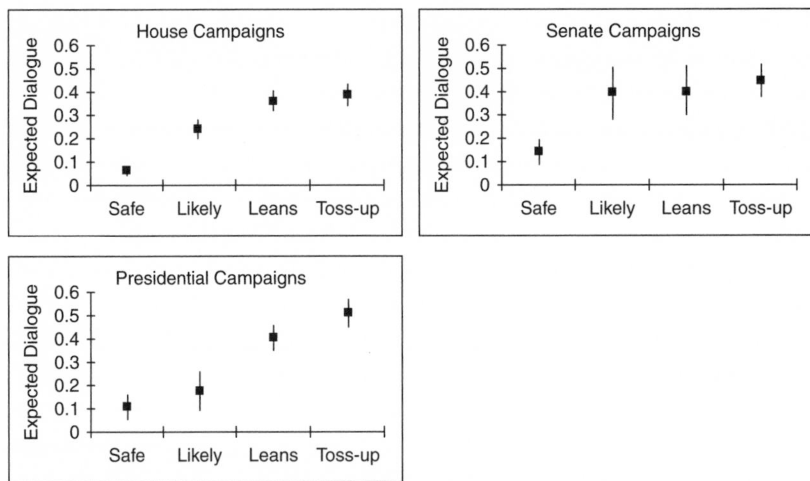

Figure 3.4. Effect of competitiveness on dialogue in House, Senate, and state-level presidential campaigns. Goldstein et al. 2002; Goldstein and Rivlin 2005, 2007. House and Senate campaign data from 2000, 2002, and 2004; presidential campaign data from 2000 and 2004. Vertical lines indicate upper and lower bounds of 95 percent confidence intervals. Full models can be found in Models 1–3 of Table A.3.

of campaign information, we see that modest levels of state competitiveness do not yield any improvement in the information environments of voters. The third graph in Figure 3.4 shows the same amount of dialogue, approximately .20, is expected in states that are safe and those that are likely to favor one candidate. Moreover, just as in the earlier sections, the most significant increase in the dependent variable occurs as one moves from media markets in modestly to those in moderately competitive states. The expected level of dialogue nearly triples from .20 to .59 ($p < .001$). And unlike congressional contests, we see that dialogue is even more likely to occur in the most tightly contested races with the expected level of dialogue jumping an additional .20 ($p < .01$). The issues the candidates and their supporters discuss are expected to overlap a whopping 80 percent of the time in media markets serving battleground states. Further analysis reveals that George W. Bush and Al Gore's ads focused on five issues in battleground states: taxes, education, social security, health care, and the budget. In 2004, Bush and John Kerry turned their attention in battleground states almost exclusively to taxes, jobs, health care, and defense.

The analysis clearly shows that electoral competitiveness—even modest levels in congressional elections—encourages candidates and their supporters to focus on the same issues. The reasons for this are not clear from this analysis, however. Scholars have suggested that dialogue is prevalent in competitive campaigns because candidates need to be viewed as being concerned and informed about the major issues of the day (Sigelman and Buell 2004; Ansolabehere and Iyengar 1994) and they are often forced to respond to the issue agenda set by the media (Sigelman and Buell 2004). Moreover, many issues are not owned by a single party, especially those having to do with the performance of the government and the economy (Kaplan et. al. 2006; Petrocik 1996). In short, the pressure of close contests makes it all the more imperative that candidates offer their views on and solutions for the problems facing voters. We also know from existing research that competitiveness increases campaign negativity. Perhaps negativity and dialogue are related. If this were the case, it would suggest that when candidates attack each other, they criticize each other's positions on the same set of issues.

The Share of Attack Ads

Although there is ample research to suggest that negative ads are beneficial for voter knowledge, there is no question that Americans detest them. Whether one is interested in the edifying effects of such ads or in banning them altogether, it is worthwhile to consider how competitiveness is related to negativity. As mentioned in the previous chapter, research has found that competitiveness generally leads to more negativity but it has not given us a nuanced picture of what that relationship looks like.

Figure 3.5 shows how competitiveness is related to the share of attack ads in House, Senate, and presidential contests. In the case of House contests, the relationship is linear with the expected share of attack ads starting out at just .10 in safe contests and increasing to .20, .33, and .48 at successively higher levels of competitiveness. The story is different in Senate races, however. The largest increase in the expected share of negative ads, from .09 to .22, occurs between safe and moderately competitive contests. The expected share then increases to .34 ($p < .10$) and levels off thereafter. Why might competitiveness have a stronger relationship with negativity in House than in Senate campaigns? The main difference is the level of negativity in toss-up House and Senate races. Perhaps Senate candidates and their supporters feel it would undermine the candidate's stature if they attack too much. Another reason has to do with experience. House candidates and their campaign staffs often have less campaign experience than Senate campaign teams. This may result

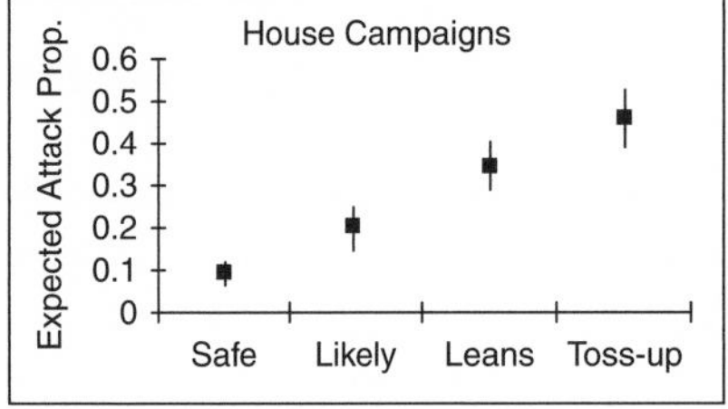

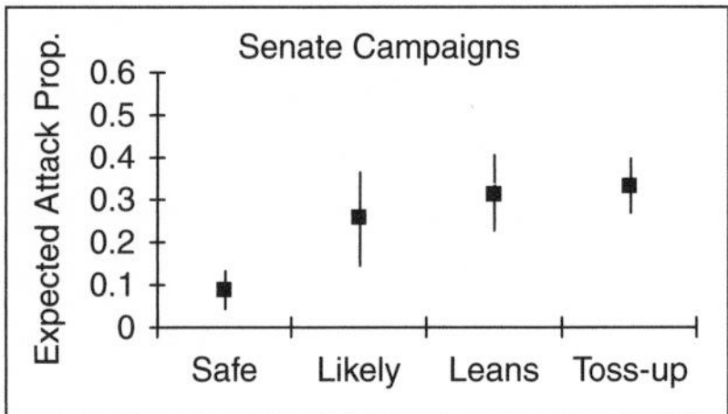

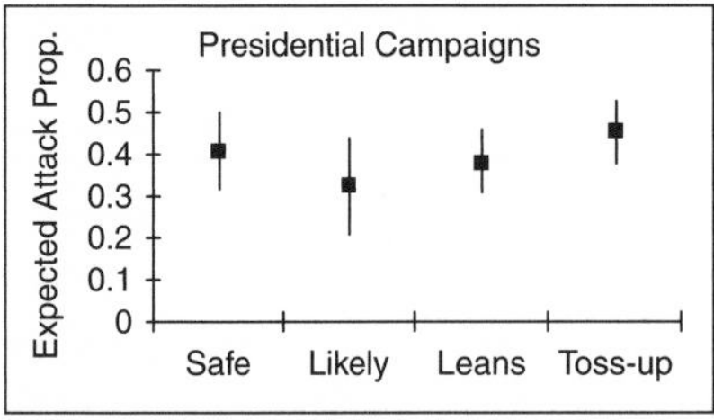

Figure 3.5. Effect of competitiveness on share of attack ads in House, Senate, and state-level presidential campaigns. Goldstein et al. 2002; Goldstein and Rivlin 2005, 2007. House and Senate campaign data from 2000, 2002, and 2004; presidential campaign data from 2000 and 2004. Vertical lines indicate upper and lower bounds of 95 percent confidence intervals. Full models can be found in Models 4–6 of Table A.3.

in different strategies in the face of a tough challenger. For example, House candidates might go on the attack earlier in the campaign than Senate candidates, or they might be more likely to respond to an opponent's attack ad with one of their own.

The most surprising graph is the one for presidential campaigns, which shows that competitiveness is not related to the share of attack ads. There is no statistically significant difference in the level of attack ads in media markets serving safe state residents and those serving battleground states. This finding is especially surprising because the analysis includes all the ads that were aired in the race, even those sponsored by interest groups, which are typically quite negative (West 2005). One might speculate that the reason the tone of ads in safe states and battleground states is the same is that the only ads that people in safe states are seeing are those that spill over state boundaries from swing states. If this were the case, however, we would have seen the same kind of relationship, that is, the absence of one, between competitiveness in state-level presidential elections and our other measures of advertising content (diversity and dialogue). Since there are considerably more sponsors airing ads in moderately and highly competitive states, and we know that interest groups ads tend to be more negative, the chart suggests that the candidates themselves, who are the primary sponsors of ads in less competitive states, are airing especially negative ads. If this is the case, then the fact that ads in safe states and battleground states are equally negative may suggest that candidates rely more on negative ads when they are trying to mobilize their base in safe states.

In the previous section, I speculated that dialogue is higher in competitive contests because it is a by-product of negativity. When candidates go negative, they attack each other on the same set of issues. In House and Senate campaigns, the relationship between competitiveness and both dialogue and negativity is quite similar, which suggests there may be something to this argument. To test this hypothesis, I simply examined the correlation between the proportion of attack advertising in a campaign and dialogue measures. The strength of the relationship between these two is quite high. In House campaigns, the correlation is .41 ($p < .001$), while it is .62 in Senate campaigns ($p < .001$), and .21 in state-level presidential contests ($p < .10$). Further analysis, which included the negativity measure in the regression models explaining dialogue and controlled for competitiveness, confirmed that there is a strong positive relationship between negativity and dialogue in House and Senate races and a marginally positive relationship in presidential contests. Thus, competitiveness drives both dialogue and negativity in House and Senate races, but the two measures are positively related irrespective of how competitive a race is. In state-level presidential contests, both competitiveness and negativity appear to drive dialogue. That said, more research is needed to establish causality; it is possible that dialogue drives negativity. Perhaps when candidates start to focus on the same issues they feel the need to distinguish themselves on those issues and do so by clarifying their own position and attacking their opponent's. Still, this unexpectedly strong relationship between dialogue and negativity opens up new avenues for research.

Conclusion

As expected, the analysis confirms that the relationship between electoral competitiveness and the quantity of information provided to voters is linear in House and Senate campaigns. The analysis also shows, however, that the relationships between electoral competitiveness and the quality of information provided to voters, that is, information diversity, information equality, and dialogue—are distinctly nonlinear. In House elections, we consistently find diminishing returns to competitiveness for each of these measures, while in Senate elections increasing competitiveness yields diminishing returns in terms of information equality and dialogue. The relationship between electoral competitiveness and both information quantity and quality in state-level presidential contests is of an entirely different sort. One might describe the relationship as something of a "threshold" effect, that is, gains in information quantity and quality are seen only at moderate and high levels of competitiveness. Finally, the analysis also reveals that the relationship between competitiveness and attack advertising is linear only in the case of House races. In Senate races, attack advertising reaches its highest levels in moderately competitive contests and does not increase after that, while it appears to have no relationship with how competitive a state is in a presidential contest.

The findings concerning House and Senate campaigns should be heartening to political reformers because they demonstrate that modest improvements in electoral competitiveness may yield significant informational benefits for voters. In terms of improving the information environment of voters in presidential contests, reformers face a more difficult battle because higher levels of competitiveness are needed. Still, the analysis suggests that a media market does not have to be located in a battleground state to attract the attention of candidates and their supporters. Media markets in states that lean toward a candidate appear to offer enough of an incentive for these interests to provide better information.

Although competitiveness does encourage candidates and their supporters to generate better information for voters from a normative standpoint, the question is whether this information affects voters in the manner expected. Does information diversity, equality, and candidate dialogue help voters learn? And what about attack ads? Do they enhance voter knowledge or lead them astray? The next two chapters tackle these questions in the context of House, Senate, and state-level presidential contests.

CHAPTER 4

Competitiveness and Campaign Knowledge in Congressional Elections

It is widely believed that competitive elections have a host of salutary effects on voters. Studies of Senate elections have concluded that competitive elections, "enliven and enrich people's political life" by making citizens more knowledgeable about their political choices (Kahn and Kenney 1999, 7), while studies of House campaigns have found that competitive races generate similarly positive but slightly more muted effects (Huckfeldt et al. 2007; Gronke 2000). This chapter will examine the relationship between electoral competitiveness and voter knowledge in these contexts but with the goal of understanding how competitive a race needs to be to generate knowledge effects. It also examines how the information generated by electoral competitiveness, that is, information that is diverse, balanced, engages in dialogue, and is more negative, affects knowledge. If competitiveness drives voter knowledge, as many scholars have asserted, but the information generated by such contests does not fully explain its effect, it would suggest that citizens in a close district or state feel obligated or motivated to inform themselves about the candidates. This would indeed be a positive side-effect of increased competitiveness.

Given the relationship between electoral competitiveness and both information quantity and quality described in the previous chapter, what should we expect the relationships between competitiveness and political knowledge in House and Senate campaigns to look like? Recall that the relationship between electoral competitiveness and the quantity of information was linear, but the beneficial effects of competitiveness on the quality of information often seemed to plateau. Thus, if the quantity of information matters more for knowledge, then we might expect to see something of a linear relationship between electoral competitiveness and knowledge. If information quality matters more, however, then we should find diminishing returns to electoral competitiveness.

Information, Interest, and Voter Knowledge

The question whether interest or information explains the effect of electoral competitiveness on voter knowledge suggests it has the potential to affect voters in both direct and indirect ways. The more direct route involves a citizen being cognizant of how close the race is and altering her behavior accordingly. For instance, she might think that under such circumstances her vote has more weight and that she has more of an obligation to weigh her choices seriously. This may lead her to pay more attention to the candidates and actively seek out information about them. Under such circumstances, it might be said that a voter is acting "instrumentally." The extant literature is somewhat mixed on the degree to which voters actually behave instrumentally, especially in House elections. One study of House elections found evidence that there is "at least some direct response on the part of ordinary citizens to the closeness of elections" (Cox and Munger 1989: 226), but a more recent study examining the effects of competitiveness on turnout is more pessimistic about the instrumental behavior of voters. According to these scholars, "neither the perception nor the reality of a competitive race produces a direct effect on turnout" because only the most politically knowledgeable understand how competitive their district is, and they are already likely to turn out (Huckfeldt et al. 2007: 809). Similarly, the politically knowledgeable are already more likely to inform themselves about their vote choice, so it is unlikely that competitiveness will have a direct effect on political knowledge.

It seems to be more likely that voters passively absorb the information generated by competitive contests (Zukin and Snyder 1984). This means that the effect of competitiveness on voter knowledge is very likely indirect; candidates respond to electoral uncertainty by providing more information to voters through television ads, radio spots, direct mail and the like, while journalists respond to it by providing more media coverage of campaigns (Jerit et al. 2006; Kahn and Kenney 1999; Just et al. 1996). Voters then inadvertently encounter this information when they are watching the evening news or listening to their favorite radio station. If political knowledge is gained in this manner, then it suggests that the quality of campaign information environments is extremely important for democratic decision-making.

Advertising and Political Knowledge

Although the conventional wisdom is that television advertisements are vacuous and devoid of information, there is a growing body of research that argues voters learn from them (Franz et al. 2007; Ridout et al. 2004; Goldstein and Freedman 2002; Zhao and Chaffee 1995; Zhao and Bleske 1995; Atkin and Heald 1976; but see Huber and Arceneaux 2007). Martin Gilens, Lynn Vavreck, and Martin Cohen even go so far as to argue that the increased volume of television advertisements in presidential campaigns accounts for why political knowledge remains high in such elections despite the fact that the informational content of news coverage in them has declined (Gilens et al. 2007). Thus, I expect to find that television advertisements help voters learn. The analysis in this chapter differs from these earlier studies, however, because it seeks to understand how certain aspects of television advertising that are driven by electoral competitiveness, namely its volume, balance, diversity, level of dialogue, and negativity, affect knowledge. It may not be immediately apparent why these information qualities should aid learning, so in the next section I offer some theoretical reasons for why they might.

Information Volume

The volume of campaign communication matters most for exposure to political information. The more candidates and their supporters try to communicate with voters, the more likely it is that voters will encounter some portion of that information. It is true that advertisers hope a commercial might be seen or heard a number of times to ensure that it sticks in voters' minds, but the primary purpose of buying so many advertisements is make sure people actually see them. As another political communication scholar argues, "Ads are not repeated *ad nauseam* so that an individual finally surrenders just to stop the pain. They are repeated to guarantee that the ad gets seen in the first place—and perhaps a few more times—by an audience that is not motivated to seek it out" (Johnston et al. 2004: 82).

Thus, the main way advertising volume affects political knowledge is by increasing the likelihood that people are simply exposed to it. This line of reasoning suggests that the relationship between advertising volume and knowledge should be mostly linear, because each time an ad is aired it is seen by someone new. It is possible, however, that at extremely high levels of advertising, when a market or state becomes saturated by ads, the positive effect of volume on political knowledge might disappear. Examples of such saturation are probably fairly rare and more likely to occur in only the most competitive Senate races. As a result, the following analysis will test for the possibility that advertising has diminishing returns for knowledge at extremely high levels.[1]

Information Equality

Robert Dahl argued that it is important for voters in an election to hear "identical information" from both parties. In Chapter 2, I made the case that he meant that voters should hear equal amounts of information because he was concerned about a party winning an election simply by holding a monopoly or near-monopoly on information provision. In this section, I turn to the question of whether the equality of information in a campaign matters for voter knowledge. Dahl was the first to admit that "identical information" in a campaign is "no guarantee of cosmic rationality" (1956: 70), but it might prove beneficial for voters nonetheless.

Numerous studies, however, have shown that people are resistant to information that is inconsistent with their partisan predispositions (e.g., see Zaller 1992). If this is the case, then why should receiving information from individuals and organizations in support of the opposing candidate increase knowledge at all? Wouldn't we expect such information to "bounce" off a non-supporter? If this is what indeed happens, then the only information that should matter for voters is information provided by their preferred candidate. This suggests that greater equality of information at the same overall volume might actually hurt knowledge because it would mean there is less information to absorb from the preferred candidate. John Zaller argues, however, that the only people who are capable of processing information in such a biased manner are those who are politically sophisticated enough to interpret the cueing or contextual messages which communicate the partisan or ideological implications of a message (42). Unsophisticated individuals cannot interpret such cueing messages, so "they tend to uncritically accept whatever ideas they encounter" (45). Some contextual information is obscure in the sense that its partisan implications are unclear even for political sophisticates. For example, a study of advertising in midterm elections found that only a third of them mentioned the party or ideology of the candidate (Vavreck 2001). If it is unclear from a candidate's ad what her party or ideology is, then the information in the ad might be accepted and processed by both political sophisticates and nonsophisticates. Thus, people can learn from an opposing candidate's advertisements.

Even though we have established that people might process information provided by an opponent, we still have not answered the question of why balanced information might aid voter learning. Some research has found that two-sided arguments are more easily comprehended and that dissent motivates thinking (Mutz 2002, 2006; Price et al. 2002). Keep in mind, however, that balance is different from dialogue; a voter might be hearing equally from both candidates in a campaign, but the candidates might be "talking past" each other, with each emphasizing issues on which he has an advantage. Yet, it is still possible that simply hearing from an opposing candidate motivates thinking and engagement. It is also possible that because so many races are uncompetitive, exposure to information from two candidates alerts voters to the fact that their race is contested and, as a consequence, merits closer attention.

Information Diversity

Why might hearing from a wide range of voices in a campaign promote learning? From the perspective of deliberative democratic theory it is normatively desirable for voters to be exposed to a wide range of opinions and arguments so that the information they possess about the candidate is as full and complete as possible. This suggests that each new source of information will convey different information or at least a different perspective on information that has been conveyed earlier in the campaign. The question is whether there is any reason to believe that different advertising sponsors will offer different information to voters.

We do know from the literature on campaign strategies that candidates and parties often issue "talking points" to their supporters during campaigns so that voters will hear the same message from different sources. But parties do not have total control over the campaign information environment. In the contemporary campaign finance era, parties and interest groups that run ads expressly advocating the election or defeat of a candidate must run those ads without that candidate's knowledge or consent. This means the content of their messages is likely to differ from those of the candidate. Moreover, political observers have noted that issue advocacy ads, which do not expressly support one candidate over the other, are typically used by interest groups (and parties before BCRA outlawed their airing of such communications) to force candidates to discuss topics that they would rather avoid (Herrnson 2005). This also suggests that as the sponsors of campaign communications in a campaign multiply so will the diversity of messages aired in the information environment.

From the perspective of voters, then, increasing the number of sponsors in a campaign should increase the diversity of information to which they are exposed, but there is research that suggests they should be better able to retain that information as well. As the sources of information multiply, the more likely it is that citizens will hear from one they find credible or from one with which they can identify. A source is credible when the audience perceives the individual as being someone "who knows the truth . . . or is likely to tell the truth" (Kelman 1961: 68). A person identifies with a source, or a source is deemed as being "attractive," when that source has qualities that individuals wish to identify with themselves (68). One study has applied this theory specifically to television advertising and found that people are indeed more likely to recall information from an ad when they perceive the person speaking in it as being credible and attractive (Chebat et al. 1995). If this is the case, then it is logical that the more sources sponsor advertisements, the more likely it is that voters will encounter a source they find credible, and the more likely it is that they will cognitively process and retain the information in that source's advertisement.

Dialogue

From the perspective of normative political thought, there may be a whole host of reasons for wanting politicians to engage in dialogue. Some argue that dialogue or deliberation may lead to better decisions or simply more agreement as competing parties work out their differences. Others go farther, arguing that dialogue legitimates democratic decision-making by requiring political victors to offer reasons for holding the positions they do. Such reasons provide political losers (those in the minority) with an understanding of why the majority voted against their wishes, which should leave a better taste in their mouth than believing they lost simply because they did not have the numbers. From the perspective of political psychology, the general argument is that dialogue will promote more thoughtful, considered opinions in voters; this has been confirmed by the studies mentioned earlier that show exposure to disagreement promotes thinking (Mutz 2002, 2006; Price et al. 2002).

These studies, however, have examined the effect of exposure to disagreement among citizens in their everyday lives. It is unclear whether hearing disagreeable views from an opposing party's candidate via advertisements in a campaign promotes the same kind of thinking. The critical difference between a personal conversation and exposure to an exchange between candidates in a campaign is not only one's personal involvement, but also the depth and sincerity of the discussion. Obviously, people who are discussing politics and disagreeing have more time to defend their views and get to the root of their differences than candidates in a campaign do. Citizens who are disagreeing also rarely have an incentive to misrepresent their views, while candidates in a campaign often find it helpful to obfuscate and prevaricate, if not outright lie. Thus, even if candidates are engaging in dialogue about certain issues in a campaign, the dialogue is likely to be far less enlightening than watching two individuals debate a subject. One might object that this is a problem of obfuscation, prevarication, and lying, not of dialogue itself. Yet dialogue does not guarantee candor. Nor does it guarantee eloquence, for that matter. Some candidates may botch the presentation of their arguments, or fail to clearly explain a complex issue, thereby rendering any dialogue they are engaged in unhelpful. It is true that when we imagine dialogue between two candidates, we imagine a more ideal exchange, but the term has been defined in the campaign literature simply as two candidates discussing the same issue, not as two candidates discussing an issue clearly and honestly.[2] Perhaps this is why the two studies that have examined dialogue's effects on political knowledge have found conflicting results (Simon 2002; Wichowsky 2008).

In addition, the argument that campaign dialogue is beneficial for voters hinges on the faulty assumption that voters cannot learn a candidate's position from his or her opponent. Of course, it is quite likely that a candidate will do a better job of representing his or her own position and reasons for maintaining that position than the opponent, but that does not mean that voters cannot learn what that position is from the candidate's challenger. From the advertising literature, we already know that people learn from negative ads—ads that mention an opponent—and may even learn more from them than ads in which a candidate talks exclusively about him- or herself (Geer 2006). In addition, scholars argue that contrast ads—a subset of negative ads in which a candidate contrasts her position with her opponent's position—are the most desirable type of ad precisely because a viewer can learn both candidates' positions from a single ad. People learn even more from these ads than from positive ones. If it is true that people can learn one candidate's issue positions from information provided by an opponent, then it is possible that voters might learn less in a campaign where there is a large amount of dialogue than from one where the candidates talk past each other about positions on different issues. In other words, more issues are likely to be discussed in a campaign when the candidates talk past each rather than when they engage in a dialogue on just a handful of issues. It is true that dialogue might lead to a *deeper* understanding of the candidate's positions on the issues discussed, but this deeper understanding might come at the price of a *broader* understanding of the candidates' positions in general.

Information Negativity

There has been a great deal of debate about whether campaign negativity is good for democracy. This area of research has been growing so rapidly that the authors of a 1999 meta-analytic study of 117 articles on the topic (Lau and Sigelman 1999) found it necessary to publish another meta-analytic study, which reviewed the findings of an additional 111 studies, just eight years later (Lau et al. 2007). In terms of whether negativity promotes learning, the two studies reported similarly positive but modest evidence that negative ads are more memorable than positive ads. In addition, the 2007 study reviewed 15 studies that examined the relationship between negativity and campaign information. The authors of the meta-analytic study found that 11 of the 15 studies reported positive effects, although they were usually quite small.

In his book, *In Defense of Negativity*, John Geer contends the reason negative ads promote learning is that they are actually more issue-oriented than positive ads and more likely to provide evidence for their claims.[3] Moreover, the attacks in negative ads typically reflect real world problems. For example, if unemployment is on the rise, candidates—challengers in particular—are more likely to attack their opponents on this issue. By doing so, candidates that are being negative not only draw the public's attention to an important issue, but serve a democratic purpose by holding those in power accountable. Geer argues, "If the public wants to have accountability, someone has to do the accounting and that accounting is not done through positive, feel-good appeals, but through harsh political attack" (2006: 110). Perhaps the most important conclusion to draw from these studies is that negative campaign information has not been found to undermine voter knowledge and may in fact help it by increasing the odds that voters will pay attention to it and process the substantive information it contains.

Competitive elections generate campaign information environments that are richer in terms of both the quantity and the quality of information they provide to voters. The discussion suggests that greater information volume and equality increase the chances that voters will be exposed to information from both sides of the electoral divide, while higher levels of information diversity and negativity should increase the odds that voters will pay attention to and process that information. Although scholars often assume that dialogue does the same, the assumption has not been tested in a campaign setting and, as I have suggested here, there are reasons to believe that dialogue will not help voter knowledge. The analysis in this chapter and the next tests these hypotheses in House, Senate, and state-level presidential contests.

A Brief Word About Advertising Effects in House and Senate Campaigns

There is reason to expect that different information environment characteristics will matter for voter learning in House and Senate campaigns. House elections are low visibility elections, that is, voters typically know less about House candidates than they do about Senate candidates and are less likely to follow a House campaign closely. The significance of this difference is that it suggests advertising volume may be more important in House campaigns than Senate campaigns for voter learning. In Senate campaigns, where voters are already familiar with the candidates, we may see that advertising volume matters less for political knowledge than being exposed to a higher quality flow of information that represents a diverse range of viewpoints, discusses the candidates in a more balanced fashion, and involves a high level of dialogue.

Data and Methods

This analysis begins by first assessing how the competitiveness of an election affects citizen knowledge overall and then proceeds to an examination of the factors that are responsible for generating those effects by using the measures of the information environment I employed in Chapter 3. In the first part of the analysis, I examine how the level of competitiveness in House and Senate elections is related to several different measures of voter knowledge in 2000, 2002, and 2004 using data from the American National Election Study (NES). The strength of the NES survey is that it asks the same campaign knowledge questions for the three years the CMAG advertising data are available.[4] It has two weaknesses, however. First, it uses a national sample, which is appropriate for House and presidential elections, but less appropriate for Senate elections (Westlye 1983). The main problem is that the NES sample draws disproportionately from large states. Those who have criticized the use of the NES for the study of Senate elections do so because the elections in large states tend to be more competitive than those in small states. Thus, studies which have concluded that voters were highly knowledgeable about Senate candidates were making claims based on an examination of data that oversampled voters who were exposed to competitive elections. Although it is still true that the NES oversamples respondents in large states, it is much less of a concern for this study because I am specifically interested in the effects of electoral competitiveness and, as such, categorize the respondents according to how competitive their Senate race is.

The other problem with the NES is that it asks very few political knowledge questions about House and even fewer about Senate contests. Moreover, it stopped asking some of its traditional knowledge measures after 2000. Through 2000, respondents were asked whether they could recall the names of House and Senate candidates, and to list their "likes" and "dislikes" for each House candidate. These knowledge measures were not used in 2002 and 2004, and so could not be used in this analysis. Even so, it is still the best survey available for the three years in which the CMAG advertising data are available.[5] Specifically, I use a measure of the respondent's ability to rate candidates on a feeling thermometer. Respondents who could rate both candidates received a "2," those who could rate one candidate received a "1," and those who could not rate either received a "0."[6]

Even though the ability to rate candidates is frequently used in the literature as a measure of political knowledge in congressional races, there are some obvious problems with it. The first is that a respondent who is uncomfortable admitting that he does not know enough about a candidate to rate him or her can still offer a rating. Moreover, a person can think she knows quite a bit about a candidate when in fact much of it is erroneous. Such a respondent might confidently offer a rating of a candidate, but do so based on poor information. This measure then is perhaps better conceived of as a confidence measure than as a political knowledge measure.

To gauge how much a respondent actually knows about a candidate, I use a different measure. In 2000 and 2004, the NES asked respondents to place House candidates on a 7-point ideology scale with a "1" indicating that the respondent believes the incumbent is "extremely liberal" and a "7" indicating that the respondent believes the incumbent is "extremely conservative." I developed the accuracy measure by comparing the respondents' placement of the incumbent in their district with the ideology score the incumbent received from the liberal lobbying organization Americans for Democratic Action (ADA) (Coleman and Manna 2000). Each year, the ADA issues a score for how liberal or conservative a member of the House is based on his or her voting record the previous year. The score ranges from "0" for a member who is very conservative to "100" for one who is very liberal. For example, in 2004, House Majority Leader Tom Delay (R-Tex.) received a "0" indicating extreme conservativism while House Minority Leader Nancy Pelosi (D-Calif.) received a score of "100" indicating extreme liberalism. I divided the ADA score by 14.3 and rounded to the nearest whole number to make it comparable to the NES ideology scale. The accuracy measure is coded so that a respondent receives a "1" if he or she correctly identifies the incumbent as a conservative ("1" or "2"), moderate ("3," "4," or "5"), or liberal ("6" or "7") and a "0" if not. The NES does not ask respondents to place Senate candidates on an ideology scale, so this measure only exists for House races.[7]

All the models control for demographic and political variables that are typically associated with political knowledge, including education, gender, race, income, strength of partisanship, partisan identification, general interest in politics, and media exposure. I also include an age variable, as well as a quadratic term for age, since recent research has shown that the relationship between age and political knowledge is nonlinear (Lau and Redlawsk 2008). In the case of knowledge concerning House candidates, I control for whether there is a statewide race. For Senate candidates, the models include a dummy for whether there is a gubernatorial race in the state, as well as a control for the competitiveness of the respondent's House race. All the models also include dummy variables for the election year.

Finally, a word needs to be said about information exposure, that is, how do we know that voters are actually seeing the campaign information that candidates and their supporters are generating? This has been a major preoccupation of scholars who use the CMAG data to try to isolate the effects of television advertising because ads will have the strongest effect on those who have actually seen them (Ridout et al. 2004; Freedman and Goldstein 1999). Yet the types of measures that have been advocated for measuring ad exposure are not included in the NES (used in this chapter) or in the National Annenberg Election Study (used in the next chapter). This is a problem confronted by all scholars using these data sources and will not be remedied until these studies include appropriate measures for gauging exposure. Others scholars have advocated dividing respondents into low, medium, and high levels of political awareness with the expectation that information effects will be strongest among those with moderate levels of awareness (Zaller 1992). Yet my question is not who benefits most from campaign information, but whether competitive elections and the kinds of information they generate create an electorate that is more politically knowledgeable overall.[8]

Electoral Competitiveness and Campaign Knowledge

Figure 4.1 displays how electoral competitiveness affects the predicted probability that a respondent could rate both House candidates, both Senate candidates, and correctly identify the House incumbent's ideology.[9] The first and third charts show that although a respondent's ability to rate House and Senate candidates increases with electoral competitiveness, it ultimately offers diminishing returns. In House elections, the predicted probability of being able to rate both candidates increases from .44 in safe districts to .64 in districts that are just modestly competitive ($p < .001$).[10] The predicted probability continues to increase with district competitiveness, but the differences between the remaining categories are not statistically significant, meaning that the crucial threshold for a voter's ability to rate—or to feel confident enough to rate—both candidates in a House contest is whether the race is at least

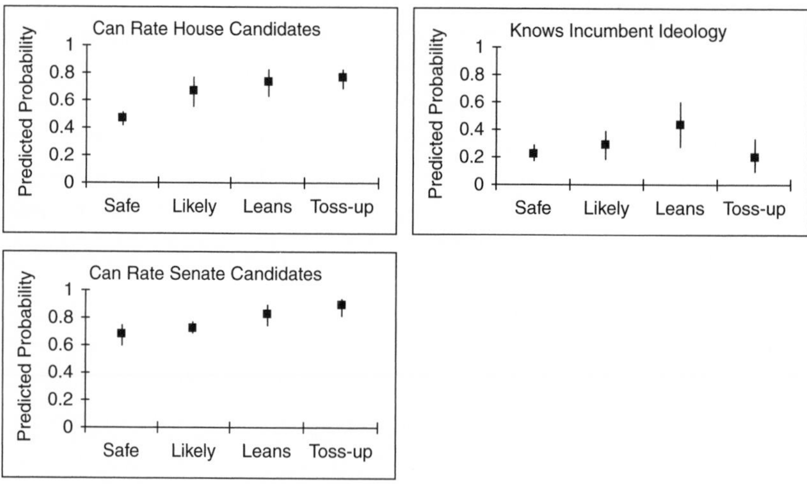

Figure 4.1. Effect of competitiveness on ability to rate House candidates, identify House incumbent ideology, and rate Senate candidates. NES Cumulative File; Goldstein et al. 2002; Goldstein and Rivlin 2005, 2007. Vertical lines indicate upper and lower bounds of 95 percent confidence intervals. Full models can be found in Models 1–3 of Table A.4.

minimally competitive. This is not true for Senate races, however. The ability of voters to rate candidates increases significantly from .50 in safe races to .58 ($p < .10$) in those who are likely to favor a candidate and then to .70 ($p < .05$) in those who lean toward a candidate. The difference in knowledge between those in the latter category and people residing in the most competitive states is not significantly different. These two charts, which demonstrate electoral competitiveness' marginal returns for knowledge, suggest that quality—not quantity—may matter more for campaign knowledge in House and Senate campaigns. We learned in Chapter 3 that the volume of advertising in House and Senate races increases in a linear fashion with competitiveness. If advertising volume was driving knowledge, we would see knowledge increase in the same way, but we do not.

The second chart confirms this finding, at least for House contests. This chart depicts the way a voter's actual knowledge of House candidates—as opposed to the ability to rate them—increases with competitiveness. It shows that the accuracy of placing an incumbent on an ideology scale is highest in "leans" or moderately competitive races. The predicted probability of placing an incumbent correctly doubles from .17 in safe races to .34 in districts that lean toward one party. Accuracy plummets in toss-up districts (.15). These findings echo those of Coleman and Manna (2000), who contend that the drop-off in accuracy among respondents exposed to the most competitive races is due to higher levels of negative advertising on the part of challengers. Their analysis uses campaign spending as a proxy for negative advertising. In the next section, I will test their hypothesis using actual negative advertising data.

The findings of these studies are at odds with others that argue knowledge is highest in the most competitive elections. Minimally and moderately competitive elections generate information that is helpful for voters and, in the case of accuracy, moderately competitive elections—not toss-ups—seem to help citizens the most. The most puzzling finding that emerges from the charts is that even though voters who are exposed to close House contests are more confident about their ability to rate the candidates, what they actually know about the candidates might be lower than in moderately competitive contests.

Accounting for Higher Knowledge in Competitive Contests

As discussed earlier, many scholars who study how voters respond to competitive elections have argued that such events engage and excite citizens, encouraging them to pay more attention to the election and to educate themselves about their vote choice. Political interest is the single most important predictor of political knowledge, so if it is higher in competitive contests, it might explain why the ability to rate candidates is high as well (we will leave aside the issue of accuracy in House races for the moment). Yet, as Figure 4.2 demonstrates, the political interest of voters is not substantially higher when they are exposed to competitive contests than when they are exposed to noncompetitive ones. The predicted probability of a respondent saying that he is "very much" interested in the upcoming election increases from .28 if he lives in a safe district to .33 if his district's election is expected to be a toss-up, but the change is not statistically significant. Strangely enough, campaign interest is actually significantly lower in moderately competitive districts than in safe districts, dipping to .23. The difference in interest between moderately and highly competitive districts appears to be large but is only marginally significant ($p < .10$, one-tailed). The competitiveness of Senate elections has no effect at all on voter interest. The chance of a respondent saying she is very much interested in the election increases slightly as the competitiveness of a race increases slightly (from .28 in safe states to .29 in toss-up states) but, again, the difference is statistically insignificant.[11]

If citizens are no more interested in competitive contests than in noncompetitive ones, it suggests that the higher levels of political knowledge in the former have little to do with internal motivation on citizens' part and more to do with the particular information environment generated by the contests in their district or state. This finding might be somewhat disheartening to reformers who are interested in making elections more competitive, because they suggest that even though competitive elections might increase the ability

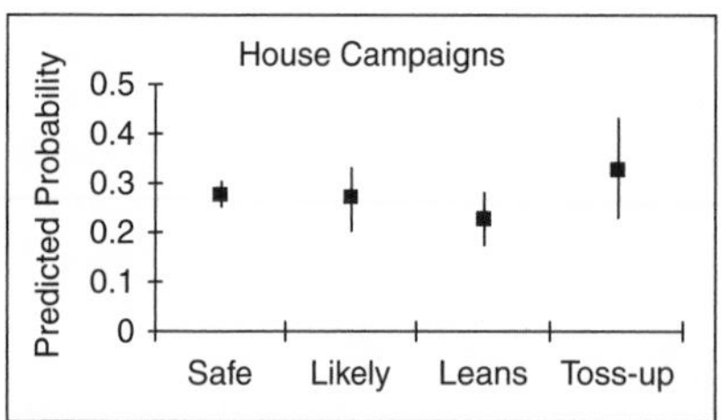

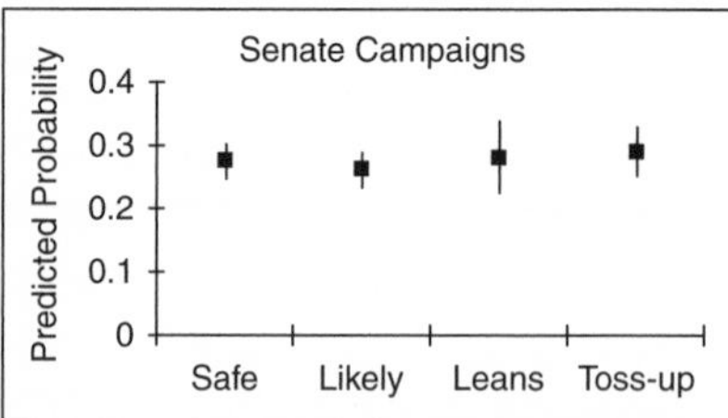

Figure 4.2. Effect of competitiveness on campaign interest in House and Senate elections. NES Cumulative File; Goldstein et al. 2002; Goldstein and Rivlin 2005, 2007. Vertical lines indicate upper and lower bounds of 95 percent confidence intervals. Full models can be found in Models 4 and 5 of Table A.4.

of voters to rate House and Senate candidates, there is no evidence that they "excite and enliven" the electorate. If citizens learn anything during a House or Senate election, it is because they passively absorb information from their environment.

Before moving on to determine whether it is the quantity or quality of information generated by competitive elections that matters more for voter learning, it is worth pausing for a moment to consider why such elections do not interest voters. One possibility is that voters may recognize that even though their House or Senate race is close, the chances of casting the deciding ballot in the election is still infinitesimal. Yet, this is a highly sophisticated line of reasoning for the average person. A second possibility is that voters are well aware that the election in their district or state is close, but other characteristics of close races, particularly their purported negativity, turn them off and erode their interest in the election. A meta-analytic study of the effects of campaign negativity, however, found no relationship between it and campaign interest (Lau et al. 2007).

What is more likely, although it may be difficult for some to believe, is that voters simply do not know that the race in their district or state is close. In a recent study, Robert Huckfeldt and his colleagues found that the perceived closeness of a House race is driven largely by partisan optimism, rather than the political realities in their district (2007: 805–6). A 2006 Pew study found that 71 percent of the voters in competitive House districts and 55 percent in safe districts said their race was close (Pew Research Center 2006). This is cautiously good news from the standpoint that people in closely contested districts were more likely to say their race was close, yet it is somewhat disconcerting that more than half of the people living in noncompetitive districts believed their race was a toss-up. In addition, 21 percent of the survey respondents admitted to not knowing their race's status. These studies suggest that many people really have no idea whether their House race is competitive, which explains why their interest is unmoved by electoral competitiveness. One might expect voters to be more aware of their Senate race's competitiveness, given the greater prominence of such contests. Yet the Pew study reveals their awareness is not much better. Although the percentage of people who recognized their race was not competitive was higher (55 versus 24 percent in the case of safe House districts), voters in states with a competitive Senate race were actually slightly less likely to recognize their state's status (69 versus 71 percent).

What this means is that those who promote reforms to enhance electoral competitiveness may want to think creatively about ways to educate voters about how close their races are. Volunteers participating in get-out-the-vote drives might be instructed to tell the people they are contacting that their race is one of the closest in the country, for example.[12] As this chapter and the others that follow will show, a voter does not have to be aware that their election is competitive for electoral competitiveness to affect their behavior, but it is possible that this awareness might lead to an extra boost in knowledge and participation.

Information Environment Quality and Voter Knowledge

If the richness of campaign information environments explains why voters learn from campaigns, especially those that are competitive, then the question is what characteristics of that information environment account for this learning. Is it the volume of information that matters or some qualitative characteristic of the information that matters more? It is also possible that a combination of quantity and quality aids learning because individuals are more likely to learn from good information if more of it is available. Recall that the relationship between electoral competitiveness and campaign knowledge that we explored earlier seemed to suggest that the salutary effects of competitiveness in House races leveled off and perhaps even declined in the most hotly contested ones. Competitiveness also appeared to yield diminishing returns for voter knowledge in Senate elections, although there was a significant jump in the ability of individuals to rate the candidates as the level of competitiveness increased from safe to modest, and then again from modest to moderate. The following analysis identifies which characteristics of the campaign information environment in competitive elections explain the peculiar twists and turns of these relationships. In doing so, it also identifies which characteristics of campaign information environments account for voter learning in general.

Voter Learning During House Campaigns

In the previous chapter, we saw that the information generated by competitive House races was more abundant, equal, diverse, and negative. In addition, candidates seemed to be more inclined to engage one another on issues as electoral outcomes became less certain. This section examines which of these information environment characteristics accounts for the ability of voters to rate their candidates and correctly identify incumbent ideology in competitive and moderately competitive contests. It also tries to explain why there is a drop-off in the ability of people to pin down their incumbent's ideology as House races become highly competitive.

Table 4.1 contains a series of regression models examining which information environment characteristics account for an individual's ability to rate House candidates on a feeling thermometer. The first model does not contain any of the information environment characteristic measures and serves as a baseline against which the subsequent models can be compared. In Models 2–6, I include the volume measure and each of the information environment measures. Then, in Models 7–10, I examine whether including an interaction term for the volume and quality measure improves the explanatory power of the model. Including such a term allows us to test the intuition that the benefits of equality, diversity, or dialogue will be felt more strongly at a higher volume of information.

In Table 4.1, we see that Model 1 explains 9.6 percent of the variation in the dependent variable. Models 2 through 6 reveal that the only measure that provides a significant explanatory boost to the model is information volume.[13] Including the measure in the model increases the explained variation to 10.3 percent. Perhaps more important, comparing the "likely" and toss-up race coefficients in Models 1 and 2 shows that including the volume measure soaks up most of their effect. This means that exposure to more information explains why people in moderately and highly competitive contests are better able to rate House candidates. As advertising volume increases from the 20th to the 80th percentile, the predicted probability of a person being able to rate both House candidates increases from .56 to .67. Surprisingly, none of the information quality measures appear to matter for this ability. The equality, dialogue, and negativity measures are all positive, but never achieve statistical significance.[14] This confirms how important it is for voters to receive information—any information—from the candidates and their supporters in House elections.

In Models 7, 8, 9, and 10, I test the intuition that the effects of information quality might be felt only at higher levels of advertising volume. Information must be received to affect its target, and higher levels of information increase the odds of reception. If this is the case, the direction of the interaction terms would be positive, indicating that the effect of both information quantity and quality receives a boost in the presence of the other. Yet, it is also possible that less information is needed when the information is of a higher quality. In this case, the coefficient for the quality measure would be positive and significant

Table 4.1. Effect of Information Environment Characteristics on Ability to Rate House Candidates

	Model 1	*Model 2*	*Model 3*	*Model 4*	*Model 5*	*Model 6*	*Model 7*	*Model 8*	*Model 9*	*Model 10*
Leans	.571***	.442***	.417***	.443***	.420***	.435***	.385**	.397**	.408**	.393**
	(.110)	(.119)	(.125)	(.119)	(.123)	(.119)	(.129)	(.124)	(.126)	(.124)
Likely	.621***	.274	.204	.271	.227	.252	.229	.160	.203	.206
	(.148)	(.182)	(.201)	(.188)	(.190)	(.186)	(.203)	(.201)	(.195)	(.189)
Toss-up	.556**	−.062	−.107	−.065	−.088	−.111	−.052	−.079	−.078	.033
	(.179)	(.250)	(.260)	(.257)	(.253)	(.261)	(.264)	(.264)	(.255)	(.274)
Volume	—	.014**	.013**	.013**	.012*	.014**	.024*	.019**	.017	.024**
		(.004)	(.004)	(.005)	(.005)	(.004)	(.011)	(.006)	(.012)	(.008)
Equality	—	—	.151	—	—	—	.266	—	—	—
			(.188)				(.208)			
Diversity	—	—	—	.003	—	—	—	.063	—	—
				(.036)				(.051)		
Dialogue	—	—	—	—	.272	—	—	—	.325	—
					(.280)				(.299)	
Negativity	—	—	—	—	—	.145	—	—	—	.319
						(.234)				(.266)
Volume*equality	—	—	—	—	—	—	−.018	—	—	—
							(.014)			
Volume*diversity	—	—	—	—	—	—	—	−.002	—	—
								(.001)		
Volume*dialogue	—	—	—	—	—	—	—	—	−.010	—
									(.020)	
Volume*negativity	—	—	—	—	—	—	—	—	—	−.031
										(.021)
N	**1,233**	**1,233**	**1,233**	**1,233**	**1,233**	**1,233**	**1,233**	**1,233**	**1,233**	**1,233**
Log likelihood	**−1036.83**	**−1029.67**	**−1029.28**	**−1029.13**	**−1029.67**	**−1029.34**	**−1028.13**	**−1028.10**	**−1028.94**	**−1027.91**
Pseudo-R^2	**.096**	**.103**	**.103**	**.103**	**.103**	**.103**	**.104**	**.104**	**.103**	**.104**

*** $p<0.001$; ** $p<0.01$; * $p<0.05$; # $p<0.1$; two-tailed. Sources: NES Cumulative File; Goldstein et al. 2002; Goldstein and Rivlin 2005, 2007. All models are estimated using ordered probit. The dependent variable is coded “2” if the respondent could rate both candidates, “1” if the respondent could rate one candidate, and “0” if neither. All the models control for standard demographic and political variables. See Table A.5 for the full models.

while the direction of the interaction term would be negative. Although the coefficients for all the measures of information quality in Models 7 through 10 are positive, none of them achieve statistical significance. The models that stand out are 7, 8, and 10 because including the interaction term in these models improves their overall fit. The equality coefficient is marginally significant using a one-tailed test, while the diversity and negativity coefficients just miss statistical significance. Overall, the models suggest that information quantity and quality may actually substitute for one other, that is, when advertising is more balanced, diverse, and negative, voters need less information to achieve the same increase in knowledge that a greater volume of poor information achieves.

Correctly Identifying House Incumbent Ideology

One common concern about increased electoral competitiveness is that it might provide candidates with an incentive to lie about their opponents. If this is the case, then competitive contests may provide voters with richer information environments in terms of information volume but poorer ones in terms of information quality. The findings of one study (Coleman and Manna 2000), which examines how increased spending affects voter knowledge in House races, suggest this possibility. The authors found that voters are less capable of correctly identifying an incumbent's ideology as challenger spending increases and concluded that challengers have an incentive to confuse voters about the incumbent's ideology as races become closer.[15] Coleman and Manna arrived at this conclusion by examining the effects of campaign spending on voter knowledge rather than any kind of advertising data.[16] The second graph in Figure 4.1 seems to confirm that what they found in the House elections of 1994 and 1996 still held in 2000 and 2004. The only difference is that the independent variable being used in the graph is a measure of electoral competitiveness rather than spending. Voter knowledge decreases in the most competitive contests, which are the ones in which challenger spending is the highest. The following analysis will determine whether challenger advertising is to blame, as Coleman and Manna suggested.

In addition to explaining the odd decline in voter knowledge that occurs in the most competitive House races, the results in Table 4.2 also help explain what accounts for the higher levels of knowledge in modest and moderately competitive contests in Figure 4.1. My first stage of explanation involves a similar approach to the one used in the previous section to explain the ability to rate House candidates. Table 4.2 contains a series of regression models that

Table 4.2. Effect of Information Environment Characteristics on Ability to Identify Incumbents' Ideology

	Model 1	*Model 2*	*Model 3*	*Model 4*	*Model 5*	*Model 6*	*Model 7*	*Model 8*	*Model 9*	*Model 10*	*Model 11*
Leans	.448#	.535#	.546#	.522#	.537#	.502#	.727*	.724*	.801**	.816**	.824**
	(.262)	(.293)	(.297)	(.292)	(.289)	(.287)	(.325)	(.315)	(.309)	(.299)	(.306)
Likely	1.125***	1.379**	1.409**	1.353**	.901	1.173*	1.207*	1.681***	1.953**	1.263**	.456
	(.315)	(.453)	(.482)	(.452)	(.688)	(.464)	(.520)	(.481)	(.690)	(.460)	(.528)
Toss-up	–.192	.184	.205	.169	–.400	–.204	–.037	.106	–.123	–1.180	–1.822#
	(.467)	(.588)	(.607)	(.587)	(.831)	(.625)	(.669)	(.653)	(.939)	(.885)	(1.029)
Volume	—	–.010	–.009	–.011	–.020	–.014	–.067*	–.083*	–.050**	–.067**	—
		(.012)	(.014)	(.015)	(.013)	(.013)	(.030)	(.034)	(.017)	(.021)	
Equality	—	—	–.068	—	—	—	–.681	—	—	—	—
			(.519)				(.581)				
Dialogue	—	—	—	.194	—	—	—	–.454	—	—	—
				(.763)				(.868)			
Diversity	—	—	—	—	.182	—	—	—	–.196	—	—
					(.179)				(.193)		
Negativity	—	—	—	—	—	1.062	—	—	—	.280	—
						(.693)				(.739)	
Volume*equality	—	—	—	—	—	—	.095*	—	—	—	—
							(.042)				
Volume*dialogue	—	—	—	—	—	—	—	.145*	—	—	—
								(.064)			
Volume*diversity	—	—	—	—	—	—	—	—	.008***	—	—
									(.003)		
Volume*negativity	—	—	—	—	—	—	—	—	—	.162**	—
										(.058)	

Incumbent attack	—	—	—	—	—	—	—	—	—	—	−.013 (.075)
Challenger attack	—	—	—	—	—	—	—	—	—	—	.139** (.053)
Incumbent contrast	—	—	—	—	—	—	—	—	—	—	−.035 (.070)
Challenger contrast	—	—	—	—	—	—	—	—	—	—	.206* (.088)
Incumbent positive	—	—	—	—	—	—	—	—	—	—	−.083* (.042)
Challenger positive	—	—	—	—	—	—	—	—	—	—	−.078 (.085)
Intercept	−3.03** (.983)	−3.07** (1.003)	−3.07** (1.001)	−3.04** (1.006)	−3.24** (1.035)	−3.13** (.987)	−3.18** (1.073)	−2.82** (1.024)	−2.91** (1.038)	−3.19*** (.966)	−3.53*** (1.031)
N	**709**	**709**	**709**	**709**	**709**	**709**	**709**	**709**	**709**	**709**	**709**
Log likelihood	**−369.34**	**−368.85**	**−368.84**	**−368.81**	**−368.07**	**−367.59**	**−364.53**	**−365.38**	**−362.20**	**−363.00**	**−355.39**
Pseudo-R^2	**.085**	**.087**	**.087**	**.087**	**.089**	**.090**	**.098**	**.095**	**.103**	**.101**	**.120**

*** $p<0.001$; ** $p<0.01$; * $p<0.05$; # $p<0.1$; two-tailed. Sources: NES Cumulative File; Goldstein et al. 2002; Goldstein and Rivlin 2005, 2007. All models are estimated using logit regression and control for standard demographic and political variables. See Table A.6 for the full models. The dependent variable for all models is the ability to correctly identify an incumbent's ideology with "Don't know" coded as "incorrect" or "0."

include each of the information environment characteristics and interaction terms between volume and different quality indicators.[17]

Given the findings of the previous section, I expect information volume to increase knowledge, and given Coleman and Manna's argument, information negativity to decrease it. Yet Table 4.2 reveals that the coefficient for advertising volume is always negative and occasionally significantly so.[18] Moreover, in Model 6 negativity appears to have a positive effect on knowledge, albeit one that barely misses statistical significance. In terms of the other variables of interest, Models 4, 5, and 6 seem to demonstrate that equality, diversity, and dialogue do not have a significant independent effect on the ability of respondents to place an incumbent's ideology. Thus, Models 1 through 6 suggest that campaign information—even its volume—does not matter much for voter knowledge one way or the other.

Models 7 through 10 tell a different story, however. They all suggest that campaign information can help or harm voter knowledge depending on its content. The positive direction of the interaction terms in Models 7, 8, 9, and 10 indicates that House advertisements that are one-sided, lack diversity, refrain from engaging in dialogue, or are positive will harm a survey respondent's ability to identify the incumbent's ideology. In Model 7, the -.067 coefficient for the volume measure represents its effect when campaign information presents just one party's views. Recall that a House race scores "0" on equality if only one party's views are presented and, in almost every instance, indicates that only the views of the incumbent's party are being presented. Thus, one can interpret the negative coefficient for advertising volume in Model 7 as an indication of what happens when only the incumbent's views are represented; respondents are misled about the incumbent's ideology. This is the first finding suggesting that deceptive challenger advertising is not the cause of the odd decline in voter knowledge we saw in the most competitive races. The positive interaction term in Model 7 indicates that as equality increases, that is, as the views of the challenger's party are represented more equally, the negative coefficient for advertising volume gets smaller and eventually disappears completely when equality reaches .40 (its 70th percentile). Similarly, the interactions in Models 8 and 9 indicate that the negative effect of advertising volume disappears when the number of individuals or organizations sponsoring ads exceeds three (its 95th percentile) or when the dialogue level reaches .40 (its 90th percentile). Model 10 shows that negativity has an even stronger positive interaction with volume, as illustrated in Figure 4.3. When a respondent is exposed to no negative advertising, the coefficient for the volume measure indicates that her ability to identify an incumbent's ideology declines significantly. The predicted probability that a respondent can correctly identify an incumbent's ideology when there is no negative advertising hovers around .30 at a very low level of advertising and declines precipitously as the volume of advertising increases such that the predicted probability is less than .10 when the volume exceeds 2,000 ads. The middle line in Figure 4.3 shows that at a moderate level of negativity—approximately 30 percent—the negative effect of ad volume is no longer significant. When the proportion of negative advertising exceeds 60 percent, however, the effect of ad volume actually becomes significantly positive. The top line illustrates how the predicted probability of correctly identifying an incumbent's ideology responds to an increase in ad volume when the proportion of negative ads is 60 percent. At 0 ads, the predicted probability is .31, increasing to .34 at 500 ads and .46 at 2,000 ads. Thus, all these models suggest that the edifying effect of advertising in House races crucially hinges on the quality of information provided and that negative information is a form of quality information.

In the final model of Table 4.2, I confirm the finding that deception in challenger ads is not the cause of the dip in knowledge that occurs in the most competitive House races by using the most straightforward measure possible: the number of challenger attack ads. The model also includes measures of the number of positive and contrast challenger ads, as well as the number of

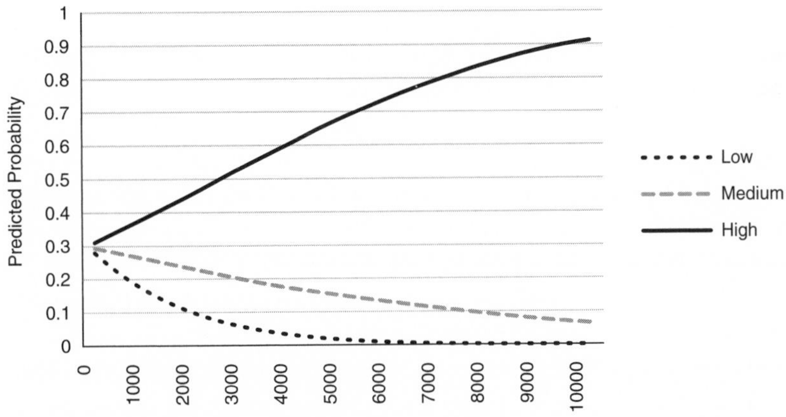

Figure 4.3. Effect of advertising volume on the ability to rate House candidates at low, medium, and high levels of negativity. NES Cumulative File; Goldstein et al. 2002; Goldstein and Rivlin 2005, 2007.

positive, contrast, and attack incumbent ads.[19] The analysis once again confirms that challenger attack ads do not harm knowledge. In fact, they appear to be quite helpful. As the number of challenger attack ads increases from 0 to 500, the predicted probability of correctly identifying an incumbent's ideology increases from .20 to .34.[20] Challenger contrast ads are even more helpful for voters. As the number of contrast ads increases from 0 to 500, the predicted probability of a respondent offering a correct response more than doubles from .20 to .47. Thus, contrary to Coleman and Manna's argument, I find no evidence that challenger communications deceive voters. In fact, I find evidence that incumbent communications do. Model 11 indicates that positive incumbent ads actually have a significant negative effect on knowledge. As the number of these ads increases from 0 to 500, the predicted probability of correctly identifying their ideology declines from .30 to .23.[21]

Despite the fact that this analysis exonerates challenger advertising, the astute reader will notice that the deficiency in knowledge among the residents of toss-up districts persists. In fact, when one accounts for the beneficial effects of challenger ads, the knowledge dip among these residents is even greater (given that challenger ads are more frequent in toss-up races). Thus, the findings of this analysis cannot fully explain the pattern first observed by Coleman and Manna. The findings, however, do shed light on why knowledge in moderately competitive races is so high. Notice that the coefficient for "likely" races in Model 11 is an insignificant .46. In Model 1, it is a highly significant 1.13, which means that contrast and attack challenger ads account for the majority of the moderately competitive race effect.[22]

If challenger ads are not the culprit, what is? Coleman and Manna believed it was challenger spending on deceptive communications. Since the majority of House races do not feature television ads, it is possible that other forms of challenger communications are misleading voters. House candidates use a variety of media to communicate with voters, including radio and newspaper advertisements, billboards, and mass mailings. In contrast to television ads, which are visible and for which the sponsoring organization must take credit, many of these communications fly below the radar of the local media, making it easier for candidates to use them in nefarious ways. Direct mail, in particular, is notorious for its deceptiveness. Perhaps such media explain the toss-up race effect. Unfortunately, it is extremely difficult—if not impossible—to collect data on these forms of communication. Thus, the mystery of what suppresses knowledge in the most competitive House races remains unsolved. This analysis has eliminated one obvious suspect, but others remain.

This study of voter knowledge in House races has shown that even though voters who are exposed to highly competitive House races might feel more confident about rating the candidates, voters exposed to moderately competitive House races actually know more about them. Moderately competitive House contests then appear to offer the right combination of information quantity and quality to voters. The study also shows that, although a high volume of advertising might ensure that voters can offer a judgment about their House candidates, that judgment will not be informed unless the information communicated is balanced, diverse, involves dialogue, and is—perhaps surprisingly—highly negative.

Rating Senate Candidates

As we saw earlier in this chapter, voters' ability to rate Senate candidates is significantly higher in moderately and highly competitive contests than in those that are safe or modestly competitive.[23] In Chapter 3, information volume and equality seemed to exhibit a similar relationship with competitiveness: the biggest jump in these two measures occurred between likely and leans states. Thus, we might expect these two measures to explain increasing knowledge. We also saw in the analysis in the previous section that volume increased the ability of voters to rate House candidates. Yet there are reasons to believe that the quality of information might matter much more than the quantity of information for the gains in knowledge associated with electoral competitiveness in the context of Senate campaigns. People are generally much more familiar with Senate than House candidates because the individuals running for statewide office typically have made a name for themselves in the state already. Between 2000 and 2006, 72 percent of NES respondents in states with a Senate race were able to rate both candidates on a feeling thermometer, while only 51 percent were able to rate both House candidates. In addition, campaign information on Senate races is much more widely available than on House races for a variety of factors. First, Senate candidates are simply better funded than House candidates, enabling them to communicate more with voters. During the years examined, the average Senate candidate spent twice as much per voter as the average House candidate did ($4.25 versus $2.07). In addition, local news organizations may feel statewide races are more worthy of coverage than House races, particularly if their audience spans more than one congressional district (Althaus and Trautman 2008). Because the name recognition of Senate candidates is so high and information about them so pervasive, the additional information provided by a general election campaign may have much less impact on this measure of knowledge than it would during a House race. This means that the availability of better information, as opposed to more information, may be more consequential for voter knowledge in Senate contests.

Here I use the same approach as I did with the House knowledge measures; I estimated a series of models that included the volume measure along with each measure of information quality. In addition, I estimated a series of models that included an interaction between advertising volume and the information quality measure of interest. Just as expected, the analysis reveals that information quality matters more than information quantity in Senate elections. Dialogue and negativity, in particular, play a significant role in boosting the ability of voters to rate Senate candidates.

In Model 1, we see that a regression model with no campaign information environment measures explains 12 percent of the variation in the ability of respondents to judge Senate candidates.[24] Adding the volume measure in Model 2 does not boost the explanatory power of the model, nor does it explain any of the "likely" or "toss-up" race effect. In fact, their coefficients increase slightly because the volume measure has a small negative effect on knowledge. Equality appears to aid knowledge significantly in Model 3, but the effect disappears in Model 7 when the other measures of information quality are included in the model.[25] Models 4, 6, and 7 suggest that diversity and negativity have no effect on knowledge, while dialogue stands out as the information quality measure that matters most, boosting the explained variation in the dependent variable to nearly 13 percent in Model 5. It continues to have a significantly positive effect on knowledge even when the other information quality measures are added in Model 7. Based on the .82 coefficient in Model 7, the predicted probability of being able to rate both candidates increases from .70 to .83 as the measure of dialogue increases from the 20th to the 80th percentile. From the standpoint of trying to understand why competitive elections boost the ability of voters to rate Senate candidates, however, the advertising dialogue measure stands out because including it in the model explains nearly half the effect on knowledge in moderately competitive elections and approximately a fifth of the effect in toss-up elections.

In Models 8 through 11, the volume and information quality measures are interacted to determine if the benefits of information quality are felt at higher or lower levels of advertising. Two substantive interactions occur between information volume and dialogue and between information volume

Table 4.3. Effect of Information Environment Characteristics on Ability to Rate Senate Candidates

	Model 1	*Model 2*	*Model 3*	*Model 4*	*Model 5*	*Model 6*	*Model 7*	*Model 8*	*Model 9*	*Model 10*	*Model 11*
Leans	.136	.148#	.081	.119	−.071	.146#	−.088	.029	.092	.131	.167*
	(.084)	(.085)	(.091)	(.085)	(.104)	(.085)	(.104)	(.104)	(.093)	(.112)	(.085)
Likely	.505***	.539***	.333#	.497***	.288#	.502**	.301	.294	.453**	.461**	.497**
	(.126)	(.142)	(.175)	(.144)	(.167)	(.160)	(.187)	(.183)	(.169)	(.167)	(.157)
Toss-up	.752***	.835***	.633***	.697***	.603**	.807***	.532*	.654***	.669***	.806***	.793***
	(.091)	(.157)	(.184)	(.178)	(.186)	(.168)	(.208)	(.189)	(.191)	(.193)	(.165)
Volume	—	−.001	−.001	−.001	−.001	−.001	−.001	.001	−.001	−.008***	−.004*
		(.001)	(.001)	(.001)	(.001)	(.001)	(.001)	(.002)	(.002)	(.002)	(.002)
Equality	—	—	.379*	—	—	—	−.002	.562*	—	—	—
			(.172)				(.209)	(.245)			
Diversity	—	—	—	.034	—	—	.026	—	.049	—	—
				(.023)			(.022)		(.034)		
Dialogue	—	—	—	—	.834***	—	.820**	—	—	−.198	—
					(.232)		(.274)			(.296)	
Negativity	—	—	—	—	—	.165	−.181	—	—	—	−.454
						(.273)	(.291)				(.389)
Volume*equality	—	—	—	—	—	—	—	−.003	—	—	—
								(.003)			
Volume*diversity	—	—	—	—	—	—	—	—	−.0001	—	—
									(.0002)		
Volume*dialogue	—	—	—	—	—	—	—	—	—	.016***	—
										(.003)	
Volume*negativity	—	—	—	—	—	—	—	—	—	—	.013*
											(.006)
N	**2,285**	**2,285**	**2,285**	**2,285**	**2,285**	**2,285**	**2,285**	**2,285**	**2,285**	**2,285**	**2,285**
Log likelihood	**−1501.10**	**−1500.87**	**−1497.98**	**−1498.68**	**−1491.06**	**−150061**	**−1489.84**	**−1497.18**	**−1498.44**	**−1473.67**	**−1497.72**
Pseudo-R^2	**.123**	**.123**	**.125**	**.125**	**.129**	**.124**	**.130**	**.126**	**.125**	**.139**	**.125**

*** $p<0.001$; ** $p<0.01$; * $p<0.05$; # $p<0.1$; two-tailed. Sources: NES Cumulative File; Goldstein et al. 2002; Goldstein and Rivlin 2005, 2007. All models are estimated using ordered probit regression and include controls for standard demographic and political variables. See Table A.6 for the full models. The dependent variable is coded “2” if the respondent could rate both candidates, “1” if the respondent could rate one candidate, and “0” if neither.

and negativity.[26] The significantly negative coefficients for volume in Models 10 and 11 indicate that a high volume of advertising that is bereft of dialogue or negativity actually harms the ability of voters to rate candidates.

The two charts in Figure 4.4 illustrate the impact of advertising on respondents at different levels of dialogue and negativity. The first chart shows how the predicted probability of being able to rate both candidates in a Senate race changes as the volume of advertising increases. The lower line indicates the effect of increased advertising when the candidates talk past one another (dialogue = 0), while the middle and top lines show the predicted probabilities at moderate and high levels of dialogue.[27] I used the 50th and 80th percentiles of dialogue, .35 and .60 respectively, to calculate the predicted probabilities at moderate and high levels of dialogue. The first chart in Figure 4.4 clearly demonstrates citizens find it more difficult to rate the candidates when they talk past one another in their advertising. The solid black line shows that the

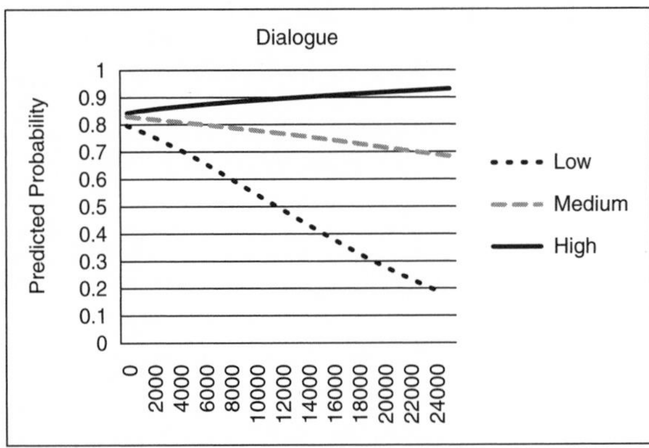

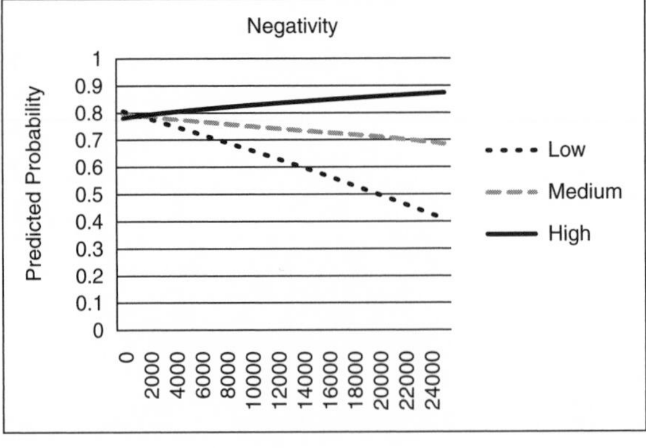

Figure 4.4. Effect of advertising volume on the ability to rate Senate candidates at low, medium, and high levels of dialogue and negativity.

candidates' advertising must feature a high level of dialogue for it to help voters judge candidates.

The second chart in Figure 4.4 indicates that a similar interaction occurs between advertising volume and negativity, although the substantive effect on the ability to rate Senate candidates is considerably weaker. Again, the three lines show how the predicted probability of being able to rate both Senate candidates in a race changes as advertising increases at low, medium, and high levels of negativity. To calculate these predicted probabilities, the 20th, 50th, and 80th percentiles of negativity were used, 0, .20, and .40 respectively. The bottom line (dotted gray) indicates that positive advertising has a significantly negative effect on the ability of people to rate the candidates. A high level of negativity changes the direction of the volume measure's coefficient in a positive direction, although it does not achieve statistical significance. Further analysis reveals that only when the proportion of negative advertising hits extremely high levels—above 60 percent—does volume have a significantly positive effect on voter knowledge. In Chapter 3, we saw that approximately 8 percent of all ads involve attacks in safe races, versus approximately 25 percent in "leans" and 30 percent in "likely" and "toss-up" contests. According to this analysis, the level of negativity that increased competitiveness produces in Senate contests ensures that advertising does not harm the ability of voters to rate candidates.[28]

Conclusion

Chapter 3 showed that even modest amounts of electoral competitiveness generate campaign information environments that we should care about from a normative perspective. In this chapter, we have explored whether these information characteristics actually have a positive impact on voter knowledge, because it cannot be assumed that they do. Aside from the anomaly of toss-up House races, the analysis confirms that electoral competitiveness boosts levels of political knowledge among voters. The unique contribution of this analysis has been to show that these higher levels of knowledge are the result of not only more but higher quality information, specifically, information that exhibits characteristics that are desirable from a normative perspective. The analysis of two of the three dependent variables shows that advertising bereft of dialogue actually harms voter knowledge. In the case of identifying a House incumbent's ideology, advertising that is one-sided or lacking in diversity is also harmful. Although negativity is rarely lauded by normative theorists, the analysis in this chapter suggests that it is a vital characteristic of a high quality information environment. In fact, the findings suggest that voters would benefit from even more attack advertising in campaigns.

The analysis in this chapter leaves two questions unanswered. The first is why certain forms of knowledge take a nosedive in highly competitive House races. We have exonerated one suspect—misleading challenger attack ads—but the question remains. The other puzzle is why certain qualities of the information environment matter for knowledge of House races and not for Senate races, or vice versa. The goal of this chapter was to confirm that electoral competitiveness contributes to higher levels of knowledge among the public and to understand the features of the campaign information environment that are responsible for those higher levels of knowledge. Thus, the question why information volume, for instance, might matter in House races but not Senate races is beyond the scope of this analysis. Yet it is an area of study that calls for more attention since this analysis has made it quite clear that campaign information effects cannot always be generalized across different types of elections. The analysis of advertising in presidential campaigns presented next will further reinforce this point.

CHAPTER 5

Competitiveness and Campaign Knowledge in a Presidential Election

The information environments generated by presidential elections are incredibly rich compared to those in congressional contests and other down-ticket races. In addition to the information generated by major campaign events such as the conventions and debates, presidential candidates and their supporters have far more resources for communicating with voters than down-ticket candidates do. For example, in the 2008 presidential race, John McCain and Barack Obama spent nearly as much on their campaigns as all the U.S. House and Senate candidates did combined.[1] Layered on top of the presidential campaign efforts are those by national media organizations who doggedly report every twist and turn of the race and local media who are quick to report on candidate or surrogate (e.g., vice presidential candidates, spouses, or major advisors) visits to their home state. As if this were not enough, voters must also process the constant chatter about the election by family, friends, and coworkers. For this reason, voters are generally more knowledgeable about presidential candidates than any other kind of political candidate.

The fact that voters are exposed to higher levels of political information during presidential campaigns is relevant for our discussion of competitiveness. Since it is virtually impossible for an American to avoid information about the candidates during a general election campaign, most voters will find it difficult *not* to learn something during the election season. These higher levels of knowledge across the country might mean that the extra information heaped on voters in more competitive states will add little to what they already know. The analysis in Chapter 3 demonstrated, however, that moderately and highly competitive states do have significantly richer campaign information environments than those that are safe or modestly competitive. Voters in battleground states may also be more interested in the campaign. If they are, the combination of more information and more interest may work together to produce higher levels of knowledge in battleground states despite the steep rise in knowledge across the country generally.

Competitiveness and Campaign Knowledge in Presidential Elections

Although there is a considerable amount of research demonstrating that the residents of presidential battleground states are more knowledgeable than the residents of non-battleground states, there is no consensus on how important this difference is (Wolak 2006; Benoit et al. 2004). The knowledge-gap argument has been made by simply categorizing survey respondents as living in a battleground state or not and then comparing campaign knowledge across those categories. It has also been made by examining the effects of political advertising in presidential elections, finding that ads promote knowledge, and then arguing that if ads promote knowledge and more advertisements are aired in battleground states then the residents of battleground states must be more knowledgeable. Although it is probably safe to assume that swing state residents are more knowledgeable than the residents of other states, we need to know more. First, it would be helpful to understand when this gap forms during a campaign and to confirm that it endures through Election Day. For example, it may be that the gap in campaign knowledge opens up in late September and early October but disappears by November. If the gap no longer exists or is substantively small on Election Day, is there any reason to be worried about it? Second, is the knowledge difference large enough to be of concern? For instance, how does it compare to the general rise in knowledge that occurs nationally over the course of a campaign?

Most of these studies use the National Election Study survey for their analysis. Although the NES is a well-designed and well-executed survey, it is not the best for capturing the day-to-day dynamics of a campaign because it typically surveys fewer than 1,500 people nationally during the entire election season. In contrast, the National Annenberg Election study interviews approximately 300 people nationally every day of the general election campaign. This makes it possible to see how the difference in campaign knowledge that has been observed between the residents of battleground and non-battleground states evolves over the course of the election.

In addition to gaining a better understanding of how the relationship between state competitiveness and voter knowledge evolves during presidential elections, this analysis will provide readers with a sense of how concerned they should be about any knowledge gap that might be observed. Opponents of the Electoral College (EC) base their arguments in part on the fact that the EC encourages presidential candidates to focus their attention almost exclusively on battleground states and to ignore the residents of states that are not in play. Any study that identifies a large and substantively significant gap in knowledge between the residents of battleground and non-battleground states would bolster their arguments. The handful of studies that have explicitly addressed this question, however, have offered contradictory opinions on the matter. One study of the 2000 presidential election seems to support the arguments of EC opponents. After analyzing NES data and discovering that the issue knowledge levels of battleground state residents are indeed higher than those of non-battleground state residents, the study's authors conclude that the "Electoral College may have unintended deleterious effects on democracy. Eliminating the archaic institution of the Electoral College could have beneficial effects on our representative democracy" (Benoit et al. 2004: 187).

Yet a more recent study that also finds a difference in knowledge levels between the residents of battleground and non-battleground states concludes that the difference is not big enough to be cause for concern. It describes the effects of presidential campaign intensity as "limited" and argues that those "living in noncompetitive states are not as disadvantaged in activation and engagement as media reports might suggest" (Wolak 2006: 360). Clearly, this is a question that has not been resolved.

Accounting for the Knowledge Gap

If the difference in campaign knowledge between the residents of battleground and non-battleground states is sufficiently high to be cause for concern, then the next question is what accounts for this difference. Does the higher volume of information that floods the media markets of swing state residents account for the difference, or does some other aspect of the information environment matter more? For example, in Chapter 3, we learned that the diversity and equality of information, as well as the level of dialogue, are also much higher in moderately and highly competitive races. Perhaps one of these characteristics, or even the interaction of one of these characteristics with a higher volume of information, accounts for the difference. If the knowledge gap turns out to be of little consequence, however, the question then becomes, why is the difference so small given the incredible richness of campaign information environments in battleground states? Answering either question will require examining how the different characteristics of campaign advertising affect voter knowledge.

As in the previous chapter, I will examine how information volume, equality, diversity, negativity, and campaign dialogue affect voter knowledge in an effort to understand whether quantity or quality of information has a greater impact on voters. In the previous chapter, I discussed why the various information characteristics might be beneficial for knowledge in congressional elections. Is there any reason to expect them to affect presidential campaign knowledge differently? One thing that is different about presidential campaigns is that most voters are familiar—sometimes quite familiar—with the candidates. The other difference is that there is an abundance of information available about presidential candidates aside from the information generated by candidates and their supporters. I would argue that both of these differences should reduce the impact of information volume on voter knowledge. If voters already know a considerable amount of basic information about the candidates, only new information that is relatively sophisticated and substantively rich should make a difference. Moreover, if information is abundant, as it often is in presidential elections, then hearing more information should not matter as much as hearing higher quality information.

Data and Methods

In this chapter, I use the 2004 Annenberg rolling cross-sectional national survey to assess the effect of electoral competitiveness, and campaign information environments more generally, on individual-level political knowledge in presidential elections. The general purpose of the Annenberg surveys is to gain a better understanding of presidential campaign dynamics by providing scholars with a daily assessment of how media exposure and other kinds of communication affect the knowledge, beliefs, and behavior of voters (Romer et al. 2004). Between October 2003 and November 2004, more than 100,000 people were surveyed, with daily samples of approximately 300. The rolling cross section design, large sample size, and duration in the field make it ideal for tracking changes over time, and for the purposes of this analysis, a more appropriate dataset for gauging campaign effects than the National Election Study.

I merged the Annenberg dataset with data on television advertising collected by the Campaign Media Analysis Group (CMAG). In 2004, CMAG monitored ads in the top 100 local media markets. Because CMAG's monitoring does not cover all media markets, however, approximately 15 percent of the Annenberg sample does not live in a media market monitored by CMAG. Although the non-CMAG markets are more likely to be in a noncompetitive state, there is no reason to believe that ads will affect the political knowledge of respondents differently in markets monitored by CMAG and those that are not.

As in Chapter 4, I use several different measures of the campaign information environments generated by the 2004 presidential general election in each media market, including the total numbers of ads aired, the number of unique sponsors airing ads, the equality of ads aired in terms of volume, the amount of dialogue that occurred between Democratic and Republican interests, and the proportion of the ads that were negative. To take advantage of the Annenberg survey's rolling cross-sectional design, I used a measure that captured the level of each measure during the previous week.[2] Thus, to create the volume of information measure, I counted the total number of ads aired by the candidates, the parties and their supporters in the previous week. For the diversity measure, I counted all the individuals and organizations—including parties—sponsoring ads during the previous seven days. The equality of information measure reflects the ratio of ad airings in favor of one candidate to ad airings in favor of the other in a given media market during the previous week, while the measure of negativity reflects the proportion of all advertising in the previous week that was devoted to attacking the opponent.

To create the dialogue measure, I used the same method employed in Chapter 3, but instead of calculating the amount of dialogue occurring over the entire general election campaign, I calculated the amount of dialogue occurring in a respondent's media market in the week prior to their interview. To the best of my knowledge, this is the first time a dynamic measure of candidate dialogue has been used in any study. Until now, researchers studying political campaigns have calculated a measure of candidate dialogue for an entire campaign (Kaplan et al. 2006; Sigelman and Buell 2004; Simon 2002). A dynamic measure is preferable for the simple reason that candidates and their supporters may discuss an issue at any point during a campaign and not necessarily at the same time. A dynamic measure can capture this, while one that calculates issue convergence for an entire campaign cannot. Imagine that two candidates in a campaign spend 20 percent of their time talking about their plans for Medicare, but one focuses on the topic in September while the other discusses it in October. Noah Kaplan and Travis Ridout (2007) find that it takes a candidate an average of 39 days to respond to an opponent on a given issue in Senate races, with response time ranging widely from 1 to 234 days (15). Response times would very likely be shorter in presidential campaigns, but they could be substantial nonetheless. Only the politically sophisticated, who possess the resources to store and retain political information for long periods of time, will be able to compare and contrast the candidates' positions over long periods of time. This is why using a dynamic measure of dialogue makes more sense.

Using a lagged version of the equality, negativity, and dialogue measures raises an interesting question. How should we treat weeks in which there was no advertising? Should seven days in which there was no advertising be coded the same as seven days in which only one side advertised? In other words, should they both be coded as "0"? Because I am theoretically interested in comparing the effects of one- and two-sided information flows, I have chosen to code weeks in which there was no advertising as missing and, thus, to exclude them from my analysis of how information equality affects knowledge. Similarly, I have opted to exclude respondents whose media market saw no advertising in the previous week from the analysis of the effects of negativity and dialogue.[3]

One of the strengths of the Annenberg survey for measuring campaign effects on political knowledge is that it asks respondents to identify the candidates' positions across a wide range of issues each day, allowing researchers to assess how individuals acquire knowledge about the candidates across the duration of the campaign cycle.[4] I restricted my analysis to five issue knowledge measures, which were asked during the entirety of the general election campaign. These questions covered a variety of issues that were actually discussed by the candidates. Each asked the respondent the question in the following format: "To the best of your knowledge . . . George W. Bush, John Kerry, both or neither?"

- who favors the federal government helping to pay for health insurance for all children and helping employers pay the cost of workers' health insurance . . .
- who favors changing the recently passed Medicare prescription drug law to allow re-importing drugs from Canada
- who favors eliminating tax breaks for overseas profits of American

corporations and using the money to cut taxes for businesses that create jobs in the United States
- who favors making the recent tax cuts permanent
- during the presidential campaign, who is urging Congress to extend the federal law banning assault weapons

Each measure was coded "1" if respondents answered the question correctly and "0" if they answered it incorrectly or responded "Don't know" to the question. More than half the respondents were able to answer each of these questions correctly: 56 percent knew that Kerry favored the federal government helping children and workers pay for health insurance, 57 percent knew he favored allowing the re-importation of drugs from Canada, and 53 percent knew he also favored eliminating tax breaks for overseas profits. Given the popularity of Bush's 2001 and 2003 tax cuts, it is not surprising that considerably more respondents—66 percent—knew that he favored making those cuts permanent. Finally, 55 percent knew that Kerry wanted Congress to extend the Assault Weapons Ban. [5]

The analysis will examine how the competitiveness of a respondent's state affected their ability to answer each of these questions individually. It also examines how it affected their ability to answer these questions in tandem by creating an index ranging from 0 to 5 from the five questions. The distribution of the index is slightly skewed toward the upper end of the range with 7 percent scoring zero on the scale, 13 percent scoring "1," 19 percent scoring "2," 22 percent scoring "3," 23 percent scoring "4," and 16 percent receiving a perfect score.[6] Perhaps the best way to think of this measure is as an indicator of how generally knowledgeable a person is about the candidates' issue positions.

The following analysis controls for a range of independent variables that mirror those used in the previous chapter, including age, sex, education, race, partisan identification, strength of partisanship, and the number of days remaining until the election. I also expect knowledge of presidential issue positions to be elevated during the weeks of the campaign that featured televised debates. To control for this effect, I created a dummy variable for the period that began on the day following the first debate (October 1) and ended seven days after the final debate (October 20). As the reader will soon learn, political interest and consumption of news media vary across battleground and non-battleground states. Thus, I have left these measures out of the initial analysis to capture the full effect of electoral competitiveness on voter knowledge.

Competitiveness and Presidential Campaign Knowledge

In Chapter 3, we saw that presidential campaign information quantity and quality were significantly higher only in the most competitive states, that is, those that lean toward a party or are considered battleground states. Over the course of a presidential general election campaign, then, we might expect voter knowledge to start out at similar levels across all states and then to diverge as residents of competitive states reap the rewards of their richer information environments. In Figure 5.1, the first five graphs show how the ability to answer the specific knowledge questions changes over the course of the campaign for respondents living in each category of state. Only in one case, which candidate favors re-importing drugs from Canada, do we see something approaching the pattern we might expect. On June 1, the percentage of residents living in each kind of state who can answer the question correctly hovers around 40 percent. As the campaign progresses, more and more respondents in every state can answer the question correctly, but by the end of the campaign those living in battleground and moderately competitive states are significantly more capable of answering the question correctly than those in less competitive states.

The stories are very different in the four other graphs. In the case of the ability to identify which candidates support eliminating overseas tax breaks and federal support for health insurance, knowledge is higher in battleground states for much of the campaign while the knowledge of people in "leans" states tends to look more like the knowledge levels of those in less competitive states. In the case of the Assault Weapons Ban question, the ability to answer it correctly remains remarkably flat during the entire campaign in all states, increasing slightly in the last month of the campaign in battleground states. Finally, the ability to identify Bush as the candidate who wants to make his earlier tax cuts permanent starts out high and remains relatively flat until the end of the campaign when it declines, strangely enough, in safe states and battleground states.

Why doesn't electoral competitiveness affect all these knowledge measures in a similar fashion? The answer almost certainly has to do with when and how much the issue was specifically discussed in the media markets of each type of state. At times when the ability to answer the question appears to increase equally across the country, it may mean that the national news media are discussing the issue. If there is improvement in one or two categories of states—most likely the most competitive ones—then it means that

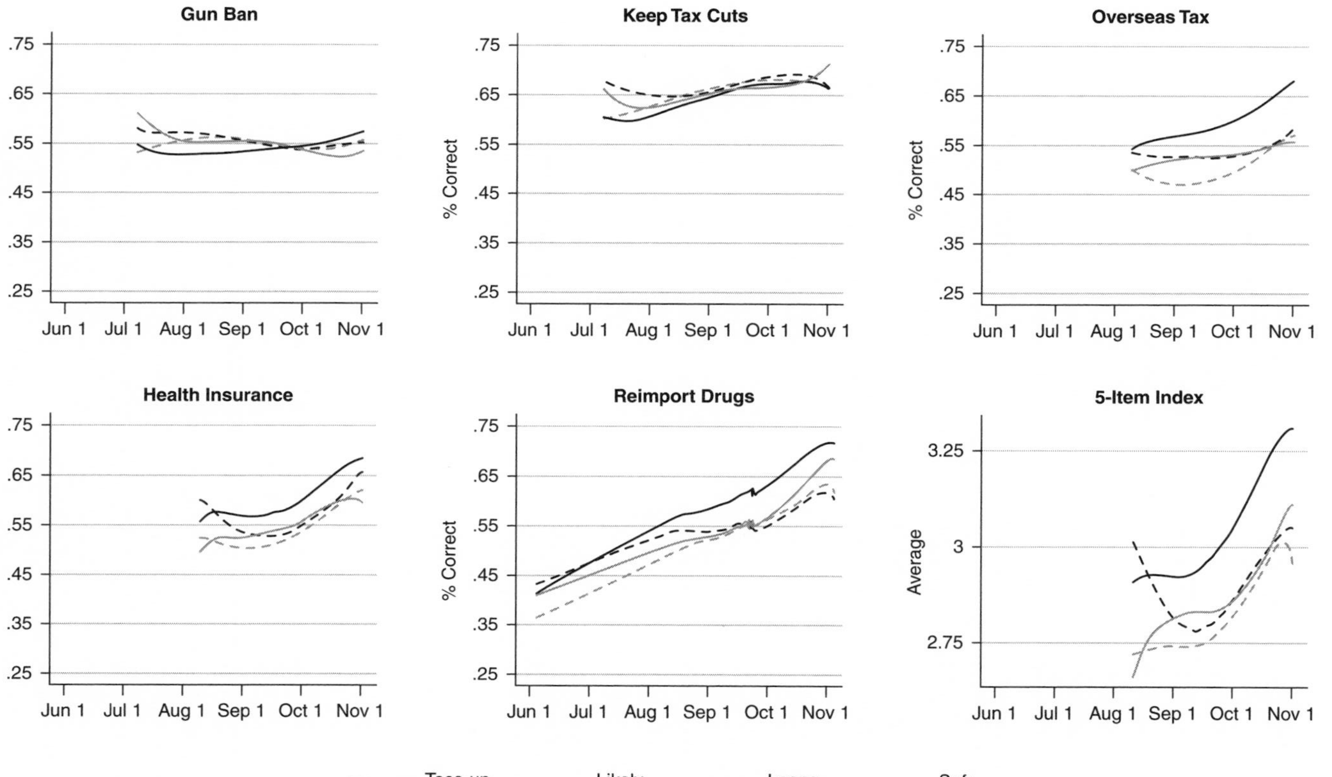

Figure 5.1. Knowledge of candidate issue positions by state competitiveness in the 2004 presidential election. Solid black line = "Toss-up"; solid gray line = "Likely"; dashed black line = "Leans"; dashed gray line = "Safe." 2004 National Annenberg Election Study; Goldstein et al. 2002; Goldstein and Rivlin 2005, 2007. Generated using lowess (bandwidth = .8).

locally available news and information sources in those states are focusing on the issue. For example, one or both of the candidates may be airing advertisements about the same issue in key media markets. It is also possible that the candidates and their surrogates are touring competitive states and discussing the same issue, which would be communicated to voters through their local television and radio news programs. A number of reasons might explain why knowledge about a given issue declines in one category of states and not others. This occurs in the case of the question concerning which candidate supports extending recent tax cuts. In this case, the ability to answer the question appears to decline rather precipitously in safe states and battleground states at the same time. It is possible that the candidates stopped discussing the issue because they decided to focus on other issues. It is also possible that the voters are being confused or possibly even deceived by whatever information they are receiving about the issue.

In the final graph in Figure 5.1, I chart how the ability to answer all five of the questions, which I am using as a measure of general campaign knowledge, changes over the campaign in each category of state. In August, respondents living in battleground and modestly competitive states score better on the index than those in the other two categories of states, but by September 1 knowledge in modestly competitive states converges with the lines of the other non-battleground states.[7] During the general election campaign, knowledge increases steeply across the nation. The rate of increase is slightly higher in battleground states but for the most part the campaign knowledge levels of everyone improve.[8]

Most people across the country learn during the campaign season, but people living in battleground states tend to learn slightly more. Given how rich the information environments of competitive states are, this final graph raises two interesting questions: (1) Why doesn't the line for moderately competitive states look more like the line for battleground states given that the information environments in states that lean toward a candidate are quite similar to those in battleground states?; and (2) Why doesn't knowledge in battleground states rise even more steeply?[9] In terms of the first question, the analysis in Chapter 3 revealed that even though the information environments in states that leaned toward one of the candidates looked more like the information environments of battleground states, there were significant differences between the two. Both the volume and diversity of information were significantly higher in battleground states, while the equality of information and level of dialogue were marginally so. The level of negativity was also slightly higher in battleground states. It is also possible that voters in battleground states are more interested or feel more invested in the campaign because they know their state will be a key player in choosing the next president. Living in an "almost" battleground simply does not have the same luster. In terms of the second question, about why knowledge is not higher in swing states given the richness of their campaign information environments, one explanation is suggested by many of the graphs in Figure 5.1: information is so prevalent nationally that the disproportionate amount of information lavished upon competitive states simply does not make much of a difference. Another reason might be that some characteristic of the information environment is depressing citizen knowledge in battleground states. The following analysis reveals that battleground state residents are indeed different in important ways from people living in moderately competitive states and that a certain aspect of the campaign information environment in swing states, namely its high volume of dialogue, is confusing for certain kinds of citizens.

Competitiveness and Interest

In Chapter 4 we saw that voter interest was unaffected by the competitiveness of House or Senate races, which meant that the campaign knowledge gains we saw among respondents could be attributed mainly to the information environment. I argued that voters exposed to such contests are often unaware of how competitive their congressional races are, but it is hard to imagine that a battleground state resident is completely unaware of how important their state is for the fortunes of presidential candidates. Candidates ardently woo such states, inundating them with appeals in the form of television and radio ads, praising their greatness and promising to cherish them long after the election has passed. The local media follow the courtships with paparazzi-like intensity, documenting candidate visits to the state and voter reactions, making it impossible for anyone living in a battleground state to turn on the local news without being reminded of the impending election. How could residents of such states not be more interested in the election than the residents of stepsister safe states?

There is no question that political interest is higher in presidential elections than in midterm elections and that certain presidential elections raise interest levels higher than others. For example, voters were significantly more interested in the 2008, 2004, and 2000 presidential contests than in the 1996 contest between President Bill Clinton and Senator Bob Dole or the 1988 race between Vice President George H. W. Bush and Governor Michael Dukakis (Lipsitz 2009). Yet recent research suggests that the elevated levels of political interest that generally accompany presidential elections tend to swamp the effects of state-level campaign efforts by the candidates. In other words, an individual's interest in a presidential election is determined by how competitive it is nationally—not by the competitiveness of one's state. This has been confirmed by some recent research that has found political interest is no higher in battleground states than in safe states (Wolak 2006; Benoit et al. 2004). These studies, however, base their claims on data from the American National Election Study post-election survey, which asks respondents to report how interested they are in the campaigns *after* the election has ended. The post-election survey typically goes into the field the day after Election Day and is administered for the next six weeks. For example, the 2004 post-election survey, which was one of the surveys used in these earlier studies, was administered from November 3 until December 20. Yet, it is possible that differences emerging in campaign interest during the general election campaign between those living in battleground and non-battleground states fade rapidly after Election Day. As a result, the National Annenberg Election Study with its rolling cross section design is more appropriate for understanding how campaign interest is affected by electoral competitiveness in presidential campaigns.

Figure 5.2 demonstrates that this is indeed the case. The Annenberg study asks voters two political interest questions. The first gauges their general interest in politics by asking respondents to indicate how often they follow politics: "most of the time," "sometimes," "now and then," and "hardly at all." These responses are coded "3," "2," "1," and "0" respectively. The second question is designed to gauge how interested respondents are in the current election. It asks respondents how closely they are following the campaign, to which they can respond "very closely," "somewhat closely," "not too closely," and "not at all." Again, these responses are coded "3," "2," "1," and "0" respectively. The first two graphs in Figure 5.2 show how general political interest and campaign interest changed over the course of the summer and general election campaign in 2004. As Figure 2 demonstrates, both forms of interest rose significantly over the six months examined with campaign interest rising more steeply. The question is whether either form of interest rose more steeply in battleground states. General political interest rises across all states from approximately 2 on the 0 to 3 scale at the beginning of the summer to around 2.3 by Election Day. The only difference across the four kinds of states

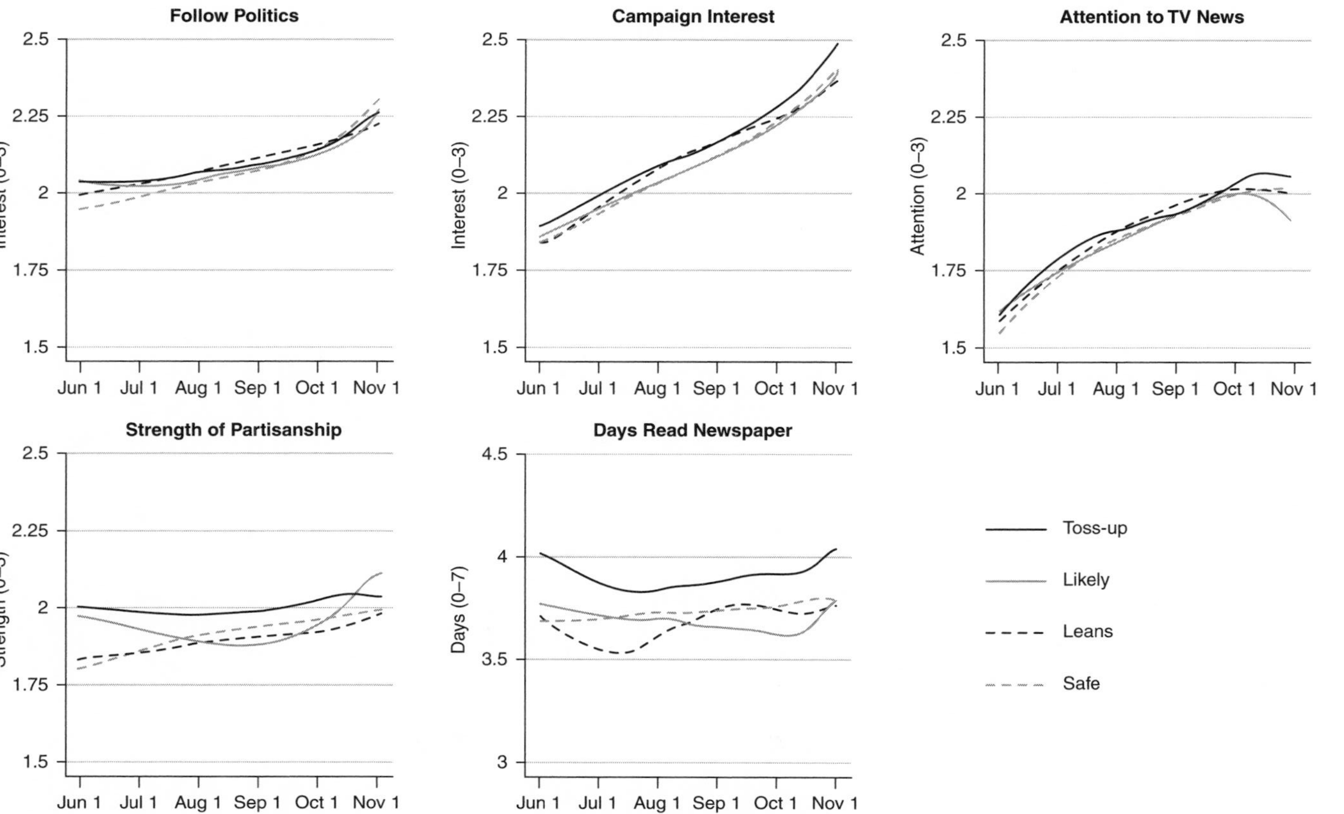

Figure 5.2. Political attentiveness measures by state competitiveness in the 2004 presidential election. Solid black line = “Toss-up”; solid gray line = “Likely”; dashed black line = “Leans”; dashed gray line = “Safe.” 2004 National Annenberg Election Study; Goldstein et al. 2002; Goldstein and Rivlin 2005, ;2007. Generated using lowess in Stata 10 (bandwidth = .8).

is that general interest is marginally lower in safe states early in the summer, but it rises in a virtually identical fashion across all states during the general election campaign. The story is slightly different in the case of campaign interest, which starts out at approximately 1.85 on the 0 to 3 scale in all categories of states at the beginning of the summer. It rises across all states through August, but at slightly higher rates in battleground and modestly competitive states. After Labor Day, however, campaign interest rises more steeply in battleground states so that by Election Day, the residents of such states average approximately a 2.5 on the scale, while those in other states average approximately 2.4. To help the reader gauge the significance of this difference, I calculated the predicted probability that a respondent would say that they were following the campaign "very closely" on the day before the election.[10] The predicted probability was .47 in battleground states and .42 across the remaining states ($p < .01$). Although the difference in campaign interest between states pales in comparison to how much interest rises across the nation after June 1, battleground states have started to distinguish themselves by October 1. The Annenberg survey also asks respondents how much attention they have paid to television news about the presidential campaign. The third graph reveals that the responses of swing state residents begin to diverge from the rest of the country starting in mid-October. Thus, while the substantive effects are not very large, it appears that toward the end of the general election, battleground state residents report being more interested and paying more attention to news about the election.

What is even more interesting is that battleground state residents are distinct in other ways that might have a bearing on their political knowledge levels. First, the fourth graph in Figure 5.2 suggests that the residents of swing states tend to be more partisan than the residents of other states, particularly safe and moderately competitive states. People living in states that lean toward a candidate have a similar level of partisanship to battleground state residents in early June and late October, but the rest of the time the strength of their partisanship lags behind as well. The final graph in Figure 5.2 reveals that they report reading newspapers more often than people in other states. The number of days they report reading the newspaper is significantly higher than the rest of the nation from June 1 to November 1.

These differences are important because media consumption and the strength of one's partisanship are usually strong predictors of one's political knowledge (Delli Carpini and Keeter 1996). The fact that swing state residents begin to distinguish themselves from the rest of the country before the general election campaign even begins might lead one to ask whether swing state residents are different in other crucial ways. For example, are they more educated than citizens of other states? They are not. In fact, residents of safe states and those that lean toward a candidate are significantly more educated than people in moderately and highly competitive states.[11] Another explanation is that John Kerry clinched the Democratic nomination early in the primary season with his victories on Super Tuesday, allowing him and President Bush, as well as members of the media, to turn their attention to the general election campaign long before the summer began.[12] Residents of the 2004 battleground states knew early on that their state would be fiercely contested by both candidates in the fall. This awareness was due not only to media coverage of the candidates' strategies, but also to the fact that the candidates were already visiting general election battleground states. For example, by the end of March President Bush had already visited the swing state of Wisconsin nine times.[13]

There are three reasons why the differences observed in the analysis between the residents of battleground and non-battleground states are important. First, the findings contradict previous studies that have argued residents of battleground states are no more interested than others in presidential campaigns. This analysis reveals that significant differences are in fact present.[14] Second, the fact that such differences are present makes the small magnitude of the battleground state effect on political knowledge all the more remarkable. If the residents of battleground states are receiving so much more information *and* they are more interested, as well as more engaged, in the election, one would expect the knowledge gap between them and the rest of the country to be even bigger. This suggests two possibilities—that information, interest, and engagement really don't matter all that much for voter knowledge, or that some other characteristic or aspect of the information environment is depressing knowledge. Finally, the differences found here also suggest that I should not control for interest, media consumption, or strength of partisanship in my models explaining voter knowledge because doing so will mask some of the state competitiveness effect. Thus, such variables will be omitted from the regression models in the next section.

How Voter Knowledge Responds to Presidential Campaign Information Environments

As Chapter 3 demonstrated, both the quantity and quality of information provided by candidates and their supporters is substantially higher in competitive states than in safe states but, as we saw earlier in this chapter, the knowledge levels of voters are not correspondingly higher. In this section I try to understand why this is the case by examining the relationship between campaign information and knowledge in presidential elections. Using an approach similar to that in the previous chapter, I examine how information volume, equality, diversity, dialogue, and negativity affect voter knowledge.

Table 5.1 includes a series of regression models explaining political knowledge. Model 1 serves as a baseline, while the subsequent models show how the information quantity and quality measures affect knowledge individually and in tandem.[15] Perhaps the most telling finding from the table is how little of the variation in knowledge is explained by the information environment measures. The R^2 value in the baseline model is .158, and the most it increases in any of the first 11 models is .003.[16] In the previous chapter, adding the information environment measures to the models explained significantly more of the variation in campaign knowledge. This suggests that advertising in presidential elections is not as important for acquiring knowledge about the candidates as it is in sub-national elections. The subsequent models provide an explanation of why the information provided by candidates and their supporters in presidential elections seems to matter so little for voter knowledge in presidential elections.

First, if there is one characteristic that stands out about the campaign information that is provided to voters in battleground states, it is its abundance. Recall the analysis in Chapter 3, which showed that the average number of advertisements aired in a battleground state media market is more than 20 times higher than in a safe state media market. Yet Model 2 shows that the volume of information provided to voters in presidential elections has a relatively small effect on the ability of voters to identify candidate issue positions.[17] The largest coefficient for the volume of ads in any model (not including those with an interaction term) is .012. To put this effect into perspective, the expected increase in a respondent's political knowledge score as the volume of advertisements increases from the 20th percentile (160 ads in the previous week) to its 80th percentile (1,150 ads) is .13 on 6–point scale.[18] As we see in Model 7, however, even this small effect disappears when the other covariates

Table 5.1. Effect of Information Environment Characteristics on Knowledge of Presidential Candidate Issue Positions

	Model 1	*Model 2*	*Model 3*	*Model 4*	*Model 5*	*Model 6*	*Model 7*	*Model 8*	*Model 9*	*Model 10*	*Model 11*	*Model 12*	*Model 13*	*Model 14*	*Model 15*
	5-Item Knowledge Index (0–5)											Soph.	Nov.	Nov. (DK)	Nov. (Wrong)
Leans	.038	.033	.037	.040	.033	.044	.050	.038	.042	.030	.042	–.012	–.132	.040	.092
	(.070)	(.066)	(.064)	(.066)	(.068)	(.069)	(.067)	(.065)	(.064)	(.064)	(.069)	(.059)	(.129)	(.123)	(.130)
Likely	.046	.017	.002	.031	.022	.038	.029	.005	.023	.009	.041	–.025	–.135	–.087	.223#
	(.082)	(.077)	(.074)	(.075)	(.079)	(.078)	(.074)	(.075)	(.073)	(.073)	(.079)	(.074)	(.136)	(.155)	(.116)
Toss-up	.163**	.085	.074	.077	.095	.093	.079	.078	.063	.079	.099	.085	–.041	–.052	.093
	(.061)	(.059)	(.057)	(.058)	(.063)	(.061)	(.061)	(.058)	(.059)	(.060)	(.063)	(.059)	(.136)	(.117)	(.122)
Volume	—	.011*	.008	–.004	.012*	.010*	–.003	.003	.001	.024**	.003	.017#	.061***	–.034*	–.027*
		(.005)	(.005)	(.006)	(.005)	(.005)	(.006)	(.010)	(.007)	(.007)	(.010)	(.009)	(.016)	(.014)	(.011)
Equality	—	—	.129*	—	—	—	.143*	.098	—	—	—	—	—	—	—
			(.056)				(.059)	(.075)							
Diversity	—	—	—	.045**	—	—	.030*	—	.056**	—	—	—	—	—	—
				(.014)			(.014)		(.020)						
Dialogue	—	—	—	—	–.093	—	–.066	—	—	.107	—	.177	.575#	–.884**	.309
					(.082)		(.091)			(.120)		(.163)	(.291)	(.259)	(.259)
Negativity	—	—	—	—	—	.215***	.176**	—	—	—	.172*	—	—	—	—
						(.060)	(.059)				(.079)				
Volume*equality	—	—	—	—	—	—	—	.008	—	—	—	—	—	—	—
								(.014)							
Volume*diversity	—	—	—	—	—	—	—	—	–.001	—	—	—	—	—	—
									(.001)						
Volume*dialogue	—	—	—	—	—	—	—	—	—	–.039**	—	–.033	–.111*	.080*	.031
										(.014)		(.020)	(.044)	(.037)	(.039)
Volume*negativity	—	—	—	—	—	—	—	—	—	—	.013	—	—	—	—
											(.013)				
Intercept	.943***	.869***	.848***	.792***	.883***	.762***	.716***	.853***	.772***	.845***	.782***	1.631***	.943**	1.421***	2.636***
	(.138)	(.142)	(.142)	(.148)	(.144)	(.139)	(.146)	(.141)	(.149)	(.143)	(.142)	(.222)	(.278)	(.264)	(.264)
N	**7,261**	**7,261**	**7,261**	**7,261**	**7,261**	**7,261**	**7,261**	**7,261**	**7,261**	**7,261**	**7,261**	**3,000**	**1,477**	**1,477**	**1,477**
R^2	**.158**	**.159**	**.159**	**.160**	**.159**	**.160**	**.161**	**.159**	**.160**	**.159**	**.160**	**.184**	**.088**	**.040**	**.046**

*** $p<0.001$; ** $p<0.01$; * $p<0.05$; # $p<0.1$; two-tailed. Sources: 2004 National Annenberg Election Study; Goldstein et al. 2002; Goldstein and Rivlin 2005, 2007. OLS was used to estimate the coefficients; all models include controls for standard demographic and political variables. See Table A.8 for the full models. The dependent variable in Models 1–13 is the respondent's score on a 5-item campaign knowledge index, ranging from 0 to 5. The sample in Model 12 is restricted to political sophisticates (Soph.); the sample in Model 13 is restricted to political novices (Nov.). The dependent variable in Model 14 is how many "Don't know" responses were offered (0–5); the dependent variable in Model 15 is the number of incorrect responses offered (0–5). The samples in Models 14 and 15 are restricted to political novices.

are included in the model. In the complete model, we see that only the effects of certain information quality measures endure, including equality, diversity and negativity. These effects are not especially large, but they hold up to the inclusion of other covariates. As equality increases from the 20th to the 80th percentile (from 0 to .7), the expected increase in the political knowledge score is .10. The same percentile increase in diversity (in this case, from 1 to 5 sponsors) yields a .12 increase. Finally, as the proportion of negative ads increases from the 20th to the 80th percentile (from .2 to .7), the score on the scale is expected to increase by .09.[19] Although these effects are not large, what is interesting is that the analysis shows that information quantity is not as important as information quality in presidential campaigns. This suggests that the reason why political knowledge is not significantly higher in presidential battleground states than in safe states is because battleground state residents receive vast quantities of poor information, that is, information that is unbalanced, lacks diversity, and is much too positive.

In Models 8 through 11, I test the intuition that the effect of the various information environment characteristics will be stronger when the volume of information is higher. If this is the case, then the direction of the interaction term should be positive. If the direction of the interaction term is negative, however, it would indicate one of two possibilities. The first is that having a large amount of information is a substitute for lower quality information. In this case, the coefficients for the volume and quality variables should be positive and the coefficient for the interaction term should be negative, but not so large that it produces a significantly negative effect on knowledge when added to either of the main coefficients. The second possibility is that equality, diversity, dialogue, or negativity actually depresses voter knowledge when the volume of information is high. In this case, the interaction term should be negative and large enough that when it is added to either of the main coefficients it shows a significantly negative effect on knowledge.

These models reveal a number of interesting findings. Model 8 shows that the positive effect of information equality is significant only when the number of ads aired in the media market during the previous week exceeds 250. At that point, the magnitude of the equality coefficient increases to .12. As advertising volume increases, so does the size of the equality coefficient, increasing to .19 at the 80th percentile of advertising.[20] The model also reveals that advertising volume has a marginally significant positive effect on voter knowledge as long as it equally represents Democratic and Republican viewpoints. At the 80th percentile of equality, the coefficient for the volume variable is .01.[21] This means that at a high level of equality, every 100 ad increase yields a .01 increase in knowledge. While this is by no means a large effect, this is the first study to show that campaign information must represent both Republican and Democratic viewpoints for it to be in any way beneficial for voter knowledge in presidential campaigns.

The small negative coefficient for the interaction term in Model 9 suggests that the beneficial effects of information diversity are stronger at lower levels of advertising. Yet even at the 80th percentile of advertising volume, the salutary effects of diversity can still be felt with the coefficient falling only slightly to .05 (from .056). Model 11 shows that information negativity is even more helpful when there is a lot of it. At the 80th percentile of advertising, the coefficient for negativity more than doubles from .17 to .37, while at the 20th percentile it is .21. Moreover, the coefficient for advertising volume becomes larger and its effect is statistically significant when the information it is conveying is disproportionately negative. The coefficient for the volume measure increases from a statistically insignificant .006 at the 20th percentile of negativity to a significant .011 at the 80th percentile of negativity. Thus the results of Models 8 and 11 suggest that a large amount of advertising is helpful only if represents Democratic and Republican viewpoints in a balanced fashion or is disproportionately negative.[22]

Recall that I argued in Chapter 3 that there are theoretical reasons to question the alleged benefits of campaign dialogue for voter knowledge. This skepticism seems to be borne out by the results of Model 10. It indicates that dialogue is actually harmful for voter knowledge at a high volume of advertising. At the 80th percentile of advertising volume, the coefficient for dialogue is a highly significant -.38, which in substantive terms means that a respondent's expected score on the political knowledge index decreases from 3.24 to 3.09 as dialogue increases from the 20th to the 80th percentile. In fact, the coefficient for the advertising volume measure jumps to .024 when the two sides do not engage in any dialogue. Thus, it appears to be better for voters if candidates talk past each other rather than engage each other on the same issues. Another way to understand this interaction is that the volume of advertising has a strong positive effect on voter knowledge when the candidates are addressing entirely different issues.

The analysis thus far, however, has not explained exactly why dialogue harms knowledge when information volume is high. This is all the more puzzling because the analysis in Chapter 4 found that dialogue boosts the edifying power of advertisements in House and Senate races. One explanation for the different findings in these two chapters is that they use different measures of political knowledge. In Chapter 4, dialogue was especially helpful for being able to rate the Senate candidates.[23] Here we find, however, that dialogue harms knowledge of presidential candidate issue positions. Is it possible that seeing ads about the same issue from both parties in a race can make a person feel more confident that he can judge the candidates *at the same time* that it hurts his ability to identify their issue positions? The following analysis demonstrates that this seems to be the case for a certain type of person: someone who does not follow politics closely.

Earlier I offered two reasons for why dialogue might undermine voter campaign knowledge. The first started with the proposition, based on previous research, that voters can learn one candidate's issue position from information provided by their opponent. If this is the case, then voters might be more likely to learn where the candidates stand on a broad range of topics when the candidates talk past each other. By doing so, the candidates cover a wider range of issues. When the topics discussed by candidates and their supporters converge on just a handful of issues, citizens only learn about where the candidates stand on those particular issues and are left in the dark as to their positions on the issues not discussed. The second reason dialogue might be harmful for citizens is that some may find it confusing. Simply put, it may be difficult for voters to keep the candidates' issue positions straight if they are talking about the same subjects.

The first question I will address is what kinds of citizens are tripped up by dialogue. Is dialogue more harmful for voters who are generally interested in politics or for those who are less interested? In Model 12, I restrict my sample to those who indicated that they follow politics "most of the time," while Model 13 is restricted to those who indicated they follow politics "hardly at all" or "now and then." The two models reveal that the strong negative interaction we observed in Model 10 holds only among those who are politically uninterested. In Model 12, we see that the coefficient for the interaction term is an insignificant –.03, while it is a highly significant –.11 in Model 13. The coefficient for the main dialogue term in Model 13 shows that dialogue is actually marginally helpful for the politically unengaged at very low levels of advertising, but that the positive effect quickly dissipates as the volume of advertising increases. At the 80th percentile of advertising, the size of the coefficient for dialogue would be a large and highly significant –.70. The interaction also implies that the large positive effect of advertising volume for the politically unengaged decreases as dialogue increases.[24] When there is no dialogue, every 100 ads increase a respondent's score on the 5–item index by .06. This effect is reduced by half when the candidates and their supporters are discussing the same issues 30 percent (70th percentile) of the time and completely disappears when that number increases to 50 percent (90th percentile).[25] The results of Model 13 are particularly disturbing because they indicate that dialogue exacerbates the already sizable knowledge gap that exists between political sophisticates and the political novices.

Why is dialogue so harmful for political novices? If the problem is that the candidates and their supporters are discussing a narrow range of issues and ignoring others, then a high level of dialogue should make respondents more likely to offer "Don't know" responses when they are asked questions about the candidates' issue positions because many of the issues are simply not being addressed in the campaign. The logic behind this hypothesis is that if candidates and their supporters have been focusing on, say, health care and taxes in their communications with voters during the previous week, the survey respondent will offer a "Don't know" response when asked a question about the candidate's position on education. However, if dialogue simply confuses people and makes it difficult for them to keep the candidates' positions straight then it should have a particularly deleterious effect on the ability of respondents to answer questions about candidate issue positions correctly. They should be more likely to attribute the wrong positions to each candidate.

In Models 14 and 15, I again restrict my sample to people who do not follow politics closely, since they are the ones who are harmed by dialogue. In Model 14, I examine how dialogue affects the number of "Don't know" responses offered by a respondent. Model 15 examines how dialogue affects the number of incorrect responses offered. Keep in mind that most of the variables should have the opposite sign that they do in Model 13, since the dependent variables capture confusion rather than knowledge. Model 14 shows that when respondents have been exposed to a high level of campaign dialogue in the previous week, they are *less* likely to offer "Don't know" responses to questions about the candidates' issue positions at low levels of ad volume. The positive effect of dialogue gets weaker as advertising volume increases, becoming insignificant when the number of ads aired in the previous week reaches approximately 650 (75th percentile), but it never reverses signs. This finding contradicts my first hypothesis, which suggested that dialogue's negative effect on knowledge was due to restricted issue coverage in the campaign. If this were the case, exposure to dialogue should have increased the number of "Don't know" responses. Instead, it appears to significantly decrease them.[26]

Model 15 reveals that even though exposure to dialogue makes political novices more likely to offer responses to questions about candidate issue positions, those responses are more likely to be incorrect. This unfortunate effect becomes marginally significant at an advertising volume of approximately 250 ad airings and becomes highly significant around 350 airings. Taken together, these two models suggest that exposure to campaign dialogue makes political novices feel more confident that they know where the candidates stand on the issues but that this confidence is seriously misguided. Instead, it appears that campaign dialogue simply increases the odds that they will confidently offer wrong answers, which supports the hypothesis that dialogue may be confusing for people who do not follow politics closely. This may also explain why dialogue could help respondents rate Senate candidates in Chapter 4. Exposure to dialogue makes people *feel* more confident about offering judgments about the candidates, even if the grounds on which they offer these judgments are muddled. More research is necessary to confirm the robustness of these findings and to understand why dialogue is so harmful for people who are less attentive to politics, but the findings here point to confusion as the culprit.

When one considers the findings of this chapter together with those from Chapter 3, one can start to construct a story of why the knowledge gap between the residents of presidential battleground states and safe states is not larger. Part of the story is that people in safe states have ample access to information about the presidential candidates. For example, they can watch network or cable news programs or read a national newspaper for coverage of the campaign. The other part of the story is that the flood of information that inundates residents of battleground states is not substantively rich. As we learned in Chapter 3, residents of battleground states may be exposed to a volume of advertising 20 times higher than the volume in safe states; that information may be more equal and diverse, but it is no more likely to be negative than the information in safe states. The analysis above echoes the findings of others who have demonstrated that negative ads help voters learn. Positive ads typically contain little more than symbolic "fluff"—i.e. flags waving and children smiling. This means that if the ads in battleground states were *more* negative, we would see a larger knowledge gap than we do. The final reason that the knowledge gap is smaller than otherwise expected is that there is a higher level of campaign dialogue in battleground states, which this analysis shows is unhelpful for some voters, especially those who do not follow politics closely. These harmful effects are felt more strongly when the volume of advertising is high, which is precisely the case in battleground state media markets.

Conclusion

In Chapter 3, we learned that competitive campaigns give candidates and their supporters the incentive to provide voters with an information environment that has many traits that are desirable from the standpoint of democratic thought. That information environment, as measured by television advertising, is richer in the sense that it is more abundant, more balanced, and features a range of voices engaged in a dialogue about the same issues. It is also more negative in the case of House and Senate campaigns. This chapter and Chapter 4 have assessed whether and how the information generated by competitive contests actually helps voters learn and have revealed a number of interesting findings. First, electoral competitiveness appears to matter much more for voter learning in House and Senate races. The ability to simply rate House candidates on a feeling thermometer—a very low bar for voter knowledge—increases by over 40 percent as the level of competitiveness in the race increases from safe to just *modestly* competitive. The ability to rate Senate candidates on a feeling thermometer increases by 29 percent as electoral competitiveness jumps from its lowest to its highest level. By contrast, the average score on the presidential campaign knowledge index is just 8 percent higher in battleground states than in safe states. The efforts of those who advocate getting rid of the Electoral College because it creates a knowledge gap among voters in battleground and non-battleground states would be better spent seeking reforms to make House elections just modestly competitive.

Second, the reason competitiveness matters more in House elections, in particular, appears to be related to the fact that voter knowledge in these races benefits a great deal from the higher volume of information generated by more competitive contests. In Chapter 3, we learned that of all the information environment characteristics, information volume was the most responsive to competitiveness. Yet, volume matters relatively little for knowledge in Senate and presidential contests. Instead, the quality of that information—by which I mean its balance, diversity, level of dialogue, *and* negativity—matters more, and these characteristics of the information environment have a weaker relationship with competitiveness. In House races, however, where the information environment is so poor, information volume has more impact.

Third, competitive elections are important for voter knowledge because they encourage political elites to provide voters with higher quality information, not because they motivate individual voters to seek out more information. In congressional elections, voter interest was unaffected by electoral competitiveness, in part because voters were unaware of the status of their election. Even if there were a way of communicating to voters how close their election is, the findings of this chapter suggest it would not make much of a difference for their knowledge. As we saw earlier, the higher levels of interest among the residents of battleground states did not yield especially high information gains for them.

Finally, a number of lessons have emerged from these analyses for those who seek to understand how campaigns create an informed electorate. First, those who have been focusing on presidential elections to test how campaign information affects voter knowledge—irrespective of whether they are looking at the effects of news coverage or television advertisements—have been looking for effects where campaign information matters least. This analysis reveals that information provided by candidates and their supporters matters much more for voter knowledge in congressional races and, very likely, in other information-poor elections, such as those for state and local office, than in presidential elections.

Second, information quality can matter as much if not more than the quantity of information for voter knowledge. This analysis has shown that information diversity, equality, negativity, and the extent to which dialogue is occurring all have implications for voter knowledge. Information balance and diversity had a positive effect on the two dependent variables that were the clearest measures of what people knew about their political candidates, which were the ability to identify an incumbent's ideology and the knowledge of Bush and Kerry's issue positions. Negativity—even challenger negativity—had a large positive effect on these measures as well as on the ability to rate Senate candidates. The level of dialogue in campaigns, however, seemed to undermine issue knowledge even as it increased the ability of respondents to rate Senate candidates and offer answers to issue position questions. What this all means is that researchers seeking to understand how advertising affects knowledge should no longer rely simply on measures of advertising volume to gauge their effects. They also need to include measures of its quality in their models and be sure to examine their interactions, or else they will miss an important part of the story.

CHAPTER 6

Competitiveness and Political Participation

It is virtually a cliché to say that competitive elections excite and engage citizens. The images of excited youngsters canvassing battleground state neighborhoods during the 2008 campaign and voters standing in lines for hours on Election Day only seemed to confirm this widely accepted truism. The cliché may describe what happens when a presidential election is especially close nationally, but as we have learned in the previous chapters, it seems to be a much poorer description of what happens in competitive congressional races and even in many battleground states during a given presidential election year. In Chapter 4, we learned that campaign interest is unaffected by electoral competitiveness in toss-up House and Senate races. Even the slightly elevated levels of campaign interest that one observes among battleground state residents does not seem to live up to the hype, especially when one compares it to the rise in interest that one observes among Americans generally over the course of the campaign.

Yet campaign interest is only one measure of voter engagement. In this chapter, I examine how electoral competitiveness affects voting and nonvoting forms of political participation, such as going to rallies, donating, advocating a candidate, and volunteering for a campaign. Declining voter engagement is one of the main reasons why political observers and reformers decry the lack of competitiveness in American elections. For example, it is not uncommon to encounter appeals for redistricting reform on the grounds that citizens faced with uncompetitive House elections will stay home.[1] In fact, a recent report by the Democratic Leadership Council considers gerrymandered congressional districts to be a form of voter suppression for this very reason (Dunkelman 2008). One also encounters claims about the importance of competitive elections for voter engagement in arguments for abolishing the Electoral College (EC). Critics of the EC frequently contend that the

EC "focuses presidential elections on just a handful of battleground states, and pushes the rest of the nation's voters to the sidelines" ("Drop Out of the College" 2006). One magazine editor, Hendrik Hertzberg of the *New Yorker*, argues that the EC divides the nation into battleground and "spectator" states and that the EC is contributing to "the death of participatory politics" in spectator states because people believe that advocating a candidate or working on a campaign "can't make a difference" (Hertzberg 2006).

In short, most of these political observers would agree with political pundit Rhodes Cook, "If 'location, location, location' is the key to a successful business, then 'competition, competition, competition' is the key to voter engagement" (Cook 2004). This chapter will test this claim by assessing whether it applies to House, Senate, and state-level presidential elections. In addition, where electoral competitiveness matters, my analysis tries to identify why it matters. Do people participate more when elections are competitive because they are being contacted by candidates and their supporters or because they are being encouraged to vote by the quality of the information environment? If campaign information is mobilizing voters, then I try to understand if any of the information qualities produced by electoral competitiveness and identified in previous chapters as being desirable from a normative standpoint improve the mobilizing effects of that information.

Using a combination of turnout, survey, and advertising data, I find in this chapter that there is some truth in Cook's assertion, but also a great deal of exaggeration. Competitive elections do boost turnout and non-voting forms of participation, such as donating and working for a campaign. But my analysis will show that often moderate levels of competitiveness are more inspiring for voters than high levels of it, particularly in House and Senate elections. The analysis will also reveal that turnout is higher in battleground states than in non-battleground states, but not as high as one might expect given that voters in battleground states have elevated levels of campaign interest and media attention, as we learned in Chapter 5. The analysis of advertising will reveal that some of these unexpected findings can be explained in part by the diminishing—sometimes even negative—returns of advertising volume. The elevated levels of dialogue that voters are exposed to in highly competitive elections are also associated with lower levels of participation in some cases. This finding confirms the research of others who have found that two-sided information flows in campaigns and exposure to disagreement can create feelings of ambivalence, which may in turn depress participation. This study, however, is the first to show that it is dialogue, not merely two-sided information flows in campaigns that depresses turnout. The analysis in this chapter also suggests one explanation for why so many studies have found that advertising has no effect on participation: they have not considered the possibility that the effect is nonlinear.

Electoral Competitiveness and Participation

Most of the studies examining the relationship between electoral competitiveness and participation use turnout as their dependent variable. Virtually all these studies suggest that competitiveness enhances turnout in state-level presidential (Lipsitz 2009; Bergan et al. 2005), congressional (Huckfeldt et al. 2007; Jackson 1993; Cox and Munger 1989; Caldeira et al. 1985), and gubernatorial (Patterson and Caldeira 1983) elections, although the strength of the effect varies from "marginal" (Huckfeldt et al. 2007, 802) to exerting "a substantial pull upwards on turnout" (Caldeira et al. 1985, 504).[2]

The relationship between electoral competitiveness and other forms of participation is not so clear, however. While it does appear that state-level competitiveness in presidential elections increases the likelihood that a voter might attend a rally about the candidates or put up a lawn sign (Lipsitz 2009), the relationship between competitivenss and these forms of political activity in down-ticket races is far less clear, in part because few studies have addressed the issue. A recent study of the 2002 midterm election found that there was no relationship between a House race being tightly contested and non-turnout forms of participation (Huckfeldt et al. 2007). This finding seems strange, however, since campaigns that are trying to mobilize voters are also trying to mobilize volunteers to help them with their effort. When elections are competitive there are also more opportunities to participate. Even if a person has the desire to attend a political rally in a safe district or state, it may be impossible because there are no rallies to attend. Thus, I expect electoral competitiveness to drive forms of participation, such as attending a meeting or working for a campaign, as well as voter turnout.

Finally, research has found that electoral competitiveness spurs voter turnout in Senate elections only in midterm election years (Jackson 2002).[3] The logic is that anyone who can be mobilized will be mobilized by a presidential election, so the competitiveness of a Senate race matters for turnout only in off-year elections when the overriding stimulus associated with a presidential election is not present. Although this question has not been investigated in the context of House elections, it seems the same logic would hold for them, that is, competitive House contests would encourage people to turn out only in midterm election years. One would also expect the same logic to apply to non-voting forms of participation in congressional elections as well; voters should only respond to the competitiveness of a congressional race during midterm election campaigns.

Finally, we need to think about the precise nature of the relationship between electoral competitiveness and the behavior of voters. As I argued in Chapter 3, if incumbents are running scared and overreacting to threats, then we may begin to see elevated levels of participation in modestly competitive congressional elections as incumbents pound the pavement to stave off being labeled as "vulnerable" by political observers and potential challengers. Research on presidential campaign strategies shows that candidates tend to be efficient, focusing the majority of their resources on perceived battleground states. Yet candidates who adopt a more "defensive" strategy might try to mobilize voters in states that lean toward their party but are not an entirely sure bet, while candidates who adopt a more "offensive" strategy might try to mobilize supporters in states that lean toward their opponent in an effort to pick up more electoral votes (Huang and Shaw 2009). Research on the 2000 and 2004 campaigns suggests that Kerry and Gore, who were short of cash, adopted neither an offensive nor a defensive strategy, instead focusing efficiently on battleground states. Bush, however, adopted a more offensive strategy due in part to his better-funded operations. Thus, it is possible that the participation levels of respondents living in both moderately competitive states and battleground states might be elevated.

The Debate About Ads and Mobilization

The analysis in this chapter will also examine how the information environments generated by competitive elections affect voters by using the measures of television advertising that should, by now, be familiar to the reader. There is considerable debate in the extant literature about whether ads mobilize voters. Some authors argue that they boost turnout (Franz et al. 2007; Hillygus 2005; Freedman et al. 2004), while others argue that they have no effect whatsoever on whether voters go to the polls (Lipsitz and Teigen 2010; Krasno and Green 2008; Ashworth and Clinton 2006; Huber and Arceneaux 2007; Holbrook and McClurg 2005). Few of these studies, however, consider how the quality of advertising provided to voters affects participation. The bulk of the research in this area has explored how negative advertisements affect turnout. Yet, after conducting a meta-analysis of negative campaigning effects in the political science literature, Richard Lau, Lee Sigelman, and Ivy Brown Rovner conclude that "*the research literature provides no general support for the hypothesis that negative political campaigning depresses voter turnout.* If anything, negative campaigning more frequently appears to have a slight mobilizing effect" (2007: 1184, emphasis original). These scholars do find, however, that negative campaigning reduces feelings of political efficacy and trust in government, but the effects are not so large as to depress the chances that a voter actually goes to the polls. Thus, I expect negative advertising not to harm participation and possibly even to boost it.

Aside from negativity, I will also be examining how advertising volume, balance, diversity, and dialogue affect participation. One of the reasons that these studies may not be finding that advertising volume has any effect on knowledge is that they do not examine non-linear measures of it. For example, it is quite possible that advertising promotes participation until it reaches a certain level, beyond which citizens start to tune out. This effect is more likely to be seen in races that feature a high volume of ads such as Senate elections and races in presidential battleground states. As for the other advertising quality measures, there is a reason to believe that equality and dialogue might actually harm participation. Recent studies have found that exposure to disagreement and engaging in dialogue at a personal level reduce the participatory impulses of citizens at the same time that they encourage more considered opinions (Mutz 2002, 2006). Mutz cites two reasons why exposure to disagreement in social networks discourages turnout. The one that is not as relevant for exposure to disagreement in television ads is that participation poses a threat to the harmony of social relationships. The reason that is relevant is that exposure to disagreement creates feelings of ambivalence in an individual. Ambivalence is defined as holding contradictory feelings or attitudes toward an object. From the outside, such a person might look as if she has no opinion, but being ambivalent is different from having no opinion. In a campaign context, a person who is ambivalent has positive and negative feelings toward both candidates. From the standpoint of democratic theory, this might be a very good thing, because it indicates that a person has more thoughtful opinions about the candidates. At the same time, however, such ambivalence might stifle her participatory impulses because it is more difficult to muster the energy and courage needed to stump for a candidate when one has a deeper understanding of his weaknesses and his opponent's strengths. A recent study has found that the two-sided information flows that competitive elections generate do create feelings of ambivalence among the voters, especially in presidential elections (Keele and Wolak 2008). Because my analysis will examine how the balance of information, as well as the level of dialogue, affects participation, I will be able to offer some insight into whether it is hearing from both candidates that stifles participation or hearing them discuss the same issues that does.

Finally, it is possible that diversity might create feelings of ambivalence as well. Following the train of thought introduced in Chapter 3 concerning diversity, when one hears from a range of voices it increases the likelihood that one will hear from one that is credible and motivating. Yet it also increases the chances that one will hear from a credible source that favors the opponent. If this is the case, then diversity might have an effect on participation that is similar to that of equality and dialogue.

The Data

In this chapter I use a variety of data to understand how electoral competitiveness affects political participation and what accounts for those effects. To assess the effect of competitiveness on turnout, the analysis uses district and state-level turnout data, rather than self-reported voting in surveys. The reason is that people often misrepresent their voting behavior, usually erring on the side of reporting that they had gone to the polls. The analysis of how electoral competitiveness affects non-voting forms of participation must rely on survey data, however, since no objective measures exist across years and different types of elections for these forms of participation. Thus, I will turn to the two surveys used in previous chapters for this part of the analysis, the American National Election Study (NES) and the National Annenberg Election Study (Annenberg) for this part of the analysis. To mirror the analysis in Chapters 4 and 5, I use the NES to examine participation in House and Senate elections and the Annenberg study for the analysis of participation in presidential elections.

In the previous chapters, I examined data from 2000, 2002, and 2004 because the advertising data that I used to create my measures of campaign information quality are only available for those years. In this chapter, I am interested in comparing participation in congressional elections during midterm and presidential election years. Because of this concern, it is necessary to examine data from at least one midterm election besides 2002. The NES did not conduct a time series study in 2006, so I expanded the analysis to include

NES data from 1998 instead. In the case of turnout, 2006 data are available, so the analysis will consider data from that year, as well as 2000, 2002, and 2004. The presidential turnout data examine the relationship between state-level competitiveness and turnout in 2000 and 2004. For the analysis of non-voting forms of participation, however, I use the same Annenberg dataset as in Chapter 5, which is from 2004. This will also enable me to use the same measures of television advertising to ascertain whether it mobilizes or demobilizes voters and to allow for direct comparisons between the two chapters. I also examined the relationship between electoral competitiveness and non-voting forms of participation in the 2000 and 2004 NES surveys and in each year found a relationship that was quite similar to the one that emerges in the 2004 Annenberg survey. Thus, the pattern that emerges in the data is robust across surveys and recent presidential election years.

Both the NES and the Annenberg surveys ask respondents about their participation in five non-voting forms of participation: attending a political meeting or rally, trying to persuade another person to support a candidate, displaying a lawn sign or bumper sticker, working for a campaign, and donating. In the NES, the questions appear on the post-election survey, so they ask respondents if they engaged in the behavior prior to Election Day. The Annenberg survey asked these questions on its rolling cross-section survey throughout the campaign. For each activity, respondents were coded "1" if they had engaged in it and "0" if they had not. I then created an index of non-voting participation by summing the five measures, which yielded an index ranging from 0 to 6.[4]

Finally, as in Chapters 4 and 5, I try to understand why electoral competitiveness has the effect on political participation that it does. To that end, I use the same measures of advertising that appeared in those chapters, as well as measures of other forms of mobilization appearing in the surveys, to try to account for the effect of competitiveness. Because the analysis reveals that it has a similar effect on voting and non-voting forms of participation and because the determinants of non-voting forms of participation have received far less attention in the literature than voting, my analysis of the routes by which competitiveness affects voter participation will focus on non-voting participation. Given the complexity of such an analysis, this move also allows me to simplify my presentation.

Electoral Competitiveness and Voter Turnout

The competitiveness of an election drives campaign mobilization and the chief object of campaign mobilization is to get voters to the polls. Thus, we expect electoral competitiveness to have a strong effect on voter turnout. To explain turnout, the analysis in this section uses a model developed by Cox and Munger (1989), which controls for state or district urbanization, including the percent of the citizens who reside in urban areas and the jurisdiction's overall population density. The models also include standard demographic variables, including the median age of residents in the district or state, the percentage that has a B.A., the percentage that is white, and the median income. In recognition of the distinct political culture of the South, the model includes a dummy variable for whether or not the district or state is southern. In the case of turnout in House elections, the model includes a control for whether or not there is a Senate or gubernatorial election taking place in the state. In the Senate turnout model, the analysis includes a control for whether there is a gubernatorial race. Because the goal of the analysis is to capture the overall effect of competitiveness on turnout, the model does not use the wide range of expenditure and competitiveness measures that Cox and Munger included. Instead, it simply uses the *Cook Political Report* measure as the analyses in previous chapters have. To capture how congressional turnout is affected by electoral competitiveness in midterm and presidential election years, separate models are estimated for each. Finally, the presidential turnout data were provided by Michael McDonald and use the state voting eligible population (VEP) in the denominator, as opposed to the voting age population (VAP).[5] The House and Senate turnout data were collected from the Federal Election Commission. To calculate the Senate turnout rate, the number of ballots cast in the Senate race was divided by the state VEP. To calculate the House turnout rate, the number of ballots cast was divided by the voting age population in the district because the VEP data are not available for districts.

The analysis of turnout in state-level presidential contests uses a slightly different approach. Instead of controlling for standard demographic variables, the model includes a variable for the average turnout in the previous two midterm elections, which controls for a state's voting rate when presidential candidate strategies have no bearing on it. Thus, this measure captures the effects of other variables that might explain state-level differences in turnout, such as the income and education of the state's residents without having to explicitly include them in the model (Bergan et al. 2005). The models also include controls for statewide races.

In congressional elections, the expectation is that electoral competitiveness will matter more in midterm elections, but the story is more complicated, as we can see in the first and second graphs of Figure 6.1. In the first graph, we see that the expected turnout in House races is highest when elections are closest during midterm elections. The expected turnout increases from .35 in safe districts to .39 when the outcome of the election is very competitive, an increase that is both substantively and statistically significant. Yet turnout is also marginally higher in districts that favor a candidate than in safe districts (.37 versus .35). We see a different pattern in presidential election years. The expected turnout hovers around .49 in districts that are safe and those that are likely to favor a candidate. The expected turnout level is significantly higher in districts that are moderately competitive, increasing to .51. It then declines

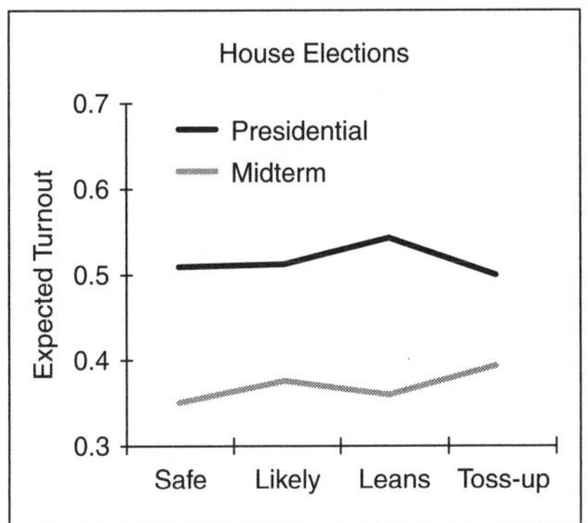

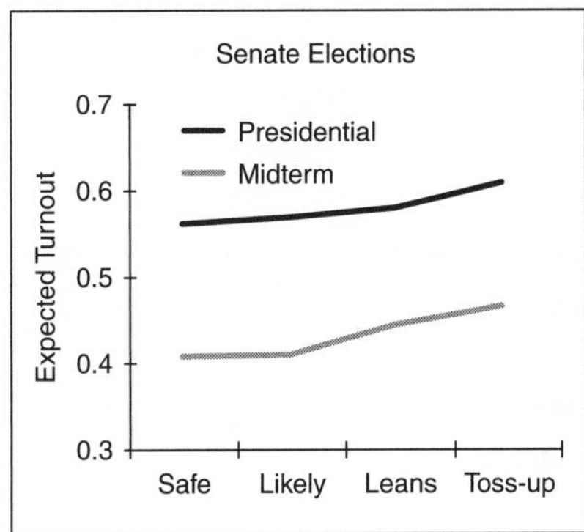

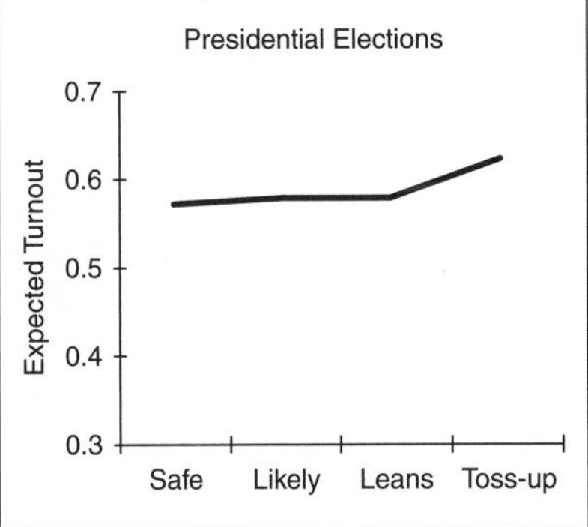

Figure 6.1. Effect of competitiveness on turnout in House, Senate, and state-level presidential elections. See Table A.9 for full models.

three percentage points in toss-up races, a decline that is statistically significant. This unexpected finding suggests that a high level of competitiveness in House races promotes participation in midterm elections but dampens it in the context of presidential elections. As we will see in the next section, this odd pattern emerges in non-voting forms of participation as well.

In the second graph of Figure 6.1, we see that turnout in Senate races is highest when the race is considered a toss-up, a finding that holds in both midterm and presidential election years. In 2002 and 2006, expected turnout increased from .41 in safe states and those that favored a candidate to .45 in moderately competitive states. Turnout received an additional boost in toss-up states, increasing to .47. Both of these increases are substantively and statistically significant, with the .06 increase in toss-up states being particularly impressive, since we will see that it rivals the turnout boost in presidential battleground states. The fact that turnout in Senate races is significantly higher in both moderately and highly competitive races also supports the idea that incumbents are running scared, at least in Senate races. What is unexpected about the effect of electoral competitiveness is that it appears to hold even in presidential election years. Expected turnout increases steadily from .56 in safe states, to .57 in those that favor a candidate, and to .58 in moderately competitive states. In states with toss-up Senate races, the expected turnout is .61. The effect of electoral competitiveness is clearly more muted in presidential elections, but is still apparent, which is good news for those advocating electoral reform in Senate elections because it suggests that the benefits of electoral competitiveness for participation extend beyond midterm election years.

In the third chart of Figure 6.1, we see that turnout in presidential elections is flat in non-battleground states, hovering around .56. It then increases to .61 in battleground states, which is in line with the findings of other recent studies (Lipsitz 2009; Bergan et al. 2005). This pattern is becoming quite familiar. In the previous chapter, we saw that the interest and knowledge levels of voters are elevated only in battleground states. The finding in this chapter suggests that, despite Bush's "offensive" strategies in the 2000 and 2004 campaigns, his mobilization efforts were in fact efficiently targeted at battleground states.

Electoral Competitiveness and Non-Voting Forms of Political Participation

Although studies have found that state-level competitiveness in presidential elections affects non-voting forms of participation, it is less clear how electoral competitiveness affects them in other types of elections. One study has found that it has no relationship to such participation in House races, but that study uses a linear measure of competitiveness (Huckfeldt et al. 2002). As we have seen in previous chapters, this is problematic because the effects of competitiveness, especially in House races, can be nonlinear. For example, in Chapter 4 we learned that the ability to place an incumbent's ideology was actually higher in moderately competitive contests than in highly competitive ones, and in the previous section we saw a similar pattern with voter turnout in House races.

The models explaining non-voting participation include a wide variety of demographic and political variables. The demographic variables include age, gender, race, education, and income, while the political variables include strength of partisanship, partisan identification, trust, external efficacy, and media exposure where appropriate. In the previous chapter, we learned that electoral competitiveness, particularly in presidential elections, has a strong effect on political interest, so I have excluded it from the models in this chapter to capture the full effect of competitiveness on participation. The models also include several measures that capture the larger electoral context. For example, the models explaining participation during House elections include controls for whether there is a Senate or gubernatorial race taking place in the state, while the models explaining participation in Senate elections include controls for the presence of a gubernatorial election, as well as the competitiveness of the respondent's House district. The analysis of House and Senate races also includes a control for whether an incumbent was competing in the election.

House Elections

In the previous section, we considered how the competitiveness of a House race affects turnout and found that it has a positive effect in midterm election years. In presidential election years, however, turnout rises with competitiveness, peaking in those that are moderately so and declining significantly in toss-up contests. Figure 6.2 shows that this strange pattern holds in non-voting

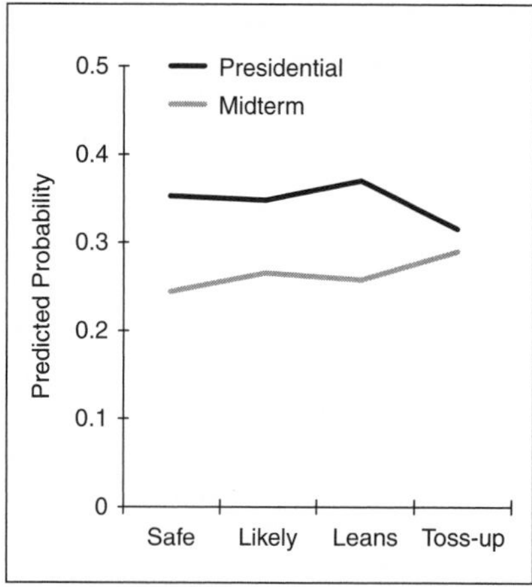

Figure 6.2. Effect of competitiveness on non-voting forms of participation in House elections during midterm and presidential election years. NES Cumulative Date File, 1998–2004. The *y*-axis shows the predicted probability that a respondent reported engaging in two acts of non-voting participation. In midterm election years, the difference in the predicted probability between safe and toss-up races is significant at the $p < .05$ level. No other differences are significant. In presidential election years, the difference in the predicted probability between "likely" and "toss-up" races is marginally significant at the $p < .1$ level. No other differences are significant. For the full models, see Models 1 and 2 in Table A.13.

forms of participation as well. The *y*-axis shows the predicted probability that a person reported participating in two non-voting forms of participation. This number was chosen because only 20 percent of the respondents reported a higher level of participation. Thus, a person who reported two political acts exhibited an elevated level of participation but not inordinately so.

As with turnout, electoral competitiveness has a positive effect on non-voting forms of participation in midterm election years. In safe races, the predicted probability that a person reported engaging in two non-voting forms of participation, such as donating or encouraging someone to support a candidate, was .25. The predicted probability rose slightly in "leans" and "likely" races, and then increased to .29 in toss-up contests. The difference in the predicted probability between safe and toss-up contests is highly significant. In presidential election years, the black line indicates that participation is elevated overall but that the competitiveness of a House race helps little. In fact, it can hurt. The predicted probability of participating in two non-voting forms of participation is .36 in safe contests, .35 in those that are likely to favor a candidate, and .37 in those that lean toward one. None of these differences are statistically significant. In toss-up contests, however, the predicted probability declines to .32. The .05 difference between moderately and highly competitive contests is marginally significant. If one compares the first chart in Figure 6.1 with this one, it is clear that House race competitiveness has a virtually identical effect on turnout and non-voting forms of participation. What is even more remarkable is that the pattern emerges in both district level turnout data and self-reported survey data. Something about highly competitive House races in presidential election years clearly demobilizes voters.

What is it about competitive House races that mobilizes voters in midterm election years and demobilizes them in presidential election years? Do certain qualities of the information environment play a role? Unfortunately, the Wisconsin Advertising Project has very limited data for 1998, and it is inappropriate, given the small number of NES survey respondents living in toss-up districts, to use only the 2002 NES data. Thus, we will only be able to explore the demobilizing effects of competitive House races in presidential election years. Fortunately, however, this effect is the more interesting of the two.

In Table 6.1, the analysis explores why highly competitive House races depress participation in presidential election years by using the advertising measures developed in earlier chapters. The method used here is similar to the one employed in Chapters 4 and 5. A series of models is estimated using the advertising volume measure and then the information quality measures individually. Models are also estimated that include an interaction between the volume measure and each of the information quality measures. The analysis also tests the role that campaign contacts play in mobilizing respondents. The contact measure is coded "1" if the respondent reported being contacted by a campaign or organization during the election season and "0" if they did not. As one examines each model, it is important to pay careful attention to how the coefficients for the competitiveness measures—especially the one for "toss-up" races—changes with the inclusion of new variables. Unfortunately, the following analysis will not identify the reason for depressed participation in competitive House races, but it will make a convincing case that without the high volume of quality information—including negative information—provided by competitive races, the demobilizing effect of such races would be much worse.

The first model in Table 6.1 serves as the base model. Here we see the marginally negative effect of toss-up House races on participation.[6] The contact measure is included in Model 2, and the large .45 coefficient indicates that being contacted by a campaign or party has a large and highly significant positive effect on participation. To put this coefficient in perspective,

Table 6.1. Effect of Advertising on Non-Voting Forms of Participation in House Races

	Model 1	*Model 2*	*Model 3*	*Model 4*	*Model 5*	*Model 6*	*Model 7*	*Model 8*	*Model 9*	*Model 10*	*Model 11*	*Model 12*
Likely	.096	.086	.034	.026	.002	.033	.033	.019	−.004	.022	.061	.045
	(.102)	(.103)	(.105)	(.107)	(.103)	(.105)	(.106)	(.103)	(.107)	(.107)	(.107)	(.106)
Leans	.006	−.012	−.173	−.200	−.253	−.178	−.156	−.229	−.258	−.201	−.111	−.212
	(.139)	(.136)	(.147)	(.163)	(.154)	(.153)	(.163)	(.152)	(.159)	(.185)	(.161)	(.151)
Toss-up	−.208	−.210	−.475**	−.477**	−.524**	−.477**	−.459**	−.533**	−.526**	−.472**	−.453**	−.555***
	(.130)	(.135)	(.159)	(.159)	(.164)	(.160)	(.173)	(.164)	(.165)	(.178)	(.163)	(.163)
Contact	—	.447***	.450***	.452***	.446***	.450***	.450***	.455***	.448***	.450***	.443***	.450***
		(.079)	(.079)	(.079)	(.079)	(.079)	(.079)	(.079)	(.079)	(.079)	(.080)	(.079)
Volume (100s)	—	—	.007*	.009	.005	.006#	.007#	.007*	.006	.009#	−.003	.001
			(.003)	(.007)	(.003)	(.004)	(.004)	(.003)	(.008)	(.005)	(.009)	(.006)
Volume*volume	—	—	—	−.0004	—	—	—	—	—	—	—	—
				(.0001)								
Equality	—	—	—	—	.204	—	—	—	.220	—	—	—
					(.180)				(.198)			
Dialogue	—	—	—	—	—	.028	—	—	—	—	−.076	—
						(.277)					(.290)	
Diversity	—	—	—	—	—	—	−.009	—	—	.012	—	—
							(.042)			(.059)		
Negativity	—	—	—	—	—	—	—	.200	—	—	—	.094
								(.174)				(.198)
Volume*equality	—	—	—	—	—	—	—	—	−.002	—	—	—
									(.010)			
Volume*diversity	—	—	—	—	—	—	—	—	—	−.001	—	—
										(.001)		
Volume*dialogue	—	—	—	—	—	—	—	—	—	—	.016	—
											(.015)	
Volume*negativity	—	—	—	—	—	—	—	—	—	—	—	.014
												(.014)
N	**991**	**991**	**991**	**991**	**991**	**991**	**991**	**991**	**991**	**991**	**991**	**991**
Log likelihood	**−1344**	**−1326**	**−1323**	**−1323**	**−1322**	**−1323**	**−1323**	**−1322**	**−1322**	**−1323**	**−1323**	**−1322**
Pseudo-R^2	**.098**	**.109**	**.111**	**.111**	**.112**	**.111**	**.111**	**.112**	**.112**	**.111**	**.112**	.112

*** $p<0.001$; ** $p<0.01$; * $p<0.05$; # $p<0.1$; two-tailed. Source: American National Election Study Cumulative File; Goldstein et al. 2002; Goldstein and Rivlin 2007. Cell entries are ordered probit coefficients with standard errors in parentheses. The dependent variable is a non-voting participation index, range. 0–5. See Table A.10 for the full models.

the predicted probability of reporting two acts of non-voting participation is .25 if a respondent did not report being contacted and .32 if he did. In the next two models, the volume measure is introduced. The difference between Models 3 and 4 is that Model 4 includes a quadratic term to allow for the possibility that the effect of advertising volume on participation is nonlinear. For example, if advertising volume has a positive effect on participation at low and moderate levels and no effect at high levels—for example, the very high levels present in toss-up races—then the coefficient for the volume measure should be positive, while the coefficient for the quadratic term should be negative. As we see, this is the case in Model 4, but neither of the coefficients is statistically significant and inclusion of the quadratic term does not improve the explanatory power of the model. In Model 3, however, the coefficient for the volume measure is statistically significant and positive. The .007 coefficient indicates that as advertising volume increases from the 20th to the 80th percentile, the predicted probability of participation increases from .27 to .30. Thus advertising volume has a much smaller mobilizing effect than being contacted, but it is a positive effect nonetheless. What is more interesting, however, is how including the volume measure in the model affects the toss-up race coefficient; the negative effect more than doubles, from −.21 to −.48. This suggests that the positive mobilizing effects of advertising in competitive House races mask other features of these races that depress participation. In other words, a competitive House race with little or no advertising will have far lower participation than one with advertising. Some readers might be concerned that this effect is the result of multicollinearity in the model. The toss-up race variable and the advertising variable are correlated at .57, but this relationship emerges very clearly in the data even when one simply compares mean levels of participation at different levels of advertising in toss-up races.

In Models 5 through 8, each of the advertising quality measures is included in the model along with the volume measure to determine if doing so improves the model's explanatory power or accounts for the demobilizing effect of highly competitive House races. Models 5 and 8 reveal that including either the equality or the negativity measure in the model does indeed improve its fit. Although the coefficients for the volume and equality measures in Model 5 are not statistically significant, they are jointly significant.[7] This suggests that the volume and balance measures are so highly correlated that the model cannot distinguish between their effects. Yet, there is no question that together they boost participation. If one did not test their joint significance, one would wrongly conclude that neither variable is beneficial, which is incorrect. Similarly, the joint significance of the negativity and volume measures in Model 8 is quite high ($p<.01$). What is also interesting about both of the models is that including the equality and negativity measures increases the magnitude of both the "likely" and "toss-up" race coefficients from their levels in Model 3. This suggests that the joint effect of advertising balance and volume, or negativity and volume in such races, mitigates the effect of whatever it is about highly competitive House contests that depresses participation more than the volume measure does alone.

In Models 9 through 12, I investigate the interaction of the volume measure with each of the advertising quality measures. Two substantive interactions emerge in Models 11 and 12, which are depicted in the two charts in Figure 6.3. Both interactions indicate that advertising, which does not have certain qualities, fails to promote participation. Contrary to our expectations concerning dialogue, the interaction in Model 11 indicates that House advertising mobilizes voters only if it features dialogue.

The first chart in Figure 6.3 shows that the predicted probability of engaging in two forms of non-voting participation changes at low and high levels of

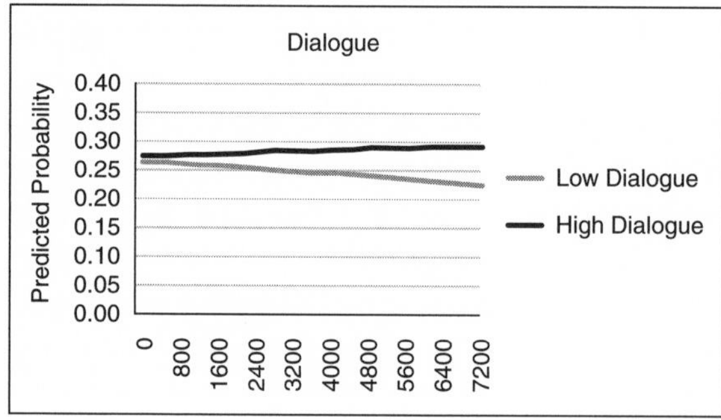

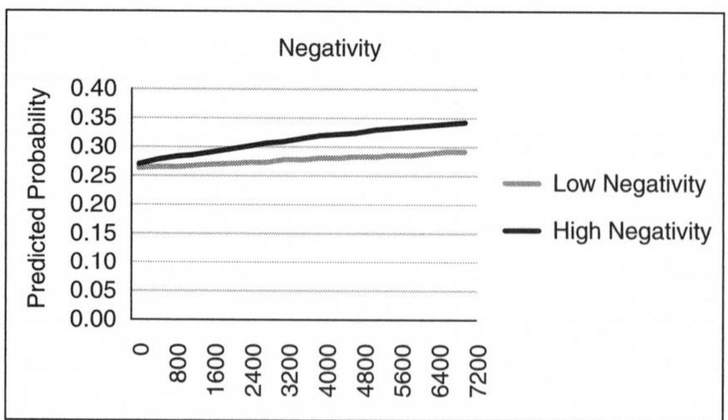

Figure 6.3. Effect of advertising volume on non-voting forms of participation in House elections at low and high levels of dialogue and negativity. National Election Study Cumulative File, 2000–2004 and Wisconsin Advertising Project. The difference between low and high dialogue is significant over 2800 ads. The difference between low and high negativity is significant over 2000 ads.

dialogue. When candidates talk past each other in their advertising and fail to discuss the same issues, the advertising does not mobilize voters as indicated by the gray line. When they engage in a high level of dialogue, advertising in a House campaign has a small but positive and statistically significant effect on participation. The difference between the two lines is significant above 2,800 ads. In the case of negativity, ads that feature no attacks do not promote participation, as indicated by the insignificant .001 coefficient for the volume measure in Model 12. When there is a high level of negativity in a campaign, which is approximately 40 percent, then advertising volume has a significant positive effect on participation. The difference between high and low negativity is statistically significant above about 2,000 ads.

Just as my analysis in Chapter 4 exonerated negative advertising in the investigation of why highly competitive House races depressed voter knowledge, the analysis in this chapter has absolved it of the blame for the demobilizing effect in presidential election years. In addition, the analysis shows that the higher levels of advertising, particularly advertising that features dialogue and attacks, mitigate the demobilizing effects of highly competitive House races. Still, I acknowledge that the analysis fails to identify the mechanisms responsible for the effect of competitiveness. A number of alternative hypotheses were explored and hint at other explanations that might be tested in future analyses with more extensive data.

(1) *Voter Fatigue.* In 1952–2000, the NES asked respondents the extent to which they agreed with the following statement: "Sometimes politics and government seem so complicated that a person like me can't really understand what's going on."[8] In 1998, one of the two midterm election years examined in this study, a person's response to this question was not significantly correlated to whether she lived in a district with a highly competitive House race. In 2000 it was.[9] It is possible that the addition of a competitive House race in a presidential election year to an individual's political universe is simply overwhelming. One would expect it to be overwhelming only for those who are less interested in politics,[10] however, and these people are least likely to participate, especially in non-voting forms of participation. Still, perhaps this measure captures some kind of voter fatigue that is engendered by too many heated political races layered on top of one another.

(2) *Changes in Campaign Strategy.* It is possible that candidates and parties rely too much on advertising when House races are highly competitive, especially in presidential election years, and neglect the grassroots campaign. In

midterm election years, 53 percent of the respondents report being contacted when House races are "likely" to favor a candidate and 51 percent in "toss-up" races. In presidential election years, 51 percent of respondents with moderately competitive House races report being contacted while only 41 percent in "toss-up" races do. In Model 2 of Table 6.1, one can see that including the contact measure in the model does not explain the toss-up race effect, as one might expect if the decline in contacts actually accounted for the negative effect of toss-up races on participation, but this pattern in campaign contacts is still striking and may be related to a larger shift in campaign strategies that explains the demobilizing effect of highly competitive House races in presidential election years.

Senate Elections

Earlier, we learned that turnout in Senate elections is highest when those elections are hard fought. This holds in both midterm and presidential election years. In Figure 6.4, however, we learn that this is not the case for non-voting forms of participation. In both midterm and presidential election years, non-voting forms of participation, such as donating and working for a campaign, are highest when elections are moderately competitive and decline when they become highly competitive. In midterm election years, the predicted probability of engaging in two forms of non-voting participation is .24. It increases to .25 in "leans" contests and then jumps to .30 in "likely" contests. It then

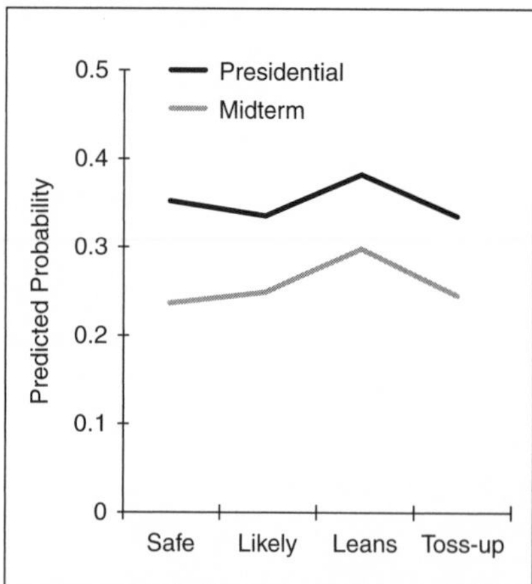

Figure 6.4. Effect of competitiveness on non-voting forms of participation in Senate elections in midterm and presidential election years. NES Cumulative Date File, 1998–2004. In both midterm and presidential election years, the difference in the predicted probability between "likely" races and all other categories of races is marginally significant at the $p < .01$ level or better. For the full models, see Models 3 and 4 in Table A.13.

falls back to .24 in toss-up races. In presidential election years, those numbers are .35, .34, .39, and .33 respectively.

In Table 6.2, we investigate this peculiar pattern in non-voting forms of participation using contact and advertising measures. Since electoral competitiveness affects participation in the same way in midterm and presidential election years, the analysis uses all the years for which the advertising data are currently available (2000–2004) and simply includes a dummy variable if the respondent was interviewed in 2002. As in Table 6.1, Model 1 of Table 6.2 serves as the baseline model and the contact measure is added in Model 2. Again, being contacted by a campaign or party has a large impact on participation. The predicted value of engaging in two non-voting forms of participation is .23 if a person did not report being contacted by the campaign and .33 if they did. Notice also that including the contact measure in the model reduces the "leans" coefficient slightly from .19 to .15, suggesting that being contacted by a campaign explains some of the effect of being exposed to a moderately competitive Senate race. Strangely, however, it does not affect the "toss-up" race coefficient at all. One might expect the magnitude of the negative effect to increase when the contact measure was included in the model, suggesting that increased contacts in such races boost participation even as other factors decrease it, but no such change occurs.

In Models 3 and 4, the advertising measures were included. Including a linear measure of advertising in Model 3 does not improve the explanatory power of the model, but including the advertising volume measure along with its quadratic form does, as we see in Model 4. The pseudo-R^2 increases from .096 to .1. This is a highly significant increase in explanatory power. Figure 6.5 depicts the effect of advertising volume in Senate races visually. Volume has a positive effect on participation as it increases to approximately 10,000 ads (approximately the 70th percentile) over the course of a campaign. This effect disappears between 10,000 and 16,000 ads (80th percentile), and then actually becomes significantly negative above that level. One might ask why this effect never emerged in House races. The reason may be that advertising volume for a single House race never exceeded 10,000 ads in a campaign season.

Perhaps more important, notice that including the volume measure along with its quadratic form completely accounts for the positive effect of being exposed to a moderately competitive election. The .15 coefficient for the "likely" measure that we saw in Model 2 completely disappears, and the magnitude of the negative effect for highly competitive races is reduced slightly from −.11 to −.09. In fact, in Model 4, the difference between the "likely" and "toss-up"

Table 6.2. Effect of Advertising on Non-Voting Forms of Participation in Senate Races

	Model 1	*Model 2*	*Model 3*	*Model 4*	*Model 5*	*Model 6*	*Model 7*	*Model 8*	*Model 10*	*Model 11*	*Model 12*	*Model 13*
Likely	–.153*	–.146*	–.119#	–.244***	–.240**	–.240**	–.142#	–.247***	–.269***	–.217**	–.131	–.248***
	(.069)	(.068)	(.069)	(.074)	(.077)	(.073)	(.086)	(.073)	(.080)	(.078)	(.094)	(.074)
Leans	.186*	.148	.220*	.004	.019	.014	.133	–.030	.006	.070	.145	–.052
	(.091)	(.092)	(.100)	(.115)	(.136)	(.115)	(.129)	(.125)	(.141)	(.121)	(.130)	(.135)
Toss-up	–.108#	–.107	.049	–.092	–.078	–.055	.039	–.119	–.045	.049	.065	–.133
	(.061)	(.061)	(.110)	(.118)	(.138)	(.130)	(.133)	(.125)	(.141)	(.140)	(.136)	(.128)
Contact	—	.568***	.567***	.557***	.557***	.556***	.561***	.558***	.551***	.556***	.561***	.559***
		(.052)	(.052)	(.052)	(.052)	(.053)	(.053)	(.052)	(.052)	(.052)	(.053)	(.052)
Volume (1000s)	—	—	–.010#	.058**	.058**	.060**	.058**	.056**	.058	.101***	.064*	.039
			(.006)	(.018)	(.018)	(.019)	(.018)	(.018)	(.036)	(.029)	(.031)	(.027)
Volume*volume	—	—	—	–.003***	–.003***	–.003***	–.002***	–.002***	–.001	–.006***	–.003*	–.002
				(.001)	(.001)	(.001)	(.001)	(.001)	(.003)	(.001)	(.001)	(.002)
Equality	—	—	—	—	–.027	—	—	—	.109	—	—	—
					(.127)				(.231)			
Diversity	—	—	—	—	—	–.008	—	—	—	–.037	—	—
						(.012)				(.039)		
Dialogue	—	—	—	—	—	—	–.404*	—	—	—	–.449	—
							(.159)				(.331)	
Negativity	—	—	—	—	—	—	—	.157	—	—	—	–.171
								(.218)				(.423)
Volume*equality	—	—	—	—	—	—	—	—	–.002	—	—	—
									(.006)			
Volume²*equality	—	—	—	—	—	—	—	—	–1.46-9	—	—	—
									(3.70-9)			

Volume*diversity	—	—	—	—	—	—	—	—	—	−.0003	—	—
										(.001)		
Volume^{2}*diversity	—	—	—	—	—	—	—	—	—	3.10-10$^{\#}$	—	—
										(2.09-10)		
Volume*dialogue	—	—	—	—	—	—	—	—	—	—	−.001	—
											(.008)	
Volume^{2}*dialogue	—	—	—	—	—	—	—	—	—	—	1.12-9	—
											(1.91-9)	
Volume*negativity	—	—	—	—	—	—	—	—	—	—	—	.010
												(.012)
Volume^{2}*negativity	—	—	—	—	—	—	—	—	—	—	—	−4.57-9
												(7.08-9)
N	**2,356**	**2,353**	**2,353**	**2,353**	**2,353**	**2,353**	**2,353**	**2,353**	**2,353**	**2,353**	**2,353**	**2,353**
Log likelihood	**−3204**	**−3131**	**−3129**	**−3118**	**−3118**	**−3117**	**−3114**	**−3117**	**−3116**	**−3112**	**−3114**	**−3117**
Pseudo-R^2	**.076**	**.096**	**.096**	**.100**	**.100**	**.100**	**.101**	**.100**	**.100**	**.101**	**.101**	**.100**

*** $p<0.001$; ** $p<0.01$; * $p<0.05$; # $p<0.1$; two-tailed. Source: American National Election Study Cumulative File; Goldstein et al. 2002; Goldstein and Rivlin 2005, 2007. Cell entries are ordered probit coefficients with standard errors in parentheses. The dependent variable is a non-voting participation index, range 0–5. See Table A.11 for the full models.

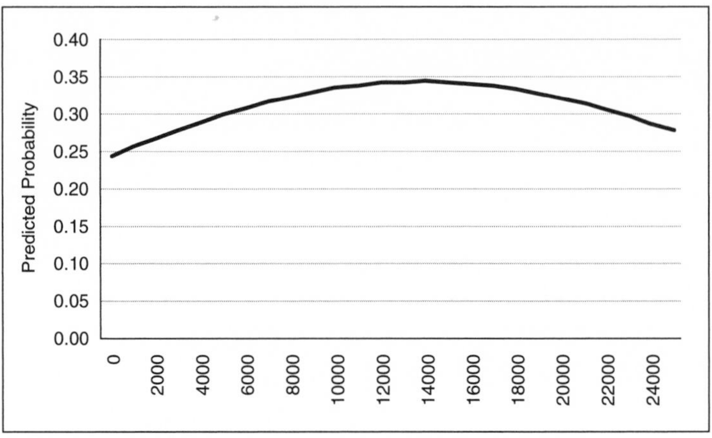

Figure 6.5. Effect of advertising volume on non-voting forms of participation in Senate elections. NES Cumulative File, 2000–2004 and Wisconsin Advertising Project. Predicted probabilities were calculated using CLARIFY.

measures is no longer statistically significant. Thus, the nonlinear effect of advertising volume accounts for much of the odd relationship we observed between competitive Senate races and non-voting forms of participation.

In Models 5 through 8, the other measures of advertising quality are added to the model to see if they improve its fit. The only one that does is the dialogue measure in Model 7, and its direction indicates that it might be creating a more ambivalent electorate because it does indeed appear to depress participation. As dialogue increases from its 20th to its 80th percentile, the predicted probability that a respondent reports taking part in two forms of non-voting participation decreases from .31 to .27. In addition, we see that the negative effect of dialogue accounts for some of the toss-up race effect. The coefficient goes from –.09 in Model 4 to .04 in Model 7 when the dialogue measure is included. Although dialogue has a negative effect on participation, Model 8 shows that negativity does not. The coefficient is not significant, but it is positive.

In Models 9 through 13, the volume measure is interacted with each of the information quality measures. None of the interactions tell an interesting story except for the one in Model 11 between volume and information diversity.[11] Because it is difficult to make sense of the interaction simply by looking at regression coefficients, Figure 6.6 depicts this interaction. Recall that I expected diversity to have a negative effect on participation if it had any at all because it might lead to ambivalence among the electorate, but the effect that Figure 6 shows is of an entirely different nature. At low and moderate levels of advertising, ads have a greater effect on participation if they have just a few sponsors.[12] The figure suggests that if there are too many sponsors at a low volume of advertising, none of them are airing enough ads to affect voters. At higher levels of advertising, however, hearing from just a few sponsors is much more harmful for participation than hearing from a wider range of voices. Recall that each candidate and group that paid for ads was counted as a sponsor. A low level of diversity is the equivalent of two sponsors, which are likely to be the candidates in Senate races. Thus, this interaction suggests that people tire of hearing from the candidates. If they are going to be inundated by Senate ads, they prefer to hear from a wider range of voices. Figure 6.6 makes it clear that a large number of ads is demobilizing even if it comes from a diverse range of sources, but it is far less demobilizing than hearing from the same sponsors over and over.

Although the analysis in Table 6.2 explains why participation is highest in moderately competitive Senate races, it fails to fully explain why participation

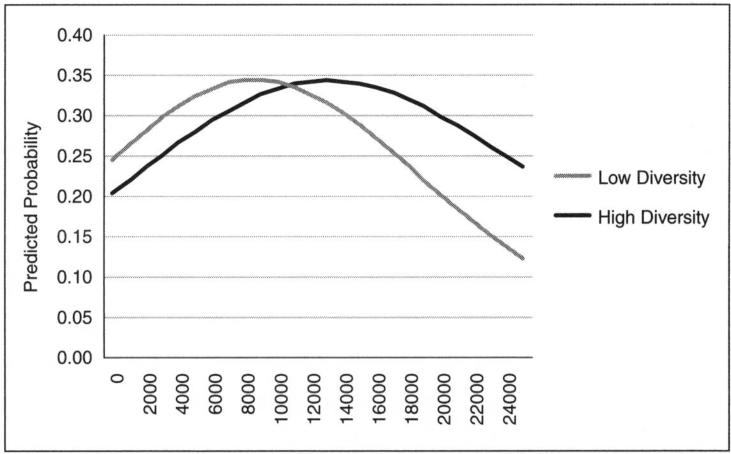

Figure 6.6. Effect of advertising volume on non-voting forms of participation in Senate elections at low and high levels of information diversity. NES Cumulative File, 2000–2004 and Wisconsin Advertising Project. The difference between low and high dialogue is significant under 8000 ads and over 14000 ads. Predicted probabilities were calculated using CLARIFY.

is so low in modestly competitive races. The magnitude of the negative effect doubled between Model 2 and Model 4 when the volume measure and its quadratic term were added, from −.12 to −.24. When the dialogue measure was added in Models 7 and 12, the coefficient for "leaning" Senate races dropped back down, again suggesting that the level of dialogue in such races is part of the problem. This is puzzling given the analysis in Chapter 3, which indicated that dialogue is extremely low in such races. More research is necessary to fully understand why the information environments of modestly competitive Senate races affect citizen participation the way they do.

The analysis shows that the higher level of participation in moderately competitive races can be explained by the nonlinear effect of advertising volume. A low or moderate level of advertising energizes citizens, while too much demobilizes them. Senate advertising that features dialogue is also enervating. Notice that hearing equally from the candidates does not have the same effect, so it is not a two-sided information flow that depresses participation but exposure to advertisements that focus on the same issue that does. More research is necessary to understand exactly why dialogue harms participation in Senate races but mobilizes voters in House contests. The analysis also reveals that too little advertising diversity exacerbates the negative effects of a high volume of advertising in Senate races.[13]

Presidential Elections

Earlier, we learned that during the 2000 and 2004 presidential elections, turnout was similar in safe, "leans," and "likely" states, and then increased significantly in battleground states. In this section, we examine how state-level competitiveness affects non-voting forms of participation and how the information environment generated by competitive elections, as measured by television advertising, affects that participation. The analysis also considers how being contacted by the campaign affects these forms of behavior.

For this analysis, I prefer to use the National Annenberg Election Study's rolling cross section survey to allow for a more nuanced analysis of how state-level competitiveness and the campaign features it drives affect participation over the course of a campaign. Recall, that Annenberg conducts more than 300 interviews nationally every day of a general election campaign. The data provided by this survey when combined with the CMAG advertising data allow the researcher to assess how advertising during a preceding period of time—this analysis uses a week-long period—affects participation. Yet, in the analysis of non-voting forms of participation in House and Senate elections, I used National Election Study data. Thus, before turning to the Annenberg study to consider how advertising and contacts affect participation, I compare participation levels across these two surveys.

Because the 2004 Annenberg survey began asking respondents about their non-voting forms of participation on September 20, while the NES typically asks such questions on the post-election survey, we expect the reported level of participation to be lower in the Annenberg survey because many respondents are interviewed relatively early in the general election campaign. Figure 6.7 shows that this is indeed the case. The three lines show how competitiveness affects the predicted probability that an individual would report engaging in two forms of non-voting participation. The top line depicts the effect in the 2004 NES survey, while the middle line shows the effect in the 2000 NES survey.[14] The lower line depicts the relationship in the Annenberg survey. If we compare the two NES surveys, we can see that participation is higher overall in the 2004 presidential campaign and the effects of competitiveness on participation are more muted than in 2000. In 2000, reported participation is much higher in battleground states than in other states with a predicted probability of engaging in two non-voting forms of participation being .31. In the next highest category of state—"likely" states—it is .26. In 2004, however, the difference between the predicted probability in "likely"

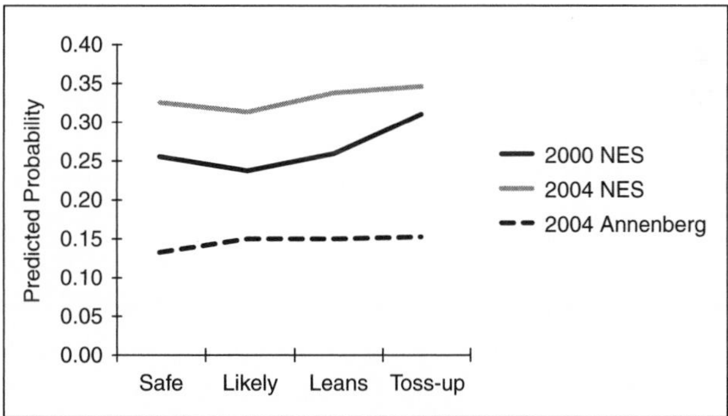

Figure 6.7. Effect of state-level competitiveness on non-voting forms of participation in presidential elections. NES Cumulative File and 2004 National Annenberg Election Study. Predicted probabilities calculated using CLARIFY. See Table A.14 for full models.

and battleground states is not statistically significant. The only differences that are significant are the ones between battleground and safe states and battleground and "leans" states, which are .02 and .03 respectively. In the 2004 Annenberg data, we see that reported participation is not only lower overall, as expected, but that participation is lower in safe states than in all other categories of states and that the level of participation in more competitive states is fairly consistent across the "likely," "leans," and toss-up categories. Even though the predicted probability of reporting two forms of non-voting participation, .14, is lower in safe states than other states—approximately .15—the difference is not substantively large. When one compares the 2004 NES and Annenberg data, the one major discrepancy is between reported participation in "leans" states. Aside from that, the relationship between competitiveness and participation is similar in the two datasets.

In Table 6.3, I use the Annenberg data to examine how advertising and campaign contacts—two campaign features that are driven by electoral competitiveness—affect non-voting forms of participation. Here I use advertising measures for the seven days prior to the interview. Thus, for example, the diversity measure captures the number of candidates and organizations that sponsored ads in the seven days prior to the day of the respondent's interview. The same demographic and political variables that were controlled for in the analysis of House and Senate data are controlled for here. I also control for the competitiveness of the respondent's House race, and whether there were any statewide races taking place. Model 1 in Table 6.3 serves as the baseline model. The astute reader will notice that electoral competitiveness does not have quite the same relationship with participation that it did in Figure 6.7. This is so because using the entire range of advertising measures on the same sample requires me to restrict my sample size since some of the measures could only be calculated from media markets in which both Democratic and Republican ads appeared. Still, one can see that even with this reduced sample size, participation in battleground states is marginally higher than in safe states (though the effect falls short of statistical significance). In Model 2, the contact measure is added, and one can see that it has a fairly large positive effect on participation. The predicted probability of reporting a high level of non-voting participation is .18 if a person has not been contacted by a candidate or party and .21 if she has. In Models 3 and 4, the advertising volume measure and its quadratic term are introduced. Neither is significant, but including the quadratic term appears to provide a slightly better fit. In addition, when the quadratic term is included in the model, the toss-up state coefficient is reduced more than if the term is not included—to .02 instead of .04. As a result, I include the quadratic term in the remaining models.

In Models 5 through 8, the advertising quality measures are introduced and just as we saw with the Senate race data, dialogue depresses participation. As the level of dialogue in a race increases from the 20th to the 80th percentile, the predicted probability of scoring a "2" on the participation index drops from .21 to .17. This is a larger effect than being contacted by a campaign. Moreover, once one accounts for the negative effect of dialogue, the volume measure becomes larger and marginally significant. The quadratic term is also marginally significant at a $p < .1$, one-tailed level.[15] This happens because more dialogue occurs with higher volumes of advertising and once one accounts for the harmful dialogue effect, one can see that advertising volume boosts participation—albeit marginally so—as long as it does not get too high, at which point its beneficial effects disappear.

In Models 10 through 13, the advertising quality measures are interacted with the volume measure and its quadratic term. A likelihood ratio test reveals that Models 12 and 13 perform significantly better than Model 4, which is the model that has the volume measure and its quadratic form alone. Model 12, in particular, performs better than any other in Table 6.3. In it, the dialogue measure is interacted with the volume measure while the negativity measure is interacted with volume measure in Model 13. The two charts in Figure 6.8 show that a person's score on the participation index is expected to change as volume increases at both low and high levels of dialogue and negativity.

When examining these figures, keep in mind that 95 percent of the media markets in which respondents lived saw fewer than 1,300 ads. The first chart shows that ad volume has a large positive effect on participation when dialogue is low but no effect when dialogue is high. The difference between low and high levels of dialogue is significant between 200 and 2,000 ads. In the analysis of Senate races, we saw that low dialogue is generally better for participation as well.

In the second chart, we see that ads featuring a high level of negativity have no effect on participation. Their effect is virtually flat, as the black line indicates. Ads that feature a low level of negativity do not necessarily boost participation, however. When ad volume is less than 400 ads (75th percentile), a low level of negativity is actually more harmful than a high one. Ads featuring a low level of negativity are very helpful when ad volume is extremely high; low negativity is significantly better when the ad volume in

Table 6.3. Explaining Effect of State-Level Competitiveness in Presidential Elections on Participation

	Model 1	*Model 2*	*Model 3*	*Model 4*	*Model 5*	*Model 6*	*Model 7*	*Model 8*	*Model 10*	*Model 11*	*Model 12*	*Model 13*
Likely	.079	.068	.064	.063	.065	.062	.042	.060	.053	.074	.050	.059
	(.124)	(.123)	(.124)	(.125)	(.126)	(.125)	(.121)	(.122)	(.133)	(.130)	(.118)	(.117)
Leans	.011	–.019	–.025	–.036	–.051	–.041	–.015	–.039	–.038	–.032	–.024	–.003
	(.083)	(.087)	(.090)	(.090)	(.088)	(.091)	(.090)	(.091)	(.090)	(.094)	(.087)	(.093)
Toss-up	.089	.055	.037	.021	.026	.020	.025	.020	.030	.023	.029	.031
	(.072)	(.075)	(.109)	(.116)	(.116)	(.116)	(.114)	(.115)	(.119)	(.119)	(.112)	(.119)
Contact	—	.238*	.237*	.238*	.243**	.239*	.237*	.239*	.245**	.240*	.239*	.237*
		(.094)	(.094)	(.094)	(.094)	(.094)	(.095)	(.095)	(.094)	(.095)	(.096)	(.096)
Volume	—	—	.002	.008	–.005	.011	.024#	.009	–.045	–.005	.060*	–.084
			(.006)	(.015)	(.019)	(.018)	(.016)	(.016)	(.040)	(.026)	(.025)	(.053)
Volume*volume	—	—	—	–.0003	.0001	–.0003	–.001	–.0003	.002	.001	–.003*	.006*
				(.001)	(.001)	(.001)	(.001)	(.001)	(.002)	(.001)	(.001)	(.003)
Equality	—	—	—	—	.178	—	—	—	–.178	—	—	—
					(.143)				(.185)			
Diversity	—	—	—	—	—	–.008	—	—	—	.075	—	—
						(.020)				(.063)		
Dialogue	—	—	—	—	—	—	–.534*	—	—	—	–.246	—
							(.211)				(.317)	
Negativity	—	—	—	—	—	—	—	–.078	—	—	—	–.217#
								(.103)				(.116)
Volume*equality	—	—	—	—	—	—	—	—	.095	—	—	—
									(.061)			
Volume²*equality	—	—	—	—	—	—	—	—	–.004	—	—	—
									(.003)			

Volume*diversity	—	—	—	—	—	—	—	—	—	−.006	—	—
										(.006)		
Volume²*diversity	—	—	—	—	—	—	—	—	—	1.97^{-5}	—	—
										(.0002)		
Volume*dialogue	—	—	—	—	—	—	—	—	—	—	−.117#	—
											(.061)	
Volume²*dialogue	—	—	—	—	—	—	—	—	—	—	.006*	—
											(.003)	
Volume*negativity	—	—	—	—	—	—	—	—	—	—	—	.160*
												(.078)
Volume²*negativityy	—	—	—	—	—	—	—	—	—	—	—	−.010*
												(.004)
N	**1,624**	**1,624**	**1,624**	**1,624**	**1,624**	**1,624**	**1,624**	**1,624**	**1,624**	**1,624**	**1,624**	**1,624**
Log Likelihood	**−2253**	**−2249**	**−2249**	**−2249**	**−2249**	**−2249**	**−2236**	**−2249**	**−2235**	**−2248**	**−2224**	**−2234**
Pseudo-R^2	**.037**	**.039**	**.039**	**.039**	**.039**	**.039**	**.040**	**.039**	**.040**	**.039**	**.041**	**.040**

*** $p<0.001$; ** $p<0.01$; * $p<0.05$; # $p<0.1$; two-tailed. Source: 2004 National Annenberg Election Study; Goldstein et al. 2002; Goldstein and Rivlin 2007. Cell entries are negative binomial regression coefficients with robust standard errors in parentheses (clustered by media market). The dependent variable is a non-voting participation index, range 0–5. See Table A.12 for the full models.

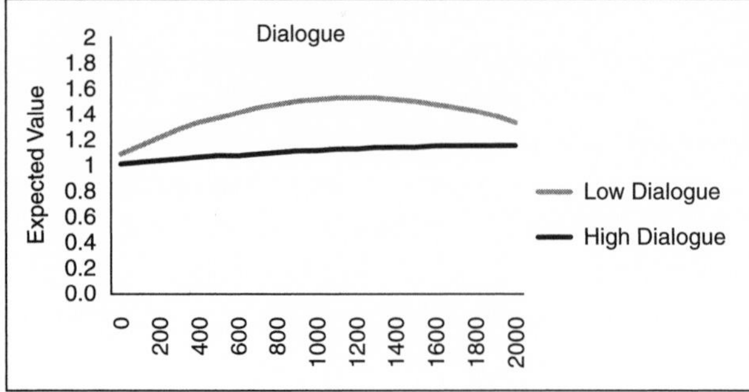

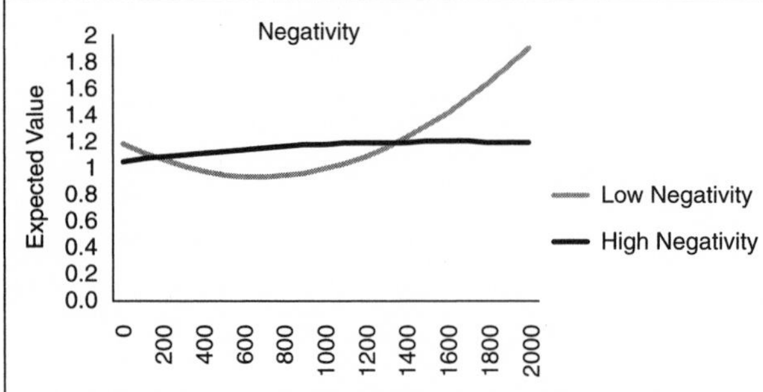

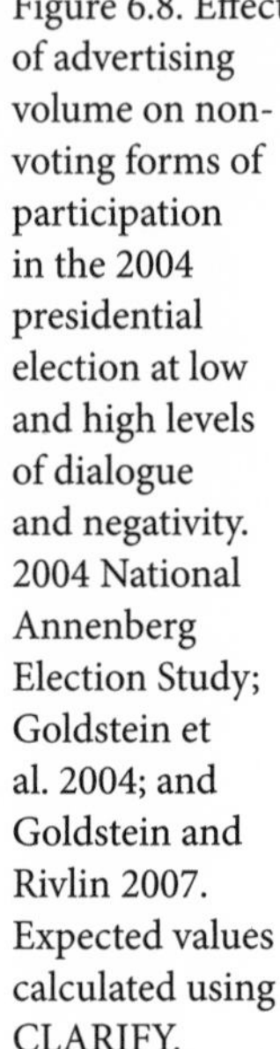
Figure 6.8. Effect of advertising volume on non-voting forms of participation in the 2004 presidential election at low and high levels of dialogue and negativity. 2004 National Annenberg Election Study; Goldstein et al. 2004; and Goldstein and Rivlin 2007. Expected values calculated using CLARIFY.

a single media market exceeds 1,600 ad airings. Fewer than 10 percent of the respondents living in battleground states were ever exposed to this level of advertising in a single week during the 2004 campaign. Thus, the second chart in Figure 6.8 indicates that most of the time it is better for advertising to feature a high than a low level of negativity, but when a media market is flooded with ads, for those ads to be positive not only is better, but may actually boost participation.

Conclusion

In this chapter, we have learned that the nature of the relationship between electoral competitiveness and participation depends on the office and sometimes even on the type of election year. For House elections, the election must be moderately or highly competitive to generate higher turnout in a midterm election year, and highly competitive to generate higher levels of non-voting forms of participation. In presidential election years both forms of participation are highest when the race is "likely" to favor a candidate and decline as a race becomes highly competitive. Are these effects "marginal" or "substantial"? In midterm election years, I would argue they are substantial. Turnout is 11 percent higher in toss-up districts than in safe districts, while non-voting participation is 18 percent higher. In presidential election years, the effects are less substantial, but what is striking is the similar pattern that emerges in turnout and non-voting participation. Clearly, citizens find something about moderately competitive contests to be engaging that is absent or obscured in toss-up contests. Perhaps the most important point, however, is simply that electoral competitiveness does indeed matter for both forms of participation in House elections.

In Senate campaigns, the surprising finding is that turnout is significantly higher in toss-up than in safe races in *both* midterm and presidential election years. In midterm election years it is also higher in moderately competitive elections. As in the case of House races, I would argue that the effects are substantial. In midterm election years, expected turnout is .15 higher in toss-up states than in both safe and moderately competitive states. In marginal elections it is .09 higher. What is remarkable, however, is that even in a presidential election year, a highly competitive Senate race also turns out more voters than a safe race. The .09 difference in expected turnout may not seem like much, but it rivals the difference in expected turnout between presidential battleground states and the rest of the country. The fact that non-voting participation is highest in moderately competitive contests might seem odd if we had not seen a similar pattern in the analysis of House races.

Finally, the pattern of participation that emerged in state-level presidential contests is hardly surprising, given what the analyses in previous chapters have revealed. Both turnout and non-voting participation are significantly higher only in battleground states. The .06 difference in expected turnout is fairly large, but the difference in non-voting participation is substantively much smaller. This may reflect the trend in 2000—and especially in 2004—for citizens in non-battleground states to seek ways to get involved in the presidential election. For example, in an earlier work of mine, I found that there was a sharp spike in donating among residents of safe states in 2004 and speculated that the reason why is that the internet has made it easy for the residents of non-battleground states to compensate for their lack of voting power by contributing (Lipsitz 2009). In 2004, Bush and Kerry supporters could also use the candidates' websites to organize "virtual meetings" and get lists of voters to call in battleground states. More work needs to be done to understand how such developments and their evolution in the 2008 election has changed the geography of participation in presidential elections, but this may explain why electoral competitiveness has a weaker relationship with non-voting participation than voter turnout.

This chapter's analysis has also tried to explain how the types of information that are generated by competitive elections and desirable from a normative standpoint affect participation. We learned that the volume of advertising does indeed boost participation but only under certain circumstances. In House races, we learned that only advertising, which features a high level of dialogue and negativity, mobilizes voters. Fortunately, as we learned in Chapter 3, advertising in House races features a high level of dialogue and is especially negative. In Table 6.1, we saw that were it not for such advertising, participation would be even lower in toss-up House races. In both Senate and state-level presidential contests, we saw that the effect of advertising volume only becomes clear if a quadratic term is included in the model to allow for the possibility that there are diminishing returns to advertising or even that a high volume of ads depresses participation. The nonlinear effect of Senate ad volume emerged very clearly in all the models in Table 6.2, but the nonlinear effects of presidential ad volume on participation emerged clearly only when the negative effect of dialogue on participation was accounted for. The reason why this nonlinear effect of advertising did not emerge in the House race analysis is that advertising in such races never reaches the point of diminishing (or negative) returns.

The harmful effect of dialogue in Senate and presidential races was not unexpected given the fact that scholars have recently discovered that two-sided information flows generated by competitive elections increase ambivalence and ambivalence has been found to depress participation. What my analysis suggests is that it may not be the two-sided information flow per se that is creating ambivalence but a particular aspect of that two-sided information flow, which is dialogue. It is not hearing balanced information that creates ambivalence but a focused exchange on the same issues that does. Presumably, when candidates talk past each other, these feelings of ambivalence do not arise and participation does not fall, but this may be because voters are learning less. More research is needed to confirm that ambivalence accounts for why dialogue has the negative effect on participation that it does in Senate and presidential elections, but these findings are certainly suggestive and in line with recent research. The other puzzle is why dialogue hurts participation in these types of elections but encourages it in House contests.

Finally, we saw that negativity can boost participation (in House races), ensure that ads do not depress participation (in state-level presidential races) or have no effect on participation (in Senate races). We saw no evidence that negative ads ever depress it. The one case where it was clear that it is better to have a high proportion of positive ads is when presidential candidates are airing an inordinately high volume of ads. The quotation from Richard Lau, Lee Sigelman, and Ivy Brown Rovner that I cited earlier could be used to summarize my findings concerning negative ads and participation.

In light of this chapter's findings, Rhodes Cook's claim that "'competition, competition, competition' is the key to voter engagement" seems a bit exaggerated. There is no question that electoral competitiveness promotes participation in midterm House races and state-level presidential contests. It also boosts turnout in Senate races. But there seems to be a darker side to it as well. In House and Senate races there is evidence that moderate levels of competitiveness create a campaign context that is more inviting to citizens. Thus, this analysis confirms the old maxim that one can have too much of a good thing.

CHAPTER 7

Improving Electoral Competitiveness Through Reform

Electoral competitiveness is not an unmitigated good, but if one seeks to improve campaigns in America, the path to their improvement involves adopting reforms to ensure that more elections are not only contested but closely contested. Without competitive elections, candidates and their supporters have no incentive to communicate with citizens and provide them with the information they need to make informed decisions in the voting booth. This also means that competitive elections are the linchpin of democratic accountability. Tough challenges force incumbents to defend their record, to describe their future policy agenda, and in doing so to heed the desires of the electorate. An unchallenged incumbent, or one who is sure of easily coasting to victory, will offer voters little more than smiles and platitudes. A healthy challenge is the only way to hold elected officials' feet to the fire and offer voters any hope of hearing a meaningful exchange between candidates.

To demonstrate the truth of this claim, this book has shown that competitive elections are more likely to generate the kinds of information that voters need to make informed decisions. Competitive elections encourage candidates to provide voters with not only more but better quality information, that is, information that is more balanced overall, more diverse, more likely to feature dialogue, and perhaps most important, more negative. The analyses in Chapters 4, 5, and 6 sought to confirm that competitive elections do in fact promote voter knowledge and engagement. In the process, these analyses also sought to confirm that these kinds of information, which appear to be wholly desirable from the standpoint of normative theory, are indeed beneficial for voters. Several key lessons have emerged that should be helpful for reformers.

First, moderate or even modest levels of competitiveness are more helpful for voters in House elections than high levels of it most of the time. In Chapter 4, we learned that political knowledge is highest in moderately competitive elections, while Chapter 6 showed us that turnout and non-voting participation in presidential election years is also highest when competitiveness is moderate. The only time toss-up races produced better individual-level outcomes was in the case of participation during midterm elections. Thus, House campaigns could be improved significantly for voters by taking steps to ensure that they are just modestly competitive. In Senate elections, elevated levels of knowledge and participation were seen consistently in moderately competitive contests. A high level of competitiveness depressed non-voting forms of participation at the same time that it provided an additional boost to voting. Thus, reformers need to aim for moderate levels of competitiveness in Senate elections to see any real gains for voters.

The relationship between competitiveness and voter engagement in presidential elections is entirely different, however. Elevated levels of interest, knowledge, and engagement were seen only in the most competitive states, despite the fact that moderately competitive states also received ample attention from the candidates. The reason very likely has to do with the fact that residents of less competitive states still have access to information about the candidates. They can also find ways to participate in the campaign if they so desire, usually via the Internet. Thus, only the extreme levels of advertising and mobilization targeted at battleground states yield levels of engagement that are distinct from the rest of the country. Recall, however, that although battleground state residents clearly exhibited higher levels of knowledge and participation, they were lower than expected, especially given their elevated levels of campaign interest. Thus, the lesson for reformers is that their efforts are better directed at subnational elections, where they are likely to yield bigger gains for the citizenry, especially given how difficult it would be to reform or abandon the Electoral College.

There are two other lessons for reformers that emerge from this analysis. First, they do not need to worry about candidates talking past one another, at least in their television ads. Dialogue does not seem to be particularly helpful for voters, especially those with less political knowledge, in high visibility elections. The analysis suggests that dialogue may be beneficial for voters in lower visibility elections, but we need to get a better sense of why it can sow confusion in the minds of some people before advocating it. Second, and perhaps more important, reformers must make peace with campaign negativity, not only because I find—like so many others—that it rarely hurts voters and usually helps them, but because making peace with negativity will allow them to fully embrace electoral competitiveness. Reformers who continue to decry the tone of American political campaigns will never feel fully comfortable with reforms that make elections more competitive.

Reforming American Campaigns

Those who are convinced by this book's argument have a host of reforms to choose from. Many of these reforms have been vetted by academic researchers, embraced by fair elections groups, and even endorsed by major media outlets. At the same time, however, most Americans are only dimly aware that these reforms are possible or even necessary. Indeed, those who seek to implement these reforms will find that a strong public education campaign is required. They will also need to be prepared for an inevitable criticism: that virtually any reform that enhances electoral competitiveness will make campaigns even more expensive than they already are.

In this chapter I discuss a wide variety of reforms for increasing electoral competitiveness at all levels of government, ranging from state legislative term limits to Electoral College reform. Although most of the reforms involve changes in election law, some causes of declining competitiveness can only be addressed by other types of public policy, such as municipal zoning and fair housing laws, which I briefly discuss. The chapter also addresses a handful of reforms that are unlikely to affect competitiveness but are likely to increase the chances that an election—usually a general election—will be contested, thereby ensuring that voters actually have a choice in the election. Although the list of reforms considered is by no means exhaustive, this discussion should give the reader an idea of what a more comprehensive reform agenda aimed at increasing electoral competitiveness might look like.

Although individuals who are concerned about declining competitiveness may be heartened by the long list of reforms at their disposal, they are likely to be discouraged by my discussion of the real prospects for change. Few political actors, including political parties, Congress, the courts, the president, and the voters, have the interest and motivation to pursue the type of reform agenda outlined here.

Reforms That Directly Help Challengers

Many scholars have documented the growing incumbency advantage in elections and its relationship with declining electoral competitiveness (Abramowitz et al. 2006). It is simply becoming harder and harder for challengers to marshal the resources necessary to mount a viable political campaign. Because the Supreme Court ruled in *Buckley v. Valeo* that nonvoluntary campaign spending limits are unconstitutional, it is virtually impossible to limit incumbent spending. Thus, reformers must find ways to funnel technical and financial support to challengers.

Encouraging Quality Challengers to Run

The problem confronting reformers is not that there is a dearth of quality candidates in noncompetitive districts and states, but that they are simply choosing not to run. Candidate quality is usually conceptualized as having previous political experience and access to resources; common sense suggests that competitive districts and states should not have a monopoly on such individuals. Moreover, researchers have actually shown that noncompetitive districts offer soil that is just as fertile for potential House candidates as the soil in competitive districts (Maisel et al. 2007: 129). The problem is that potential candidates residing in safe districts are much less likely to be contacted and encouraged to run by the parties. Since it is even more difficult for an individual to challenge an incumbent without the backing of a party, potential candidates understandably decide it is more prudent to hold on to their day jobs than to try to oust an incumbent from office without such support. This means that in order for the situation to change, reformers must enact reforms that change party incentives, encouraging them to focus more resources on noncompetitive jurisdictions, or they must advocate reforms that provide challengers in noncompetitive districts and states with the kind of support that the parties are not giving them.

Although the national party committees no longer have access to soft money, the state parties do. One potential reform would involve allowing the state parties to use this money to train potential candidates, and possibly even their staff, about how to run campaigns. Many organizations and political action committees already offer candidates classes on how to manage campaigns. This is not quite the same as having the full support of the party, but it does reduce some of the information costs associated with getting a campaign up and running. Such training would also give potential candidates contact with a party and may serve as a foundation for further collaboration once the campaign has started. Moreover, funding this kind of training with soft money is not unlike using soft money for voter mobilization, which is currently allowed for state parties. Get-out-the-vote efforts are about encouraging citizens to fulfill the role of a democratic citizen by equipping them with the information they need to vote. Similarly, candidate training equips them with the information they need to play an equally important role in the process—that of a political candidate.

There is some evidence that the parties are starting to think differently about the value of running challengers in noncompetitive districts. Former Democratic national chair Howard Dean launched his "50-State Strategy" in 2005, arguing that "If you don't show up in 60 percent of the country, you don't win, and that's not going to happen anymore." Implementation of the strategy involved hiring party organizers in every state, and while many party insiders disparaged the idea at the time, many political observers saw President Barack Obama's 2008 victory in states such as Indiana and North Carolina as a vindication of Dean. But the strategy not only paid off for the party's presidential candidate, it yielded victories in congressional districts that had been held by Republicans for some time. For example, in 2008, the Democrats picked up seats in Mississippi and Louisiana, which held special elections early in the year, and in other states such as Idaho and Alabama in November. If the Democrats stay true to this strategy, then we may see more competitive local and state races in the future. And if Republicans try to fight fire with fire by adopting the same strategy, there is a possibility that it could spawn a new era of competitive elections in America. Many party leaders, however, will resist or continue to resist the adoption of such a strategy because of its high costs and the fact that it is a risky strategy when national elections are close. Thus, those who desire more competitive elections should work with groups advocating a 50-state strategy to apply pressure to party leaders.

Public Financing

One obvious way to help candidates in the absence of party support is through campaign finance reforms, especially public financing. Although advocates of public financing claim it enhances competitiveness, there have been surprisingly few studies of the question. Some recent research has vindicated reformers' claims by demonstrating the following: (1) that public funding programs increase the number of candidates who contest elections; and (2) that public funding increases the likelihood that incumbents will face a competitive election (Mayer et al. 2006). Some of this research, however, emphasizes that these findings are conditional on the amount of public funding provided. For example, Hawaii and Wisconsin provide legislative candidates with a paltry sum for running, which renders their programs ineffective, while Minnesota and Arizona support candidates at more realistic levels and enjoy considerably more success. It is unclear whether Congress or the public would ever support public funding for Senate and House candidates, but individual states might adopt clean election programs just as Minnesota and Arizona have.

There is much more debate about the effects of spending limits on candidates who accept public financing. Although some have argued that spending limits hurt challengers who must be able to spend without limits if they are to successfully compete against incumbents (Jacobson 1978, 1990), the lion's share of more recent research in this area suggests that spending limits have no effect or a positive effect on electoral competitiveness (Gerber 1998; Green and Krasno 1988, 1990; Levitt 1994). Thus, it appears reformers can include spending limits in their arsenal of potential reforms to address declining competitiveness.

Reforming the Franking Privilege

The franking privilege, which has existed since colonial times, allows members of Congress to send mail to constituents without postage. It is frequently attacked for its expense and the fact that it gives incumbents an advantage over challengers. At the same time, many view it as a crucial mechanism linking voters and their representatives and an important way for members of Congress to spread political news that might be ignored by the media. Although there have been egregious abuses of the franking privilege in the past, its use is currently quite restricted. It cannot be used for campaigning purposes, to send holiday greetings, or to provide biographical information about representatives and their families. Members of Congress can use it, however, to send out mass mailings such as questionnaires and newsletters. The amount is limited by a formula that is based on the number of addresses in the representative or senator's district or home state. In addition, senators cannot send out mailings within 60 days of a primary or general election; the limit for representatives is 90 days.

Even with these restrictions, critics contend that members of Congress frequently spend more money on the frank than many challengers spend during their entire campaign. The costs of franked mail are also significantly higher in election than non-election years, suggesting that the mailings are being used for campaign purposes. Proposed reforms include eliminating the privilege altogether, which even most critics believe is going too far, to prohibiting unsolicited or mass mailings, or simply lowering the financial allowance for such mailings.[1] Any of these reforms has the potential to reduce the margins by which incumbents win elections.

Redistricting Reforms

There is a building consensus that gerrymandering is a factor in declining competitiveness, although there is still considerable debate about how large a factor it is (Tufte 1973; Lyons and Galderisi 1995; Monmonier 2001; Cain et al. 2005; McDonald 2006a,b,c).[2] Even those who do not believe that gerrymandering explains the increased polarization of party elites in Congress agree that political competitiveness declines after redistricting (McCarty et al. 2006: 18). Despite the growing evidence that gerrymandering and declining competitiveness are linked, it is unclear that redistricting reform will enhance competitiveness. Those who harbor such doubts point to the fact that some states that have reformed their redistricting processes have seen little in the way of increased competitiveness. Those who advocate redistricting reform, however, contend that these states have simply not enacted the right kinds of reform.

Independent Redistricting Commissions

The rules and regulations governing redistricting vary from state to state, but most states allow the state legislature to redraw congressional and state legislative district lines after reapportionment. The second most popular method is to give the job to a commission, which may take any of a number of forms. Generally, these commissions are either bipartisan, in which case the number of Republican and Democratic appointees is balanced, or composed of politically neutral appointees. State courts also have a role in the redistricting process. If the state legislature and governor cannot agree on a plan, or if a commission deadlocks, the courts can typically intercede. They can also step in to resolve violations of the Voting Rights Act or state law. Studies have found that the redistricting process yields more competitive districts when it is taken out of the hands of state legislatures and placed in the care of courts or commissions (Carson and Crespin 2004).[3]

In terms of independent redistricting bodies, research has revealed a number of characteristics that give such institutions a better chance of producing competitive districts, although they by no means guarantee them. The commissioners must be selected through a nonpartisan process. Commissions with political appointees are bound to produce district maps that protect incumbents. If the parties in a state will not accept a commission with nonpartisan appointees, then the second best option is for the commission to have a neutral tie-breaking vote.

Reforming or Adopting Redistricting Principles

Redistricting principles are typically written into state constitutions or state law. Such principles can be grouped into three categories: form-based, population-based, and politically-based principles (Forgette and Platt 2005: 936–37). Form-based criteria regulate the shape of districts and usually require a state to create districts that are contiguous, which means that all parts of the districts must be connected and/or compact. The latter is meant to prevent the drawing of oddly shaped, sprawling districts. Population-based principles require those drawing district lines to respect existing political and communal boundaries. For example, a political subdivision criterion requires states to respect county or municipal borders, while a criterion to respect the "core" of an existing district is intended to prevent the wholesale redrawing of district lines from one cycle to the next. Protecting "communities of interest" is a more nebulous concept. It can mean drawing district lines that correspond to existing political or geographic boundaries, but it is more frequently used to justify drawing district lines to take in whole ethnic or racial communities. Finally, politically-based criteria include those that explicitly state that incumbents should or should not be protected. In the latter case, states typically prevent mapmakers from considering certain information, such as the partisan affiliation of voters or the location of an incumbent's home, when drawing district lines.[4]

Some of these principles are clearly designed with the goal of weakening the grip incumbents hold on their district, which should have the effect of making elections more competitive.[5] In addition, the more criteria required by a state, the more the hands of mapmakers are tied, making it difficult to draw gerrymandered districts. Other criteria might protect incumbents, however. For example, the "communities of interest" criterion might result in creation of more homogeneous districts, which would very likely favor incumbents. The question is whether such intentions are reflected in election outcomes. Research on congressional elections does suggest that incumbents win by smaller margins in states that have more redistricting criteria than in those with fewer (146). Moreover, the more population-based and anti-incumbent principles a state adopts, the poorer incumbents do. Form-based principles, on the other hand, appear to have no effect on electoral competitiveness. These findings appear to hold for both congressional and state legislative elections.[6]

Arizona and Washington have adopted an additional type of political principle: to create competitive districts whenever possible and when doing so is not detrimental to other redistricting goals. It is unclear whether this criterion has been effective, however. The main reason is that such criteria have low priority and can conflict with higher priority principles. For instance, the desire to create more competitive districts can run up against the imperative to create majority-minority districts under Section 5 of the Voting Rights Act. Arizona's 2000 redistricting process illustrates this conflict. In 2000, Arizonans adopted a proposition that established an Independent Redistricting Commission, as well as a list of criteria that included the creation of competitive districts where doing so did not conflict with other criteria. The redistricting commission found, however, that once Native American and Hispanic (heavily Democratic communities) districts had been drawn to comply with the Voting Rights Act, few Democrats were left in the state to spread around in the interest of creating competitive districts (McDonald 2006c, 2008). As a result, the districts created by the new commission were no more competitive than the districts drawn by the state legislature in previous rounds when there was no competitiveness criterion (McDonald 2008: 150). The maps drawn by the Commission were actually challenged in court by a group disappointed by its failure to create more competitive districts. Yet the Arizona Court of Appeals eventually found in favor of the Commission, arguing that it had taken the competitiveness criterion into account, but had simply found that embracing it was detrimental to other redistricting goals.[7]

Although one is reluctant to suggest yet another criterion for redistricting, research suggests that drawing legislative and congressional districts in a manner that respects media market boundaries is beneficial for challengers. Congressional districts that are more congruent with media market boundaries increase the number of media contacts challengers have with voters, and this in turn increases the likelihood that voters will know the names of the challenger (Levy and Squire 2000). When a challenger must advertise in multiple media markets to reach voters, it raises the costs of campaigning for them considerably and puts them at a further disadvantage with respect to incumbents. Media markets might fall within the category of a "community of interest" since they are designated with the television viewing habits of people in mind. Every year, Nielsen Media assigns counties to media markets based on which television stations the inhabitants of the county watch. This means that people assigned to the same media market get their news and information from similar sources. Since the term "community of interest" lacks "a commonly accepted definition" and, therefore, allows for "creative arguments on what could and should constitute a community of interest," there is no reason why the concept could not be stretched to include media markets (Cain et al. 2005: 19). Moreover, media markets are made up of counties and, since many states already require that their redistricting bodies respect the unity of counties, this should make respecting media market boundaries even easier.

Neutral Election Administration

One mark of a healthy democracy is the professional and neutral administration of elections. As Americans learned in the wake of the 2000 election debacle, the United States falls short in this respect. In this country, elections are administered by individuals "who depend on their party for their jobs" (Gerken 2010: 16). In 33 states, the secretary of state or chief election official is elected through a partisan election process. In the remaining states, the position is usually filled by gubernatorial appointment. No state uses a nonpartisan election process (Hansen 2005: 975). As Heather Gerken, an election law scholar, points out, the most obvious consequence of having partisans occupying such positions is "political bias." She explains,

> Politics, after all, is a game devoted to helping your friends and hurting your enemies. It is possible to do both when administering elections. Most election policies have partisan consequences. Making it easier to vote is thought to help Democrats; making it harder to vote is thought to help Republicans. If you think older people are likely to vote for your candidate, you will want to make it easier to vote absentee. Because people can be deterred by long lines, you will want to reduce the number of polling places or voting machines in areas where your opponent's supporters live. (2010: 16)

The bias of election administration in the United States is widely recognized among academics and commonly referred to as a problem of "foxes guarding the henhouse." Although there is no research to the author's knowledge that shows a relationship between partisan election administration and electoral competitiveness in state and local elections, it seems logical that partisan administrators would try to protect their party's incumbents and undermine the prospects for the opposing party's candidates. They will take steps to ensure that the jurisdictions dominated by their party are less competitive and that those dominated by the opposing party are more competitive. In states that have a near partisan 50–50 split, such as Ohio or Florida, such efforts might cancel each other out, but most states these days have a clear partisan bias. If one assumes that such states will tend to elect secretaries of state and other election officials from the state's favored party, then it is likely that those election officials will take steps to ensure that the candidates for statewide office from their party are even safer, thereby discouraging competitiveness in statewide elections.

In states that favor one party over the other, the election administrator's efforts to stem competitiveness in the name of protecting incumbents will outweigh efforts to encourage competitiveness in jurisdictions where the opposing party's candidates dominate. In addition, if one considers that state and county election official positions might be occupied by the same person, or people from the same party, for a long period of time, one can see how efforts to make elections in jurisdictions dominated by the opposing party more competitive over an extended period of time might whittle away the opposition's ability to hold on to those jurisdictions. Once the favored party's candidate wins an election, then those same election officials will turn their efforts to protecting the new incumbent, which will involve making the district less competitive. Thus, partisan election officials in states that already favor a party can be expected to steadily reduce electoral competitiveness even further in their states.

Even if neutral election administration did not improve electoral competitiveness, I would still feel the need to mention it because I argued in Chapter 2 that for political competitiveness to be fair, the rules must apply to all candidates equally. It is an abomination unworthy of a mature democracy such as the United States that the partisan proclivities of an election official should in any way influence the outcome of an election. Thus, even if reforming election administration did not increase electoral competitiveness, it is imperative for fair political competitiveness.

Many hoped that Congress or the courts would address election administration reform in the wake of the 2000 presidential election, but their hopes have met with disappointment. As a result, election law scholars have tried to offer alternative methods for achieving reform. Gerken has proposed the creation of a "Democracy Index" that would rank all states and localities based on election performance. It is designed to create "pressure for reform" because "no one [will want] to be at the bottom of the list" (2010: 5–6). Rick Hansen believes Gerken's proposal is too idealistic because parts of the Democracy Index will be viewed as ideological and favoring Democrats. As a result, he recommends the more "old-fashioned" approach of trying to push election reform packages through Congress and the state legislatures when there is unified party control of the executive and legislative branches since history shows election reform can be successful under such conditions (2010, 17). He also urges election reformers to push initiatives in states with an initiative process. Irrespective of the reform path, ensuring that American elections are administered by neutral election officials is essential for creating fair political competition in this country. It is also likely to improve electoral competitiveness.

Term Limits

In the early 1990s, when many states were passing term limits, most observers would have guessed that their implementation would enhance electoral competitiveness (Fund 1991; Petracca 1991; Barcellona and Grose 1994). In fact, that was one of the major selling points of the reform; term limits would force incumbents out of office, which would create more open seats; since open seats tend to be more competitive, this would lead to more closely-contested elections.

The problem with this logic is that open seats are not necessarily competitive seats, and, as it turns out, the open seats produced by term limits appear to be slightly less competitive than open seats that occur naturally when incumbents retire or are forced from office by scandal. This fact was discovered by Bruce Cain, John Hanley, and Thad Kousser (2006), who examined the effect of state legislative term limits on election returns in 1991–2003. Although they find that term limits do in fact create more open seats and descriptive turnover (i.e., put new faces into office), they also find that the open seats created by term limits are less competitive for two reasons. First, naturally occurring open seats are often the result of forces that make the election competitive as well. For instance, if a Democratic state legislator resigns from office because of involvement in a scandal, then Republican challengers will naturally have a leg-up in the open seat created by the resignation. Such forces are obviously absent when open seats are created by term limits.

Term limits also appear to dampen competitiveness by reducing the chances that quality candidates will challenge incumbents. Such challengers are strategic actors and inclined to bide their time until incumbents are termed out, rather than run against them while they are in office. Thus, the authors conclude that "the effects of term limits on competitiveness are mild to nonexistent" (Cain et al. 2006: 201).

It is worth underscoring, however, that Cain and his colleagues do find that term limits increase contestation in state legislative elections, that is, the number of seats in which two major party candidates face off. The percentage of contested seats in states with term limits was 74 percent versus 56 percent in states without them. The explanation for this difference is that more candidates, including many political novices, tend to compete in the open seats created by term limits. It is possible, however, that the size of this difference might decrease or disappear altogether in the long run, if the higher rates of contestation in term limited seats are due to the reform's relative novelty. Thus, optimism about the effect of term limits on contestation should be cautious.

Lowering Barriers to Third Party Participation

From the perspective of this analysis, the main reason to lower barriers for third party competition in American elections is to decrease the number of uncontested elections in this country. As discussed in Chapter 2, it is not uncommon for House, state legislative, and local elections to feature a single candidate. In Chapter 2, I also made the argument that political contestation is central to both egalitarian and deliberative conceptions of democracy. One of the main objections to lowering barriers to third party competition, however, is that the participation of minor parties in our two-party system has the potential to "spoil" elections, that is, a minor party candidate might attract enough votes from a popular major party candidate to swing the election to their less popular major party opponent. Such was the popular claim about Ralph Nader's effect on the outcome of Florida's election in the 2000 presidential election. Yet the "spoiler" effect is not a pathology of minor party political participation but rather of a system that does not allow for run-off elections. If we adopted an instant run-off system, which would require voters to rank candidates or indicate their second choice, then third party candidates could never spoil elections. Moreover, even with our current system of electing candidates, it is quite rare for third parties to throw an election to the less popular major party candidate, especially in subnational elections, where reform in favor of third parties is most likely to occur. For example, research has found that House minor party candidates are more likely to run in incumbent-held seats than in open seats that are more competitive (Herrnson 2006: 113), which suggests that third party candidates are unlikely to spoil House elections.[8] If contested elections are a foundational component of democratic elections, and the spoiler threat of third parties is quite small, there is no reason to lower barriers to third party competition.[9]

Addressing the Homogenization of Political Jurisdictions

Scholars and journalists are currently debating whether declining electoral competitiveness reflects increased polarization among the electorate. In other words, increasing victory margins in elections might reflect the fact that political jurisdictions are becoming more committed to a given party. This could be the result of two trends: individuals within jurisdictions could be adopting more extreme partisan attitudes or citizens could be "sorting" themselves into more Democratic or Republican jurisdictions via migration (Fiorina et al. 2006). There is some evidence that Americans themselves are becoming more polarized (Abramowitz and Saunders 2005), but it is unclear what kind of policy prescriptions could mitigate such a trend.[10] The research concerning geographic sorting has a long history. For example, many scholars attribute the political realignment of the South to an influx of Republican northerners (Converse 1972; Wolfinger and Arsenau 1978; Wolfinger and Hagen 1985). Another line of research has concluded that people who move to the suburbs of cities have certain characteristics: they are more likely to be young, white, educated, and, most importantly for our purposes, Republican (Borjas et al. 1992). Those left behind tend to be poorer, less educated, and more committed to the Democratic Party. Such suburban migration might explain an increase in homogeneous congressional and state legislative districts within states, but it cannot explain why the states themselves appear to have become more homogeneous. Recent research that has examined interstate migration, however, has found that people who move from one state to another are also more likely to be Republican. This can result in a gain for the Republican Party in states with large migratory populations, but this depends on how Republican the state is in the first place. If the native population of a state is already

Republican, migration does not make much of a difference. Conversely, states with a large outflux of migrants should become more Democratic. However, if the state is already Democratic, one should not see much of a change in election outcomes. Although there is mounting evidence that mobility is increasing the homogeneity of political jurisdictions, there is still considerable debate about how much it is driving the decline in electoral competitiveness in this country (Klinkner and Hapanowicz 2005).[11]

If geographic sorting is occurring, the policy prescriptions for it go well beyond the realm of election law. For instance, they might involve encouraging larger cities to use zoning laws to diversify housing opportunities, as well as enforcing "fair housing" laws that are already on the books, both of which would promote integration (Macedo et al. 2005: 108–9). Short of enacting such measures, however, there really is very little that can be done—or, as many would argue, should be done—to stem the tide of such trends. Moreover, such policy changes might stem the tide of homogenizing state legislative and congressional districts, but they would do little to affect statewide homogenization, which is also occurring.

Mechanisms of Reforming Presidential Elections

Although recent presidential elections have been quite competitive at the national level, the majority of state-level presidential elections have not. This has led a wide range of journalists and reform organizations to call for the elimination of the Electoral College. Scholars tend to be more sanguine about the Electoral College, but this has not prevented them from exploring how the division of the country into "safe" states and "battleground" states affects voters (Lipsitz 2009; Gimpel et al. 2007; Wolak 2006; Benoit et al. 2004) and speculating about how the elimination of the Electoral College might change candidate strategies and tactics (Goux and Hopkins 2008). Although the lack of competitiveness in state-level presidential elections has received much attention, there are a number of reforms that could make presidential primaries more competitive as well.

Presidential Primaries

The 2008 primary season served as a reminder of why competitive presidential primaries are important, and at the same time, what their downsides are. A party with a competitive primary is more likely to draw media attention and to pique the interest of voters. It also gives Americans the opportunity to familiarize themselves with the candidates long before the general election even starts, which allows the eventual nominee to spend more time engaging their opponent rather than introducing themselves to the electorate. Competitive primaries also last longer, in the sense that it takes longer for a clear frontrunner to emerge, and this gives lesser known candidates a chance to travel around the country, building name recognition and support. At the same time, intense primaries can exhaust candidate resources and splinter parties. Voters may also grow weary of the long drawn out campaign, especially when it is followed by a competitive general election.

Before discussing reforms designed to enhance competitiveness in presidential primaries and caucuses, one must understand how they operate. The primary season starts in January with the New Hampshire primary and Iowa Caucuses and runs through the end of June. Since many states envy the candidate and media attention that is lavished on Iowa and New Hampshire as the first contests of the primary season, as well as the influence they have over early momentum in the race, they have started to move their primaries and caucuses earlier to increase the role that their state plays in the nomination process. This has led to a heavily front-loaded primary election season that has compressed the schedule of candidates. In 2008, more than 75 percent of the states held early primaries before April 1. In terms of how electoral votes are allocated at the state level, the Democratic Party requires all states to allocate delegates according to proportional representation, so a candidate who gets 40 percent of the vote should get 40 percent of the delegates (this does not include superdelegates, who are not bound by the outcome of state primaries). The Republican Party allows each state to decide whether it will allocate delegates according to a winner-take-all rule or proportional representation, with the result that most states use a winner-take-all system.

The easiest way to make more primaries competitive would be for the Republican Party to mandate that all states allocate delegates according to a system of proportional representation. Just as PR does for other elections, it would encourage candidates to continue fighting for delegates irrespective of whether they are likely to win a plurality of the votes or not. Perhaps more importantly, PR prolongs uncertainty in the primary election season. The 2008 primaries provide an excellent illustration of this. The Democratic Party's use of proportional representation allowed Senator Obama to stay in the game even after Hillary Clinton's Super Tuesday win in populous states such as New York, New Jersey, and California, while the Republican Party's preference for winner-take-all rules helped John McCain clinch the nomination early despite strong performances by candidates such as Mitt Romney. This illustration also clearly illustrates why parties might have a preference for winner-take-all systems in primaries: they produce winners earlier. It is unclear that this actually helped the Republicans in the long run, however. For months, the Republicans and McCain had to struggle for news coverage as the media focused on the contest between Clinton and Obama. This provided voters with even more time to familiarize themselves with the Democratic candidates and their positions, which may have boosted their party's chances in the general election.

Despite the importance of how delegates are allocated, the biggest complaint about the current primary system is that the outcome of later primaries is often considered irrelevant because a nominee has already been determined by earlier primaries. This is different from the complaint that they are noncompetitive because the primary in a state might be quite competitive but its outcome still irrelevant to the party's nomination. The problem is that the reforms for remedying this situation are often at odds with the goal of competitiveness. For example, some have suggested a National Primary Day, which would require all states to hold their primaries and caucuses on the same day. Such a reform would favor well-known and well-heeled candidates and make it impossible for lesser-known candidates to attract media attention by campaigning hard in early primary states and winning. Others have suggested a series of regional primaries held a month apart with the order of regions rotating each election cycle or determined by lottery.[12] A regional plan probably offers the best chance of eliminating frontloading while preserving the competitiveness of primaries over the long run.

Reforming or Abolishing the Electoral College

Electoral College reforms fall into essentially two categories: those that would abolish or effectively bypass it and those that would simply eliminate the unit rule in exchange for a more representative allocation of electoral votes. Since it would be virtually impossible to pass an amendment to the Constitution that eliminates the Electoral College, many reformers have embraced a clever reform that requires states to tie their state's electoral votes to the national popular vote. This reform has better chances than a constitutional amendment because it only requires the state legislatures—which are responsible for determining how their state allocates electoral votes—in states with a total of 270 electoral votes to pass the measure. The second class of reforms usually involves exchanging the unit rule for an allocation of electoral votes based on performance in individual congressional districts or proportional representation. Since basing electoral votes on candidate performance in congressional districts would politicize the redistricting process even more than it already is and potentially introduce biases into vote counts because the process of drawing district lines is a partisan one in most cases, most reformers prefer allocating electoral votes according to a system of proportional representation.

The question is which reform, if any, would offer more Americans a competitive election than the current system. One of the proposed reforms would actually have the opposite affect: allocating electoral votes based on performance in congressional districts. As discussed in earlier chapters, congressional districts have become less and less competitive during the past few decades because their boundaries have been drawn to protect incumbents or for partisan purposes. Imagine if the attention lavished on battleground states by candidates and the media was focused on just a handful of competitive districts! It would certainly make campaigning easier for candidates and might even reduce campaign spending since much less advertising would be purchased, but even fewer Americans would experience the full brunt of a presidential election.

The other two feasible Electoral College reforms that are often discussed—the National Popular Vote and encouraging states to allocate electoral votes based on proportional representation—would affect presidential campaigns in a similar fashion. First, the adoption of either reform would result in closer national elections because the popular vote is always closer than the vote in the Electoral College due to the unit rule. The proportional representation reform would also produce closer national outcomes. For example, if it had been adopted in 2008, Obama would have defeated McCain with 289 electoral votes to 249 (the actual result was 365 to 173).[13] If the National Popular Vote were adopted, presidential campaigns would look very different from the way they do now, but one crucial aspect of the process would not change: candidates would still have finite resources, which means they would continue their practice of targeting certain voters and not others. Since the bulk of the money in presidential campaigns is spent on advertising, and the trend in the last two decades has been to purchase advertisements in media markets, candidates may simply switch their focus from battleground states to battleground media markets. It is possible that candidates would choose the more straightforward route of simply moving their advertising back onto the national networks, but this seems unlikely given the tendency of presidential candidates to target persuadable voters as efficiently as possible (Shaw 2006).

Obama's 2008 presidential campaign is illustrative in this respect. Despite his ambitious game plan, which involved targeting many traditionally Republican states, Obama still purchased the lion's share of his advertising at the local level. There were a few notable exceptions, including the $5 million he spent on network ads to reach Olympic viewers and the half hour of ad time he purchased on CBS and NBC for his lengthy prime time commercial, but most political observers agree that this was more indicative of the vast funds he had at his disposal than a signal that presidential candidates are moving their advertising back onto the networks.

If candidates indeed targeted battleground media markets, they would focus on the media markets with the lowest cost per persuadable voter. Candidates currently focus on such media markets, but the range of viable media markets is confined to battleground states. Under the proposed reform, that constraint would be lifted. For example, Daron Shaw has calculated the cost efficiency of reaching swing voters in various media markets. The top 20 media markets include many in traditional battleground states, but also the New Orleans and Lafayette media markets in Louisiana and the Little Rock-Pine Bluff and Fort Smith-Fayetteville markets in Arkansas. Whereas these media markets have not received any advertising in recent presidential elections, they would no longer be ignored if the Electoral College did not factor into candidate strategy (2006: 61). In addition to advertising, these markets would also receive the lion's share of candidate visits, since candidates tend to concentrate their visits in competitive jurisdictions (Doherty 2007; Shaw 2006).[14] It is possible, however, that such a system might discourage candidates from making campaign appearances. Under the current system, they can focus on a single state, visiting multiple media markets in a relatively short time. It will be far more taxing and costly to hop around the country from competitive media market to competitive media market. Candidates might be unwilling to subject themselves and their families to such a grueling schedule and, instead, funnel more resources into advertising and less into making physical appearances.

If candidates focused on battleground media markets rather than battleground states, would the strategy expose more Americans to competitive presidential contests? The answer is probably "yes" because candidates who were free to focus on competitive media markets irrespective of the state they serve would be able to target their resources more efficiently than they currently do. Under the current system, candidates must purchase advertising in battleground state media markets irrespective of its cost.[15] If the Electoral

College were eliminated, presidential candidates would simply rank the media markets in relation to their cost per persuadable voter, and allocate their resources accordingly. This means that residents of media markets like New Orleans and Little Rock-Pine Bluff would see presidential ads. The funds saved from a more efficient targeting of persuadable voters would allow the candidates to air ads in additional media markets thereby reaching more voters than they currently do under the Electoral College.

What would happen if states exchanged the unit rule for a PR system? I would argue that candidates would adopt a strategy very similar to the national strategy just described. Since winning electoral votes would no longer hinge on winning the majority of votes in a state, such a system would encourage candidates to pick up votes wherever they could. State boundaries might still factor into a candidate's strategic calculations since smaller states tend to be overrepresented and large states underrepresented in the Electoral College. Thus if two media markets had the same cost-per-persuadable voter, but one was located in a state, such as Wyoming, which is overrepresented in the Electoral College, and the other was located in California, which is underrepresented, the candidates would probably prioritize the Wyoming media market.

Since it is very unlikely that every state would adopt a PR system, it might be wise to consider what would happen if the country experienced partial reform (i.e., some states adopted PR while others maintained the unit rule). States that are regularly considered battleground in presidential elections would very likely keep the unit rule to maintain their appeal, while larger states that are typically neglected might consider adopting a PR system to make their state more appealing. Such a partial reform would undoubtedly subject more Americans to the full force of a presidential campaign than the current system would, because in addition to campaigning hard in battleground states, candidates might turn some of their attention to traditionally safe states.

Electoral competitiveness can be improved in this country and, in most cases, adopting reforms to improve it will have the added bonus of also making our elections more fair. Table 7.1 lists all the reforms for which there is either some evidence that they will improve competitiveness or strong reason to believe that they will. This list is by no means exhaustive, but it does give the reader a sense of the broad range of reforms that might be adopted to enhance competitiveness. Of these reforms, the most important to pursue are those that aid high quality challengers. Increasing electoral competitiveness in

Table 7.1. Electoral System Reforms That Enhance Contestation and Competitiveness

Reforming State and Local Elections

- ➢ Help Challengers
  - Allow state parties to use soft money for candidate training
  - Encourage parties to adopt a 50-state strategy
  - Publically finance campaigns at adequate levels
  - Revoke or reform the franking privilege
- ➢ Reform the Redistricting Process
  - Adopt independent redistricting commissions
  - Adopt anti-incumbent redistricting criteria
  - Adopt a competitiveness criterion
  - Respect media markets as a "community of interest"
- ➢ Make all election administration offices nonpartisan
- ➢ Lower barriers for third party participation in elections
- ➢ Address homogenization of political jurisdictions
  - Use zoning laws to diversify housing opportunities
  - Enforce existing "fair housing" laws

Reforming Presidential Elections

- ➢ Encourage the Republican Party to adopt a rule mandating that all states allocate primary delegates based on proportional representation
- ➢ Adopt proportional representation instead of unit rule for allocation of electoral votes or tie them to the national popular vote

this country is impossible if the individuals who would make strong political candidates refuse to run for office. They must be supported and encouraged.

Agents of Change

Although there are many ways to make elections more competitive at all levels of government, it is far less clear who will advocate or support such reforms. Those that are designed to weaken the incumbency advantage or are perceived as benefiting one party over the other will inevitably face stiff opposition. In addition, there is little evidence that reformers will have much help from the courts, which have proved unwilling to take the value of competitive elections seriously. Reformers' only hope lies with American voters, but mobilizing them will require a massive education effort, since surveys suggest that few Americans know or care about declining electoral competitiveness.

State Legislatures

Since our federal system gives the power to regulate elections primarily to the states, one might be inclined to advocate for election reform at the state level. Yet the state legislatures and executives are probably the least likely of all potential agents to promote reforms that increase electoral competitiveness. Aside from the fact that incumbents are likely to resist any reform that makes their electoral prospects more shaky, the main reason is that most of these reforms weaken the power of political parties. For example, redistricting reforms would take away what many party insiders consider a legitimate prize of winning elections: the power to draw district lines in a manner that pleases your party. Term limits are particularly vexing to parties because they weaken their institutional power by throwing out long-time members, who have accrued seniority and all the legislative experience and power accumulated with it, before they are ready to go. Finally, the fact that reforms designed to enhance competitiveness will make campaigning more expensive does not sit well with the major parties because it means that much more of their organizations' time and resources will have to be devoted to prospecting for dollars. Thus, it is unlikely that legislative leaders—a term usually synonymous with "party leaders"—will embrace election reform unless the people who elect them begin to demand it. I turn to the likelihood of that happening below.

The story might be different for presidential primary and general election reform because the incentives are different. For example, in the case of primaries, Republican Party leaders in large states might be persuaded to abandon the unit rule in favor of allocating delegates according to a PR system because doing so would encourage party nominees to pay more attention to their state. On the other hand, Electoral College reform proponents might find allies among state legislatures in safe states that are generally ignored by presidential candidates. In fact, advocates of the National Popular Vote have convinced the state legislatures and governors in Hawaii, Illinois, New Jersey, and Maryland to adopt the reform.

Congress

Congress has the authority to regulate many aspects of the election process but rarely exercises it. Instead, it prefers to leave electoral regulation to the states. This does not mean that reform legislation is never introduced. It frequently is, but it typically dies a quick death in committee without the benefit of a hearing. There have been cases of Congress passing reform legislation, but they are few and far between. The most recent example was the 2002 Help Americans Vote Act (HAVA), which, in the wake of the 2000 presidential election, set new standards for voting machines and provided funds for updating voting systems and training poll workers. It passed with overwhelming support from both parties for reasons that are typically not available for other types of electoral reform: it dealt with an issue that was highly salient for the American public; and the reform was not perceived as unduly benefiting either party. Unfortunately, election reform issues typically fly below the radar screen of all but the most politically savvy Americans. More important, they rarely enjoy the support of both parties because reforms are often perceived by one party as helping the other, regardless of the normative arguments that might support them. Thus, HAVA is in many ways the exception that proves the rule.

Federalism is another issue that prevents many members of Congress from endorsing electoral reform.[16] The Constitution provides Congress with the authority to regulate elections in the "Elections Clause": "The times, places and manner of holding elections for Senators and Representatives, shall be prescribed in each state by the legislature thereof; but the Congress may at any time by law make or alter such regulations, except as to the places of choosing Senators." The second half of the sentence clearly allows Congress to override the states from time to time, but it was by no means an uncontroversial provision during the constitutional debates. During the ratification process, the anti-Federalists argued that the second clause was tantamount to giving Congress full control over the elections process, forcing Alexander Hamilton to defend the provision in Federalist No. 59. He argued that Congress would intervene in the process only under "extraordinary circumstances," suggesting that under normal circumstances the states should control the process.[17]

The Courts

Despite the fact that many election law scholars have argued that the courts should play a larger role in regulating the political marketplace, the courts have remained steadfast in their conviction that the myriad problems of election law stem from infringements on constitutionally protected individual and associational rights. This does not mean that members of the Supreme Court do not voice concerns about the country's lack of competitive elections; they do from time to time. For example, in *Veith v. Jubelirer* (2004), Justice Souter, joined by Justice Ginsberg, argued that when it comes to redistricting, "the Court's job must be to identify clues . . . indicating that partisan competition has reached an extremity of unfairness." Such opinions, however, are usually found among dissenters and rarely in majority opinions.

As the Court has itself said, much of the problem with adopting a political markets approach to election law is that it is extremely difficult to identify when a political market breakdown has occurred. In the case of redistricting, the majority in *Veith* argued that "Eighteen years of judicial effort" yielded "no judicially discernible and manageable standards for adjudicating political gerrymandering claims." In other words, no one has been able to derive a test for determining when gerrymandering has gone too far, let alone answer other arguably more difficult questions, such as what an ideal level of electoral competitiveness would look like.

Nathaniel Persily, an election law scholar, points out an additional problem. In several areas of case law, such as ballot access, campaign finance, redistricting and the regulation of party primaries, the Supreme Court has expressed its opinion that incumbent protection is acceptable, and in several of these areas, has even, "explicitly given its blessing to anticompetitive state action" (Persily 2006: 177). For example, in the area of ballot access, where some argue that the two major parties have colluded to shut minor parties out of the political marketplace, the Supreme Court has argued that "The State's interest [in political stability] permits them to enact reasonable election regulations that may, in practice, favor the traditional two-party system."[18]

In addition to the Court's unwillingness to use competitiveness as a meaningful criterion in its decisions, a number of recent opinions have generally weakened federal oversight of the election process. This trend started with a decision in 1993, *Growe v. Emison*, which held that federal judges must hold off on intervening in redistricting disputes "where the State, through its legislative or judicial branch, has begun to address that highly political task itself."

In another case, *Georgia v. Ashcroft* (2003), the Court gave states that require pre-clearance under the Voting Rights Act more flexibility in complying with such requirements. And although Section 5 of the Voting Rights Act was renewed in 2006, there is considerable evidence that the Department of Justice under President George Bush politicized the pre-clearance process by giving more deference to state leaders. President Obama, however, has expressed a desire to push back this tide of devolution. At a Brookings Institute conference on election reform, then-Senator Obama said he thought the biggest problem with Section 5 of the Voting Rights Act is that the

> Justice Department feels disempowered . . . we [need] a Justice Department that is empowered anywhere in the country—not just in areas that historically had repressed voters, but anywhere in the country that, if there is a minority group that is vulnerable, that the Justice Department is empowered to go in and look and investigate and see whether or not the voting practices and procedures that have been set up are further suppressing these voters. (Brookings Institution 2006)

Although these comments suggest that President Obama is in favor of enhancing federal power, the question is if he is in favor of using it for enhancing electoral competitiveness.

The President

In recent history, presidents have shown half-hearted support, if not outright hostility, toward electoral reform efforts. This has not always been the case. For, example, Lyndon Johnson used his ample political skills to usher the Voting Rights Act of 1965 through a reluctant Congress. Since then, however, presidents have kept election reform efforts at arms-length, particularly in the area of campaign finance reform. One might argue that presidents support election reform efforts when it is in their best interest to do so. This is only part of the story, however. The other part is that election reform is rarely high on a president or the nation's priority list. For example, the reason why President Lyndon Johnson was willing to push for the Voting Rights Act, despite believing that the Democratic Party would lose the South for a generation if it was passed, was because over half of all Americans in 1964 said civil rights was the most important issue confronting the country. He and Congress could hardly sit on their hands in the face of such widespread concern.

Since then, presidents have shown little enthusiasm for electoral reform.

President Richard Nixon vetoed the Federal Election Campaign Act of 1971 and later the 1974 Amendments to that act. In both cases, it was quite evident that the measures did not serve the president's interest. The 1971 Act was passed by a Democratic Congress concerned about the rising costs of elections and the fact that President Nixon had outspent Hubert Humphrey by 2 to 1 in the campaign. The 1974 Amendments were passed in the wake of the Watergate scandal and investigations revealing Nixon's virtually total disregard for campaign finance law in the 1972 campaign (illegal corporate contributions, undisclosed slush funds, etc.) (Corrado and Mann 1997).

Later presidents, while not as openly hostile to campaign finance reform as Nixon, were hardly supportive. When Senators John McCain and Russ Feingold, along with Representatives Chris Shays and Marty Meehan, began to push the Bipartisan Campaign Reform Act through Congress under the Clinton administration, they had little support from the White House (Mycoff and Pika 2007: 119). Although President Clinton voiced support for BCRA, many believed his support was motivated more by the fact that he was being investigated for campaign irregularities than by genuine support for the effort.[19] While scholars have argued Clinton's verbal commitment to BCRA changed the dynamics of negotiation in Congress because it was clear he would sign the bill if he had the opportunity, he was unwilling to expend any political capital on the effort.

President George W. Bush vowed to veto BCRA after he entered office because it did not include provisions he favored, such as a prohibition on unions spending members' money on political activity without the explicit permission of each member. He also did not favor the soft money ban on individuals. He changed his tune after the collapse of Enron, however, as public opinion began to favor comprehensive campaign finance reform. He ultimately signed the bill into law in 2003, but only reluctantly.

President Bush's support for HAVA was similarly lukewarm. Prior to the bill's passage in Congress, Bush's involvement with HAVA was been described by one political observer as "passive, if not indifferent" (Broder 2001)· His remarks at the signing of the bill, however, suggested that he felt the bill was important, claiming that "The vitality of America's democracy depends on the fairness and accuracy of America's elections" and that bill's passage would, "help protect the sanctity of the vote and to encourage Americans to exercise the right to vote" (Bush 2002). Yet President Bush dragged his feet on implementing the portions of the bill for which he was responsible. The legislation required the president to appoint a four-member Election Assistance

Commission, composed of two Republicans and two Democrats, within 120 days of signing the bill. Bush waited nearly a year to appoint the members, which meant that the funds appropriated for implementing HAVA were not distributed until the beginning of 2004, frustrating many state and local officials who were facing HAVA deadlines for changes that were supposed to occur before the 2004 election. Moreover, the funds eventually appropriated were far less than the amount authorized—a situation that might have been different had Bush taken more interest in the legislation.

Thus, history suggests that we should expect little from President Barack Obama in the way of election reform, unless there is a sudden outpouring of support from the public for such efforts or he suddenly finds that it is in his interest to support reform. President Obama has expressed support for some forms of election reform, such as redressing the decline in competitive elections, which he pins largely on "a system where too often, representatives are selecting their voters instead of voters selecting their representatives" (Brookings Institution 2006). He has not only said that such a system is "unacceptable" but has explicitly stated he would "encourage states to form [independent redistricting] commissions" (Midwest Democracy Network 2007). Such statements seem to suggest that President Obama might pay more than lip-service to reforms designed to enhance competitiveness, but it is unlikely that his administration would take a proactive role on the issue given the crises currently confronting the country. The fact that the issue of declining electoral competitiveness, or any of the reforms that might address it, failed to merit a mention on President Obama's campaign Website underscores the low priority of the issue for his administration.

The Voters

In 2006, the Pew Research Center for the People and the Press conducted the first survey dedicated to assessing the public's level of knowledge about the declining competitiveness of House elections and their general concern about its decline. The study concluded that the public do not share the concern of politicians and political experts about declining competitiveness, and are "only dimly aware" of redistricting debates. Moreover, they "appear to lack a clear sense of whether the elections in their own House districts are competitive or not" (Pew 2006: 1). Perhaps more important, most survey respondents fail to see the benefits of increased competitiveness. When asked what the effect of facing a tough election is for a politician, 22 percent said it "makes them work harder to represent their district better," while 62 percent said tough campaigns make politicians "focus too much on fundraising and campaigning instead of being a good representative." Such numbers suggest that the impetus for election reform is unlikely to come from the public any time soon.

A study examining whether the availability of the initiative process helps with the passage of electoral reforms that enhance accountability and competitiveness seems to confirm this. John Matsusaka argues that the initiative has not played much of a role in bringing about electoral reform. The only exception is for term limits on state legislators (but not on state executives). "The broad implication is that if reformers are looking to direct democracy as the magic bullet for electoral reform, they are likely to be disappointed" (2006: 168). The 2005 defeat of the much discussed and anticipated initiatives to turn over the redistricting process to independent commissions in California and Ohio only seem to underscore the veracity of Matsusaka's argument.

Some scholars remain optimistic, however. Michael McDonald (2008) points out that voters in Alaska, Arizona, and Idaho have adopted redistricting reform initiatives. He argues that the key to passing such initiatives is to build a coalition with broad bipartisan support, take steps to ensure that the reform is not perceived as being overtly partisan, and, finally, keep the initiative simple. The proponents of the California and Ohio initiatives violated at least one of these rules, according to McDonald. If McDonald is right, then—to use a metaphor—voters might "drink" if they are "led to water," but they cannot be expected to fight the force of status quo inertia on their own. This is arguably the most important task that lies ahead for reformers: to educate voters about the benefits of electoral competitiveness and the perils of too safe elections.

EPILOGUE

Why Voters Are Not Excited by American Campaigns

> I know nothing grander, better exercise, better digestion, more positive proof of the past, the triumphant result of faith in human kind, than a well-contested American national election.
>
> —Walt Whitman, *Democratic Vistas*

The goal of this book has been to understand how the campaigns generated by competitive elections affect voters. For the most part, my analysis has shown that competitive elections, even those that are modestly or moderately competitive, generate information environments that help voters learn. They also encourage political elites to mobilize citizens. Yet, I have found little evidence that they move voters in a psychological or emotional sense. Voters learn when elections are competitive, not because they are motivated to seek out more information, but because they cannot help but learn from the rich information environments that competitive elections generate. They are more likely to vote, not because they think their vote is more likely to matter, but because political elites prod them into doing so. I believe that using different metaphors for thinking about political campaigns may help us understand why voters are not more enthusiastic about elections generally, and competitive elections specifically.

Understanding Voter Passivity

Why aren't voters more excited about competitive elections? It is easy to blame campaign negativity and voter cynicism, but there are more creative ways to try to answer this question. In particular, I would like to return to the discussion of metaphors that was briefly introduced at the beginning of the book. Scholars have argued that metaphorical concepts help structure our experiences, enabling us to comprehend them so we know what to do and how to behave in a given situation (Lakoff and Johnson 1980: 83). We use metaphors all the time to make sense of the political world. For example, we say members of Congress have written a "blank check" when they have created a vaguely worded bill that can be exploited, or that they have adopted a "poison pill" when they have accepted an amendment that would make passage of a bill more difficult. Legislation that includes provisions specifically designed to benefit special interest groups is referred to as "pork barrel" legislation. These metaphors help us understand what an object or event means for people. Yet, different metaphors can be used for the same thing, each providing another layer of meaning.

In the following discussion, I consider three metaphors that have been used to structure our understanding of political campaigns. Each one depicts democratic citizens in a unique way and may help us understand why they do not share Walt Whitman's enthusiasm for well-contested elections.

Campaigns as "Battles"

Undoubtedly, the dominant metaphor for a political campaign is "war." The word "campaign" itself is from the Latin *campus* ("field"), and originally referred to the period of time or season an army was "in the field." It is not difficult to see why this metaphor has come to structure our experience of election seasons; the parallels abound. Candidates are viewed as generals directing troops of loyal soldiers into battle. They strategize, attack, counterattack, defend, mobilize, draw fire, return fire, retreat, advance, gather intelligence, and rally the troops. Consultants in particular seem to be drawn to the war metaphor. For example, Lee Atwater claimed that his favorite book was Sun Tzu's *Art of War* because "Everything in it you can relate to my profession, you can relate to the campaign" (Pitney 2000: 13). In Mary Matalin and John Carville's memoir of the 1992 Bush campaign, she chose the following Vietnamese battle cry for her epigraph: "Follow me if I advance. Kill me if I retreat. Avenge me if I die" (Matalin and Carver 1994: 9).

In the Introduction, I argued that this metaphor suggests that there are no rules in politics—that ethics simply do not apply in the political realm—hence, the title of Matalin and Carville's book, *All's Fair: Love, War, and Running for President*. The metaphor also suggests two possible roles for the citizen: civilian or soldier. Civilians can be viewed either as the people who stay behind tending the home front and supporting the troops or as those caught in the cross-fire, who try to avoid mortar fire and sniper shots as they scamper through the rubble looking for food and water. Soldiers and the civilians supporting them are animated by a just cause or an inspiring leader. As recent presidential elections remind us, voters can get excited about elections when they are inspired, but unfortunately this seems to happen all too rarely and only at the national level. House and Senate candidates might have the potential to be just as inspiring, but voters rarely know enough about them to be moved.

The second way of imagining the citizen suggests the conventional wisdom about why people are not excited about competitive elections: the fighting. Campaign negativity is often viewed as being the most noxious byproduct of this "war," and the solution—many argue—is to somehow get candidates to "play nice." Yet campaign reform efforts that have tried to do this have largely failed (Maisel et al. 2007) precisely because those advocating them have failed to fully appreciate the meaning of political campaigns for candidates and political consultants; one does not win a war by playing nice.

I would argue that the fundamental problem this metaphor points to is that voters do not believe the wars are just or that their leaders are inspiring. Metaphorically speaking, citizens will endure the hardships of war if they believe that their suffering is for a larger good, but most elections do not seem to measure up to that standard. In the context of a democratic election, a just "war" involves conflict over issues that are of central concern to citizens. If candidates bicker about petty matters or engage in cheap attacks, one cannot blame citizens for tuning elections out. When candidates engage in meaningful debate about issues that citizens find important and when candidates hold each other accountable for their attention to and performance on those issues, citizens should be more willing to sacrifice their time to following an election and supporting a candidate. Inspiring leaders not only can make a convincing argument about why the war is just, that is, why an election matters, but can also offer a clear vision of the future and hope that it can be achieved. I would argue that meaningful elections and inspiring leaders have not disappeared. Rather, their presence is obscured by a cynical media that covers political campaigns in an increasingly negative fashion and focuses on the twists and turns of campaign strategy rather than the substantive issues in elections (Patterson 1994). As Diana Mutz argues, the problem with such coverage "is that it suggests to news media audiences that being persuaded by a politician is a bad thing, a sign of weakness, gullibility, or stupidity" (Mutz 2007: 237). If this is the case, it is not that the current era suffers from a dearth of inspiring leaders but that we are not letting ourselves be inspired. Instead, we are encouraged to smother inspiration and to replace it with—at best—a healthy skepticism—or at worst—contempt for those seek to inspire. Yet, inspiration is central to a vibrant democracy. Sure, people may vote out of habit or a sense of duty. Countries can even adopt policies that force people to vote. Inspiration, however, is what makes a person an active and engaged citizen and what separates thriving democracies from those that merely function.

Campaigns as "Town Hall Meetings"

Others have offered a different metaphor for the election season: the New England town meeting. Even though this metaphor is drawn from the political world, it is nonetheless a metaphor when it is used to refer to the collective decision-making process we undertake during elections in a mass democracy. Voters do not meet in the local community center, debate the candidates, or attempt to reach consensus on their vote choice, unless they live in a state with presidential caucuses. Yet, the metaphor of the town hall meeting is very seductive because of the rich role it envisions for citizens in a democracy. It also emphasizes the collective nature of the decision-making process. Instead of the war metaphor, which emphasizes the adversarial nature of campaigns, the town hall meeting metaphor suggests the more cooperative aspects of elections. For instance, it forces us to acknowledge that the ultimate decision in an election reflects choices that we have made together as a body of citizens. Instead of launching attacks, candidates in a town hall meeting ideally stand before their neighbors, friends, and family and explain why they believe they should lead. In this metaphor, the role of the citizen is quite clear: it is to ask the candidates questions, to ruminate over the responses, to discuss one's thoughts with others, and to ultimately make a considered and well-informed decision.

What does the town hall meeting metaphor teach us about the engagement of citizens? First, such meetings happen periodically for brief periods of time. Yet American elections do not ask citizens to devote a few hours to making a decision; they drag on for months and sometimes even years.

This suggests that reforms that shorten the primary and general election campaigns might help voters stay interested in the election. Voters in a town hall meeting also have direct contact with their leaders. The relationship between voters and candidates in a mass democracy is almost always entirely mediated. Voters rarely get an opportunity to ask questions of candidates, while candidates rarely have the opportunity to answer the questions of voters. Instead, candidates "speak" to voters through various forms of media, hoping they are listening, while voters "speak" to candidates through polls and focus groups. Perhaps the chief lesson of this metaphor, then, is that voters feel alienated from their political leaders. It is difficult to get excited about candidates when one's sole means of experiencing them is as a talking head in a 30-second commercial. Deliberative theorists have advocated a wide array of reforms to make voters feel more connected to their leaders and fellow citizens, which need not be recounted here. Although I believe the first priority is to adopt reforms that make elections more competitive, reformers should certainly consider deliberative reforms as part of a more comprehensive reform agenda.

Campaigns as "Sporting Events"

In this section, I turn the spotlight on a less commonly used metaphor for political campaigns, one that I believe highlights other elements of the campaign process that depress voter interest: campaigns as sporting events. To be sure, this metaphor fails to capture many important aspects of campaigns: games do not end with fans deciding who the winner is and spectators are confined to their seats—there is no room for participation in such contests unless it takes the form of cheering and other forms of urging their team onto victory. Such imperfection, however, is the nature of metaphor—a metaphor is not a metaphor if it is identical to that which it describes.

Thinking about campaigns in terms of sports may help us come to terms with the role citizens often play in a mass democracy and how we can engage them better in politics. Although many political scientists and democratic theorists make their careers fighting such passivity, most citizens are simply spectators of politics. They learn about politics through news coverage, watch debates and speeches on television occasionally, maybe put a bumper sticker on their car if they are really excited about a candidate, but few rarely ever get involved. What if citizens acted more like sports fans? They would voraciously read the "politics" pages, memorize statistics about their favorite party or candidate, faithfully attend every rally and meeting on the campaign, talk about the campaigns with all of their friends, wear hats and jackets sporting the mascots—donkeys and elephants—of their favorite parties, and rejoice when their favorite candidate won. They would join informal political groups in their areas (the equivalent of joining a local softball league), take classes in "politics" (the equivalent of tennis lessons) and encourage their own children to join political youth groups (the equivalent of the American Youth Soccer League).

The most appealing aspect of the sports metaphor, however, is that it suggests that the best way to engage voters is to give them a competitive, fair fight. Few people want to watch a game where the teams are unevenly matched and the outcome is likely to be a "blowout," so competitiveness is crucial. Yet if we want to use the sports metaphor to help us understand why voters are not more excited about elections, we already know that competitiveness is not enough. Perhaps there is something else about competitive sporting events that makes them more enthralling than most elections. One aspect is that they are team efforts and that supporters are, in a sense, an extended part of the team. It is difficult to create this sense of belonging in an era of candidate-centered politics, but perhaps a concerted public relations effort on the part of the Democratic and Republican parties might help. The other aspect of competitive sporting events that makes them more engaging is the sense that they are fair. In particular, there are three aspects of fairness in sports that I want to focus on. These include ensuring that players have a level playing field, that the rules are standardized, and that they are enforced by neutral referees.

To start with, there is a major difference between how the National Football League (NFL) and Major League Baseball (MLB) do business that affects how competitive games are across the nation. In MLB, teams generate revenue through television viewership and local attendance. As a consequence, teams in large markets are much wealthier and can afford to pay players top dollar. Not surprisingly, such inequality in payrolls translates into inequalities in success across different size markets. The NFL does things differently. Since 1964, teams have shared revenue and imposed salary caps on players to level the playing field. Although teams have found ways of circumventing these limits—by providing huge signing bonuses, for instance—revenue sharing has been widely credited with maintaining competitiveness throughout the league and boosting the NFL's overall popularity. Many have blamed baseball's flat attendance rates on the increasing payroll disparities between teams. One journalist argues that, "if you're not one of the top twelve teams in terms of payroll, you don't make the playoffs. . . . And if you're in the bottom half in terms of payroll you almost never get over a .500 winning percentage" (Surowiecki 2000: 43). As a result, many contend that MLB needs to adopt a revenue-sharing scheme similar to the NFL's.

There is an obvious parallel between well-financed teams like the Yankees, who can easily defeat teams from smaller markets, and well-financed candidates who can easily defeat poorer challengers. As in MLB, the losers are not just the poorer challengers but the voters (fans) who know that their candidate or party does not stand a chance. Even people who are supporters of the winner may find the contest less interesting if there is no credible challenger. The campaigns-as-sporting-contest metaphor, then, forces us to confront the way elections are financed in this country. It suggests that equalizing candidate resources by providing publicly financed floors and/or placing spending limits on candidates not only will make elections more competitive, but might increase voter interest in electoral contests.

Another parallel suggested by the differences between the NFL and MLB is the one between better financed teams and the two major political parties. Think of the Democrats and Republicans as the New York Yankees ($184 million payroll) and the Boston Red Sox ($128 million). At the opposite end of the spectrum, imagine the Green and Libertarian parties as the Tampa Bay Devil Rays ($30 million) and the Milwaukee Brewers ($27 million). Now consider that the Yankees typically pay their top two players more than the Devil Rays or Brewers pay their entire roster. If the Devil Rays and Brewers seem to have the deck stacked against them, consider the situation of the Green and Libertarian parties in the United States: in 2008, John McCain and Barack Obama raised $1.75 billion, while Cythia McKinney (Green) and Bob Barr (Libertarian) raised less than $2 million together. As I suggested in Chapter 2, the best way to help third parties is to make it easier for them to enter the political market. Obviously, they would also benefit reforming the Federal Election Campaign Act to make it easier for them to obtain public financing.

The second aspect of fairness in sports is the standardization of rules. In other words, the rules for how a sport is played are generally the same everywhere it is played. For example, the rules for football are the same no matter where the game is played in Pennsylvania, but the rules for how one votes are not. In the 2008 election, Pennsylvania's 67 counties used five different voting methods, including paper ballots (1 percent), lever machines (65 percent), punch cards (11 percent), optical scan systems (13 percent), and electronic systems (10 percent). Seven counties used multiple methods. This is a serious issue because the systems all have different error rates: in 2000 only 1 percent of the ballots in optical scanner counties registered no choice, while 4 percent of the ballots in punch-card counties registered no choice (Holmes 2001: 237). In 2000, Florida suffered from a similar lack of standardization leading former-President Jimmy Carter to say that, "basic international requirements for a fair election are missing in Florida" (Carter 2004). The situation in Florida and the rest of United States contrasts sharply with how Canadian elections are conducted. No matter where one lives in Canada, one votes using a paper ballot and marking an "X" beside the name of the preferred parliamentary candidate (no hanging chads). This is not to say that American officials should adopt the particular system used by Canada, but to say that they should make a serious effort to standardize methods for voting across the country. To return to the sports metaphor, the current state of affairs in voting is something akin to different National Basketball Association (NBA) venues if they varied the dimensions and construction of their equipment. Obviously, the size and materials used to construct backboards and rims affect the ability of players to score. This is why the NBA Board of Governor's has created specific guidelines concerning the dimensions and construction of backboards and rims. Although some sports fanatics might disagree, I would argue that the methods for voting deserve more care and scrutiny than those for registering basketball shots.

A weak effort in this direction was made in 2002 when Congress passed, and Bush signed, the Help America Vote Act. That legislation authorized Congress to spend $3.9 billion to help the states modernize and standardize their voting technology. Specifically, the law required the states to create computerized voter registration lists, define what constitutes a vote on each type of voting machine used in the state, improve poll access for the disabled, and allow people to check their ballots and correct errors before casting their votes. The law also established new criminal penalties for anyone providing false information when registering or voting, or conspiring to deprive voters of a fair election. When he signed the legislation, Bush said, "Every registered voter deserves to have confidence that the system is fair and elections are honest, that every vote is recorded and that the rules are consistently applied. The legislation I sign today will add to the nation's confidence" (Pear 2002). Yet, of the $3.9 billion authorized by Congress, only $1.4 billion was appropriated, and states complained that they were left to "walk the reform road alone." Barack Obama has publicly stated that he supports fully funding HAVA, but thus far those funds have not been forthcoming.

Although I am arguing for increased standardization, I want to be clear that I am not necessarily contending that all states should use the same voting technologies, or that Congress should federally mandate that they do so. Standardizing voting methods within every state would be a significant improvement. In addition, every state should develop consistent standards for reviewing ballots.

The final aspect of the sports metaphor that one should appreciate is the notion that game rules should be enforced by neutral parties. Obviously, referees can always make errors and may even make partial calls on occasion, but the notion that a referee can have standing ties to a team that is playing in a game that he or she is calling is preposterous. Even a referee such as Italy's Pierluigi Collina, who was recognized for his fairness and impartiality all over the world, was never allowed to referee a soccer match that Italy played in. Yet Florida's secretary of state in 2004, Glenda Hood, was a former Republican office holder, an elector for George W. Bush in 2000, and appointed to her current position by the Bush's brother Jeb Bush. Even worse, her predecessor, Katherine Harris, was co-chairwoman of Bush's 2000 campaign in Florida at the same time that she was supposed to be overseeing the fairness of the election in that state. Moreover, she accompanied a group of Florida Republicans to campaign in the New Hampshire primary for Bush and was a delegate at the convention that nominated him. The fact that the 2000 election in Florida was not overseen by "a nonpartisan electoral commission or a trusted and nonpartisan official" is another reason Carter claimed that the elections in that state, and by extension most of the states in the union, were not fair.

The purpose of this discussion has been to use an analysis of political campaign metaphors to help us understand why voters are not more engaged by elections generally, and competitive elections specifically. The metaphor of political campaign as war—the dominant metaphor used—suggests citizens may not be engaged because they are not inspired by political leaders or do not find elections meaningful. The metaphor of political campaign as town hall meeting points to other reasons for citizen apathy. Elections drag on for far too long and offer few opportunities for candidates and citizens to interact. Finally, the metaphor of political campaign as sporting event suggests a host of reasons pertaining to the perceived fairness of elections that might undermine citizen engagement. First, fans enjoy watching a game between two well-matched rivals far more than a blow-out, which is the modal outcome in American elections. Sports are also standardized in the sense that they are played the same no matter the location. Elections in the United States are not. Finally, it is not unheard of for sports fans to storm the field if they believe a game is being refereed in a biased manner. Yet American elections are administered for the most part by party loyalists. It should come as no suprise then that most Americans do not share Whitman's enthusiasm for elections, even when they are well-contested

The analysis in the previous chapters show that reformers' first priority should be to advocate reforms that make elections more competitive because doing so is the surest and easiest way to guarantee that voters are provided with good information and encouraged to participate, in addition to the host of other reasons that competitive elections are good for democracy, such as holding representatives accountable. In the long run, however, a comprehensive reform agenda must focus on how to make the electoral process more engaging for voters. In other words, we need to seek reforms that will inspire and involve voters, and, ultimately, encourage them to jump out of their seats and cheer.

APPENDIX

Table A.1. Effect of Competitiveness on Advertising Volume in House, Senate, and State-Level Presidential Campaigns

	Model 1 H/INC	*Model 2 H/CHALL*	*Model 3 H/OPEN*	*Model 4 S/INC*	*Model 5 S/CHALL*	*Model 6 P*
Median Age/%>65	−.01	.02	.01	.09	.08	.18
	(.02)	(.03)	(.04)	(.06)	(.15)	(.11)
Percent white	.01*	.003	.01	.01	.03	.02
	(.01)	(.01)	(.01)	(.01)	(.02)	(.02)
Percent with B.A.	.0002	.01	.02	−.03	.04	.04
	(.01)	(.02)	(.02)	(.04)	(.13)	(.05)
Income (1000s)	−.01	−.01	−.02	.02	.08	.0003
	(.01)	(.02)	.02	(.03)	(.10)	(.04)
Voting Age Pop (10000s)	—	—	—	.001***	.0003	.0001
				(.0003)	(.001)	(.001)
Cost per airing	−.0004***	−.001**	−.001*	−.001*	−.0003	−.001*
	(.0001)	(.0002)	(.0002)	(.001)	(.001)	(.0003)
Year 2002	.07	−.01	−.004	.38**	1.49#	—
	(.12)	(.20)	(.24)	(.26)	(.81)	
Year 2004	.30**	.07	.17	.09	.24	.82*
	(.12)	(.20)	(.21)	(.26)	(.74)	(.40)
Toss Up	2.19***	2.67***	2.41***	1.66***	3.47***	2.93***
	(.18)	(.27)	(.24)	(.28)	(.77)	(.46)
Leans towards	1.78***	2.14***	2.03***	1.04**	2.82**	2.56***
	(.15)	(.21)	(.26)	(.36)	(.99)	(.50)
Likely to favor	1.06***	1.59***	.98**	.69*	2.13**	−.07
	(.13)	(.21)	(.35)	(.29)	(.85)	(.58)
N	**929**	**929**	**78**	**63**	**63**	**175**
R^2 or pseudo-R^2	—	—	—	**.04**	**.03**	**.022**
Log likelihood	**−2364.85**	**−1563.26**	**−490.08**	**−544.52**	**−419.25**	**−1229.55**

*** $p<0.001$; ** $p<0.01$; * $p<0.05$; # $p<0.1$; two-tailed. Sources: Goldstein et al. 2002; Goldstein and Rivlin 2005, 2007. Models 1, 2, and 3 respectively explain advertising volume for incumbents, challengers, and both candidates in open races. Models 4 and 5 explain advertising volume for Senate incumbents and challengers. The dependent variable in Model 6 is total number of ad airings in each media market. Analyses of House advertising data use zero-inflated regression models; analyses of Senate and presidential advertising data use negative binomial regression models. House and Senate campaign data are from 2000, 2002, and 2004; presidential campaign data are from 2000 and 2004.

Table A.2. Effect of Competitiveness on Information Diversity and Equality in House, Senate, and State-Level Presidential Campaigns

	Unique sponsors			*Equality ratio*		
	Model 1 *H*	*Model 2* *S*	*Model 3* *P*	*Model 4* *H*	*Model 5* *S*	*Model 6* *P*
Median Age/% Over 65	–.01	.03	.01	–.06	.05	.06
	(.01)	(.04)	(.02)	(.04)	(.04)	(.05)
Percent white	.01*	.001	.01	.01	-.001	.04*
	(.004)	(.01)	(.01)	(.01)	(.01)	(.02)
Percent with B.A.	.01#	–.001	.001	–.001	.10**	.03
	(.01)	(.03)	(.01)	(.01)	(.04)	(.03)
Median income (1000s)	–.01	.03	–.001	–.01	.04	–.005
	(.01)	(.02)	(.01)	(.02)	(.07)	(.02)
Voting age population (10000s)	—	–.00003	–.0002	—	–.0003	–.002
		(.0002)	(.0003)		(.0004)	(.002)
Cost per airing	–.001***	–.0003#	.00004	.00003	–.001#	.001
	.0001	(.0002)	(.0001)	(.00002)	(.001)	(.001)
Year 2002	–.55***	–.61***	—	.22	.17	—
	(.11)	(.16)		(.19)	(.17)	
Year 2004	–.26**	–.40**	.08	.18	–.32	–.27
	(.09)	(.16)	(.10)	(.21)	(.23)	(.28)
Open race	. –09	.41*	—	.14	.44	—
	(.10)	(.18)		(.22)	(.41)	
Toss-up	2.23***	1.53***	2.33***	2.83***	2.93***	2.00***
	(.14)	(.17)	(.15)	(.20)	(.11)	(.38)
Leans towards a party	2.00***	.83***	1.89***	2.65***	3.19***	1.50***
	(.14)	(.24)	(.16)	(.21)	(.51)	(.41)
Likely to favor a party	1.21***	.90***	.71**	1.76***	1.65***	.39
	(.14)	(.25)	(.23)	(.23)	(.25)	(.50)
N	**998**	**83**	**175**	**367**	**82**	**122**
R^2 or adjusted R^2	—	**.260**	**.218**	—	—	—
Log pseudo-likelihood	**–863.22**	**–146.03**	**–330.72**	**–145.85**	**–30.39**	**–56.44**
AIC	—	—	—	**.86**	**1.06**	**1.11**

*** $p<0.001$; ** $p<0.01$; * $p<0.05$; # $p<0.1$; two-tailed. Sources: Goldstein et al. 2002; Goldstein and Rivlin 2005; Goldstein and Rivlin 2007. Models 1, 2, and 3 explain total number of unique advertising sponsors in House, Senate, and presidential campaigns using negative binomial regression models. Models 4, 5, and 6 explain information equality using generalized linear models with a binomial distribution and logit link function. House and Senate campaign data are from 2000, 2002, and 2004; presidential campaign data are from 2000 and 2004.

Table A.3. Effect of Competitiveness on Dialogue and Negativity in House, Senate, and State-Level Presidential Campaigns

	Dialogue			Attack ad proportion		
	Model 1 *H*	*Model 2* *S*	*Model 3* *P*	*Model 4* *H*	*Model 5* *S*	*Model 6* *P*
Median age/% Over 65	–.002	–.01	.01*	.06	.07	–.02
	(.003)	(.01)	(.01)	(.04)	(.09)	(.02)
Percent white	.001#	.004**	-.001	-.01	-.004	.002
	(.001)	(.002)	(.002)	(.01)	(.01)	(.01)
Percent with B.A.	.003#	.02*	–.001	–.02	–.01	.05*
	(.002)	(.01)	(.004)	(.02)	(.04)	(.02)
Median income (1000s)	–.004*	–.01	–.002	.01	.04	–.01
	(.002)	(.01)	(.003)	(.02)	(.04)	(.02)
Voting age population (10000s)	—	–.00004	–.0001	—	–.001***	–.001#
		(.0001)	(.0001)		(.0003)	(.001)
Cost per airing	–.00003#	.000003	.0001#	.0002	–.0002	.0001
	(.00002)	(.0001)	(.00003)	(.0002)	(.0003)	(.0001)
Year 2002	.06***	.04	—	–.52**	.18	—
	(.02)	(.04)		(.18)	(.29)	
Year 2004	.05**	.004	.13	.11	–.27	.36*
	(.02)	(.05)	(.03)	(.22)	(.32)	(.16)
Open race	–.01	.13*	—	–.13	.62*	—
	(.02)	(.05)		(.22)	(.28)	
Toss-up	.32***	.30***	.26***	2.17***	1.76***	.18
	(.03)	(.05)	(.04)	(.24)	(.31)	(.30)
Leans Toward a party	.30***	.26***	.19***	1.76***	1.51***	–.14
	(.02)	(.06)	(.04)	(.22)	(.44)	(.33)
Likely to favor a party	.18***	.25***	–.03	.92***	1.42***	–.37
	(.02)	(.06)	(.05)	(.26)	(.39)	(.44)
N	**367**	**82**	**140**	**367**	**83**	**123**
R^2 **or adjusted** R^2	**.44**	**.56**	**.41**	—	—	—
Log pseudolikelihood	—	—	—	**–120.66**	**–25.91**	**–58.74**
AIC	—	—	—	**.723**	**.938**	**1.13**

*** $p < 0.001$; ** $p < 0.01$; * $p < 0.05$; # $p < 0.1$; two-tailed. Sources: Goldstein et al. 2002; Goldstein and Rivlin 2005, 2007. Models 1, 2, and 3 explain amount of dialogue in House, Senate, and presidential campaigns using OLS models. Models 4, 5, and 6 explain proportion of attack advertising in a campaign using generalized linear models with a binomial distribution and logit link function. House and Senate campaign data are from 2000, 2002, and 2004; presidential campaign data are from 2000 and 2004.

Table A.4. Models for Figures 4.1 and 4.2

	Model 1 *Rate House candidates*	*Model 2* *Know Inc ideology*	*Model 3* *Rate Senate candidates*	*Model 4* *Campaign interest*	*Model 5* *Campaign interest*
Age	.031***	.006	.013	.020*	.004
	(.008)	(.012)	(.010)	(.008)	(.009)
Age*age	–.000***	–.000	–.000#	–.000	.000
	(.000)	(.000)	(.000)	(.000)	(.000)
Education	.057**	.057*	.099***	.026	.029
	(.017)	(.024)	(.024)	(.017)	(.020)
Male	–.033	.044	.044	.054	.072
	(.051)	(.069)	(.067)	(.047)	(.058)
White	.154*	–.019	.228**	–.148**	–.096
	(.060)	(.087)	(.080)	(.058)	(.071)
Political knowledge	.116***	.159***	.131***	.218***	.244***
	(.028)	(.036)	(.036)	(.027)	(.033)
Strength of partisanship	.049	.099*	.003	.152***	.163***
	(.032)	(.042)	(.042)	(.029)	(.035)
Days read paper	.040***	.004	.041**	.005	.006
	(.009)	(.013)	(.013)	(.009)	(.010)
Republican	.145	.373*	.263#	–.017	.006
	(.111)	(.167)	(.141)	(.106)	(.127)
Democrat	.231*	.088	.343*	–.015	–.063
	(.110)	(.167)	(.143)	(.104)	(.126)
2002	.162*	—	.152	–.475***	–.469***
	(.080)		(.122)	(.072)	(.090)
2004	.279***	–.115#	.247**	.234***	.293***
	(.061)	(.069)	(.076)	(.059)	(.072)
Gubernatorial race	.014	–.031	.290**	.000	.047
	(.073)	(.112)	(.099)	(.064)	(.075)
Senate race	.016	–.002	—	.072	—
	(.053)	(.077)		(.049)	
House competitiveness	—	—	.055	—	.027
			(.046)		(.037)
House "Likely"	.517***	.284*	—	.003	—
	(.085)	(.111)		(.071)	
House "Leans"	.706***	.556***	—	–.021	—
	(.132)	(.162)		(.111)	
House "Toss–up"	.798***	–.050	—	.124	—
	(.144)	(.277)		(.104)	
Senate "Likely"	—	—	.165*	—	–.015
			(.082)		(.070)
Senate "Leans	—	—	.543***	—	.054
			(.128)		(.090)
Senate "Toss–up"	—	—	.773***	—	.064
			(.090)		(.059)
N	**3,154**	**2,129**	**2,389**	**3,792**	**2,553**
Log likelihood	**–2876.05**	**–1044.47**	**–160.06**	**–3145.89**	**–2127.43**
Pseudo R^2	**.09**	**.11**	**.12**	**.20**	**.20**

*** $p<0.001$; ** $p<0.01$; * $p<0.05$; # $p<0.1$; two tailed. Source: NES Cumulative File. Models were estimated using NES post–survey population weights. Models 1, 3, 4, and 5 were estimated using ordered probit regression; Model 2 was estimated using logit regression.

Table A.5. Effect of Information Environment Characteristics on Ability to Rate House Candidates (Full Model)

	Model 1	*Model 2*	*Model 3*	*Model 4*	*Model 5*	*Model 6*	*Model 7*	*Model 8*	*Model 9*	*Model 10*
Age	.038**	.037**	.037**	.037**	.037**	.037**	.037**	.038**	.037**	.037**
	(.014)	(.014)	(.014)	(.014)	(.014)	(.014)	(.014)	(.014)	(.014)	(.014)
Age*age	–.000*	–.000*	–.000*	–.000*	–.000*	–.000*	–.000*	–.000*	–.000*	–.000*
	(.000)	(.000)	(.000)	(.000)	(.000)	(.000)	(.000)	(.000)	(.000)	(.000)
Education	.086**	.093**	.093**	.093**	.093**	.093**	.092**	.090**	.093**	.092**
	(.030)	(.031)	(.031)	(.031)	(.031)	(.031)	(.031)	(.031)	(.031)	(.031)
Income	.103*	.105*	.101*	.105*	.102*	.105*	.098*	.104*	.101*	.100*
	(.045)	(.046)	(.047)	(.046)	(.046)	(.046)	(.047)	(.046)	(.046)	(.046)
Male	–.032	–.040	–.038	–.040	–.039	–.038	–.037	–.042	–.038	–.040
	(.086)	(.085)	(.086)	(.086)	(.085)	(.085)	(.086)	(.086)	(.086)	(.085)
White	–.020	–.016	–.018	–.016	–.014	–.016	–.013	–.021	–.013	–.028
	(.108)	(.108)	(.108)	(.108)	(.108)	(.108)	(.108)	(.107)	(.108)	(.107)
Strength of partisanship	.070	.082	.081	.082	.082	.082	.082	.085	.082	.087
	(.054)	(.054)	(.054)	(.054)	(.054)	(.054)	(.054)	(.054)	(.054)	(.054)
Republican	.123	.076	.083	.076	.075	.084	.082	.072	.073	.081
	(.181)	(.181)	(.181)	(.181)	(.181)	(.179)	(.181)	(.181)	(.181)	(.179)
Democrat	.319#	.284	.294#	.284	.283	.292#	.288	.284	.281	.288#
	(.176)	(.176)	(.176)	(.176)	(.176)	(.174)	(.176)	(.176)	(.176)	(.174)
General political knowledge	.106*	.114*	.113*	.114*	.114*	.112*	.114*	.114*	.115*	.110*
	(.050)	(.050)	(.050)	(.050)	(.050)	(.049)	(.050)	(.050)	(.050)	(.049)
Read newspaper	.046**	.047**	.048**	.047**	.047**	.047**	.049**	.048**	.048**	.049**
	(.016)	(.016)	(.016)	(.016)	(.016)	(.016)	(.016)	(.016)	(.016)	(.016)
Open race	–.162	–.168	–.166	–.169	–.163	–.184	–.179	–.197	–.170	–.220#
	(.119)	(.118)	(.118)	(.120)	(.118)	(.122)	(.119)	(.121)	(.120)	(.121)
Senate race	–.003	.007	.019	.008	.013	.009	.014	.010	.016	.010
	(.092)	(.092)	(.093)	(.094)	(.092)	(.091)	(.093)	(.094)	(.092)	(.091)
Gubernatorial race	.006	.043	.040	.043	.043	.048	.043	.042	.043	.072
	(.111)	(.110)	(.110)	(.110)	(.109)	(.109)	(.110)	(.110)	(.109)	(.111)
2002	.370*	.319#	.329#	.323#	.295	.330#	.304#	.335#	.300	.299#
	(.177)	(.179)	(.179)	(.187)	(.182)	(.180)	(.181)	(.188)	(.182)	(.181)

2004	.578***	.492***	.498***	.495***	.487***	.494***	.483***	.480***	.489***	.470***
	(.107)	(.110)	(.111)	(.112)	(.111)	(.111)	(.112)	(.114)	(.111)	(.112)
Leans	.571***	.442***	.417***	.443***	.420***	.435***	.385**	.397**	.408**	.393**
	(.110)	(.119)	(.125)	(.119)	(.123)	(.119)	(.129)	(.124)	(.126)	(.124)
Likely	.621***	.274	.204	.271	.227	.252	.229	.160	.203	.206
	(.148)	(.182)	(.201)	(.188)	(.190)	(.186)	(.203)	(.201)	(.195)	(.189)
Toss–up	.556**	–.062	–.107	–.065	–.088	–.111	–.052	–.079	–.078	.033
	(.179)	(.250)	(.260)	(.257)	(.253)	(.261)	(.264)	(.264)	(.255)	(.274)
Volume (100s)	—	.014**	.013**	.013**	.012*	.014**	.024*	.019**	.017	.024**
		(.004)	(.004)	(.005)	(.005)	(.004)	(.011)	(.006)	(.012)	(.008)
Equality	—	—	.151	—	—	—	.266	—	—	—
			(.188)				(.208)			
Diversity	—	—	—	.003	—	—	—	.063	—	—
				(.036)				(.051)		
Dialogue	—	—	—	—	.272	—	—	—	.325	—
					(.280)				(.299)	
Negativity	—	—	—	—	—	.145	—	—	—	.319
						(.234)				(.266)
Volume*equality	—	—	—	—	—	—	–.018	—	—	—
							(.014)			
Volume*diversity	—	—	—	—	—	—	—	–.002	—	—
								(.001)		
Volume*dialogue	—	—	—	—	—	—	—	—	–.010	—
									(.020)	
Volume*negativity	—	—	—	—	—	—	—	—	—	–.031
										(.021)
N	**1,233**	**1,233**	**1,233**	**1,233**	**1,233**	**1,233**	**1,233**	**1,233**	**1,233**	**1,233**
Log likelihood	**–1036.83**	**–1029.67**	**–1029.28**	**–1029.13**	**–1029.67**	**–1029.34**	**–1028.13**	**–1028.10**	**–1028.94**	**–1027.91**
Pseudo-R^2	**.096**	**.103**	**.103**	**.103**	**.103**	**.103**	**.104**	**.104**	**.103**	**.104**

*** $p < 0.001$; ** $p < 0.01$; * $p < 0.05$; # $p < 0.1$; two tailed. Sources: NES Cumulative File; Goldstein et al. 2002; Goldstein and Rivlin 2005, 2007. Cell entries are ordered probit coefficients with robust standard errors in parentheses. All models were estimated using NES post–survey population weights. The dependent variable ranges from 0 to 2 with "2," "1," and "0" indicating that respondent could rate both, one, or neither candidate on a feeling thermometer.

Table A.6. Effect of Information Environment Characteristics on Ability to Identify Incumbents' Ideology (Full Model)

	Model 1	*Model 2*	*Model 3*	*Model 4*	*Model 5*	*Model 6*	*Model 7*	*Model 8*	*Model 9*	*Model 10*	*Model 11*
Age	–.002	–.002	–.001	–.003	–.004	–.000	.000	–.003	–.005	–.004	–.003
	(.035)	(.036)	(.036)	(.036)	(.036)	(.035)	(.036)	(.036)	(.036)	(.036)	(.037)
Age*age	.000	.000	.000	.000	.000	.000	.000	.000	.000	.000	.000
	(.000)	(.000)	(.000)	(.000)	(.000)	(.000)	(.000)	(.000)	(.000)	(.000)	(.000)
Education	.186*	.182*	.183*	.182*	.188*	.187*	.200**	.212**	.190**	.210**	.214**
	(.075)	(.075)	(.075)	(.075)	(.075)	(.076)	(.075)	(.075)	(.074)	(.076)	(.077)
Income	.205#	.207#	.209#	.206#	.206#	.199#	.230#	.224#	.222#	.221#	.197
	(.118)	(.117)	(.119)	(.118)	(.117)	(.118)	(.122)	(.118)	(.119)	(.121)	(.123)
Male	.440*	.446*	.443*	.448*	.476*	.460*	.460*	.482*	.441*	.478*	.523*
	(.203)	(.202)	(.205)	(.203)	(.205)	(.204)	(.206)	(.206)	(.203)	(.206)	(.213)
White	.176	.170	.168	.176	.173	.154	.165	.139	.167	.172	.103
	(.293)	(.293)	(.296)	(.295)	(.293)	(.298)	(.305)	(.295)	(.301)	(.302)	(.307)
Strength of Partisanship	.205	.202	.202	.201	.214#	.209#	.227#	.219#	.204	.215#	.223#
	(.125)	(.126)	(.126)	(.125)	(.127)	(.126)	(.126)	(.128)	(.126)	(.127)	(.128)
Read newspaper	.017	.017	.017	.017	.015	.020	.009	.002	.011	.014	.012
	(.039)	(.039)	(.039)	(.039)	(.039)	(.039)	(.039)	(.039)	(.038)	(.039)	(.039)
Senate race	–.104	–.066	–.060	–.065	–.138	–.032	–.122	–.060	–.057	–.060	–.048
	(.229)	(.231)	(.237)	(.231)	(.243)	(.231)	(.238)	(.243)	(.234)	(.234)	(.241)
Republican	.302	.313	.314	.313	.282	.293	.316	.276	.333	.299	.368
	(.434)	(.439)	(.438)	(.438)	(.441)	(.438)	(.453)	(.445)	(.447)	(.427)	(.442)
Democrat	–.166	–.147	–.147	–.147	–.178	–.158	–.214	–.252	–.192	–.212	–.215
	(.450)	(.457)	(.456)	(.457)	(.458)	(.456)	(.464)	(.462)	(.460)	(.446)	(.460)
Gubernatorial race	–.256	–.249	–.254	–.249	–.225	–.253	–.209	–.272	–.306	–.234	–.094
	(.282)	(.285)	(.289)	(.285)	(.288)	(.282)	(.312)	(.290)	(.285)	(.276)	(.319)
Inc. Years in Office	.006	.010	.010	.009	.008	.008	.018	.022	.017	.021	.042#
	(.019)	(.020)	(.020)	(.020)	(.020)	(.019)	(.020)	(.020)	(.020)	(.020)	(.023)
2004	–.279	–.221	–.224	–.231	–.133	–.238	–.131	–.102	–.322	–.108	–.006
	(.216)	(.237)	(.241)	(.238)	(.247)	(.235)	(.254)	(.249)	(.241)	(.234)	(.239)
Leans	.448#	.535#	.546#	.522#	.537#	.502#	.727*	.801**	.724*	.816**	.824**
	(.262)	(.293)	(.297)	(.292)	(.289)	(.287)	(.325)	(.309)	(.315)	(.299)	(.306)
Likely	1.125***	1.379**	1.409**	1.353**	.901	1.173*	1.207*	1.953**	1.681***	1.263**	.456
	(.315)	(.453)	(.482)	(.452)	(.688)	(.464)	(.520)	(.690)	(.481)	(.460)	(.528)
Toss-up	–.192	.184	.205	.169	–.400	–.204	–.037	–.123	.106	–1.180	–1.822#
	(.467)	(.588)	(.607)	(.587)	(.831)	(.625)	(.669)	(.939)	(.653)	(.885)	(1.029)

Volume (100s)	—	–.010	–.009	–.011	–.020	–.014	–.067*	–.050**	–.083*	–.067**	—
		(.012)	(.014)	(.015)	(.013)	(.013)	(.030)	(.017)	(.034)	(.021)	
Equality	—	—	–.068	—	—	—	–.692	—	—	—	—
			(.519)				(.581)				
Dialogue	—	—	—	.194	—	—	—	—	–.454	—	—
				(.763)					(.868)		
Diversity	—	—	—	—	.182	—	—	–.196	—	—	—
					(.179)			(.193)			
Negativity	—	—	—	—	—	1.062	—	—	—	.280	—
						(.693)				(.739)	
Volume *equality	—	—	—	—	—	—	.096*	—	—	—	—
							(.042)				
Volume *diversity	—	—	—	—	—	—	—	.008***	—	—	—
								(.003)			
Volume *dialogue	—	—	—	—	—	—	—	—	.145*	—	—
									(.064)		
Volume *negativity	—	—	—	—	—	—	—	—	—	.162**	—
										(.058)	
Incumbent attack	—	—	—	—	—	—	—	—	—	—	–.013
											(.075)
Challenger attack	—	—	—	—	—	—	—	—	—	—	.139**
											(.053)
Incumbent contrast	—	—	—	—	—	—	—	—	—	—	–.035
											(.070)
Challenger contrast	—	—	—	—	—	—	—	—	—	—	.206*
											(.088)
Incumbent positive	—	—	—	—	—	—	—	—	—	—	–.083#
											(.042)
Challenger positive	—	—	—	—	—	—	—	—	—	—	–.078
											(.084)
Intercept	–3.028**	–3.066**	–3.068**	–3.040**	–3.238**	–3.125**	–3.175**	–2.911**	–2.819**	–3.194***	–3.528***
	(.983)	(1.003)	(1.001)	(1.006)	(1.035)	(.987)	(1.073)	(1.038)	(1.024)	(.966)	(1.031)
N	**709**	**709**	**709**	**709**	**709**	**709**	**709**	**709**	**709**	**709**	**709**
Log likelihood	**–369.34**	**–368.84**	**–368.83**	**–368.81**	**–368.07**	**–367.59**	**–364.52**	**–362.20**	**–365.37**	**–363.00**	**–355.38**
Pseudo-R^2	**.085**	**.087**	**.087**	**.087**	**.089**	**.090**	**.097**	**.103**	**.095**	**.101**	**.120**

*** $p<0.001$; ** $p<0.01$; * $p<0.05$; # $p<0.1$; two tailed. Sources: NES Cumulative File; Goldstein et al. 2002; Goldstein and Rivlin 2007. Cell entries are logit coefficients with robust standard errors in parentheses. All models were estimated using NES post-survey population weights. The dependent variable for all models is ability to correctly identify an incumbent's ideology, with "Don't know" coded as "incorrect" or "0."

Table A.7. Effect of Information Environment Characteristics on Ability to Rate Senate Candidates (Full Model)

	Model 1	*Model 2*	*Model 3*	*Model 4*	*Model 5*	*Model 6*	*Model 7*	*Model 8*	*Model 9*	*Model 10*	*Model 11*
Age	.014	.014	.014	.014	.014	.014	.014	.014	.014	.012	.015
	(.010)	(.010)	(.010)	(.010)	(.010)	(.010)	(.010)	(.010)	(.010)	(.010)	(.010)
Age*age	–.000#	–.000#	–.000#	–.000#	–.000#	–.000#	–.000#	–.000#	–.000#	–.000	–.000#
	(.000)	(.000)	(.000)	(.000)	(.000)	(.000)	(.000)	(.000)	(.000)	(.000)	(.000)
Education	.126***	.125***	.129***	.125***	.130***	.126***	.129***	.130***	.125***	.125***	.125***
	(.024)	(.024)	(.024)	(.024)	(.024)	(.024)	(.024)	(.024)	(.024)	(.024)	(.024)
Income	.135***	.136***	.132***	.136***	.133***	.134***	.135***	.129***	.136***	.139***	.136***
	(.038)	(.037)	(.037)	(.037)	(.038)	(.038)	(.038)	(.038)	(.037)	(.038)	(.037)
Male	.069	.067	.071	.072	.069	.066	.073	.070	.072	.078	.064
	(.067)	(.068)	(.068)	(.068)	(.068)	(.068)	(.068)	(.068)	(.068)	(.069)	(.068)
White	.237**	.240**	.251**	.233**	.257**	.239**	.253**	.249**	.235**	.263**	.235**
	(.081)	(.081)	(.081)	(.081)	(.081)	(.081)	(.081)	(.081)	(.081)	(.081)	(.081)
Republican	.308*	.307*	.308*	.314*	.317*	.306*	.324*	.308*	.310*	.313*	.297*
	(.141)	(.141)	(.141)	(.141)	(.141)	(.141)	(.141)	(.141)	(.142)	(.141)	(.141)
Democrat	.338*	.337*	.337*	.340*	.341*	.337*	.344*	.333*	.336*	.346*	.340*
	(.141)	(.141)	(.141)	(.140)	(.140)	(.141)	(.140)	(.141)	(.140)	(.139)	(.141)
Gubernatorial Race	.256*	.244*	.210*	.231*	.150	.236*	.151	.224*	.224*	.135	.217*
	(.100)	(.101)	(.104)	(.101)	(.107)	(.102)	(.107)	(.106)	(.101)	(.107)	(.104)
House competitiveness	0.039	0.037	0.041	0.032	0.037	0.017	0.036	0.019	0.023	0.032	0.067
	(0.048)	(0.048)	(0.048)	(0.048)	(0.048)	(0.049)	(0.048)	(0.049)	(0.048)	(0.049)	(0.049)
Read newspaper	.056***	.056***	.056***	.056***	.056***	.056***	.055***	.055***	.056***	.057***	.057***
	(.013)	(.013)	(.013)	(.013)	(.013)	(.013)	(.013)	(.013)	(.013)	(.013)	(.013)
Strength of partisanship	.053	.053	.053	.056	.055	.053	.057	.054	.056	.052	.055
	(.042)	(.042)	(.042)	(.042)	(.043)	(.042)	(.043)	(.043)	(.042)	(.043)	(.042)
2002	.524***	.530***	.529***	.621***	.603***	.533***	.667***	.519***	.614***	.604***	.544***
	(.148)	(.148)	(.149)	(.159)	(.154)	(.148)	(.161)	(.151)	(.159)	(.152)	(.148)
2004	.427***	.432***	.431***	.454***	.499***	.438***	.509***	.407***	.436***	.540***	.495***
	(.078)	(.079)	(.079)	(.079)	(.083)	(.079)	(.084)	(.084)	(.086)	(.084)	(.082)

Leans	.136	.148#	.081	.119	−.071	.146#	−.088	.029	.092	.131	.167*
	(.084)	(.085)	(.091)	(.085)	(.104)	(.085)	(.104)	(.104)	(.093)	(.112)	(.085)
Likely	.505***	.539***	.333#	.497***	.288#	.502**	.301	.294	.453**	.461**	.497**
	(.126)	(.142)	(.175)	(.144)	(.167)	(.160)	(.187)	(.183)	(.169)	(.167)	(.157)
Toss-up	.752***	.835***	.633***	.697***	.603**	.807***	.532*	.654***	.669***	.806***	.793***
	(.091)	(.157)	(.184)	(.178)	(.186)	(.168)	(.208)	(.189)	(.191)	(.193)	(.165)
Volume (100s)	—	−.001	−.001	−.001	−.001	−.001	−.001	.001	−.000	−.008***	−.004*
		(.001)	(.001)	(.001)	(.001)	(.001)	(.001)	(.002)	(.002)	(.002)	(.002)
Equality	—	—	.379*	—	—	—	−.002	.562*	—	—	—
			(.172)				(.209)	(.245)			
Diversity	—	—	—	.034	—	—	.026	—	.049	—	—
				(.023)			(.022)		(.034)		
Dialogue	—	—	—	—	.834***	—	.820**	—	—	−.198	—
					(.232)		(.274)			(.296)	
Negativity	—	—	—	—	—	.165	−.181	—	—	—	−.454
						(.273)	(.291)				(.389)
Volume*equality	—	—	—	—	—	—	—	−.003	—	—	—
								(.003)			
Volume*diversity	—	—	—	—	—	—	—	—	−.0001	—	—
									(.0002)		
Volume*dialogue	—	—	—	—	—	—	—	—	—	.016***	—
										(.003)	
Volume*negativity	—	—	—	—	—	—	—	—	—	—	.016***
											(.003)
N	**2,285**	**2,285**	**2,285**	**2,285**	**2,285**	**2,285**	**2,285**	**2,285**	**2,285**	**2,285**	**2,285**
Log likelihood	**−1501.10**	**−1500.87**	**−1497.98**	**−1498.68**	**−1491.06**	**−1500.61**	**−1489.84**	**−1497.18**	**−1498.44**	**−1473.67**	**−1497.72**
Pseudo-R^2	**.123**	**.123**	**.125**	**.125**	**.129**	**.124**	**.130**	**.126**	**.125**	**.139**	**.125**

*** $p<0.001$; ** $p<0.01$; * $p<0.05$; # $p<0.1$; two tailed. Sources: NES Cumulative File; Goldstein et al. 2002; Goldstein and Rivlin 2005, 2007. Cell entries are ordered probit coefficients with robust standard errors in parentheses. All models were estimated using NES post–survey population weights. The dependent variable ranges from 0 to 2 with "2" indicating that respondent could rate both, one, or neither candidate on a feeling thermometer.

Table A.8. Effect of Information Environment Characteristics on Knowledge of Presidential Candidate Issue Positions (Full Model)

	Model 1	*Model 2*	*Model 3*	*Model 4*	*Model 5*	*Model 6*	*Model 7*	*Model 8*	*Model 9*	*Model 10*	*Model 11*	*Model 12*	*Model 13*	*Model 14*	*Model 15*
Age	.037***	.037***	.037***	.037***	.036***	.036***	.036***	.037***	.037***	.036***	.036***	.039***	.019#	–.005	–.014
	(.005)	(.005)	(.005)	(.005)	(.005)	(.005)	(.005)	(.005)	(.005)	(.005)	(.005)	(.007)	(.011)	(.011)	(.011)
Age*age	–.000***	–.000***	–.000***	–.000***	–.000***	–.000***	–.000***	–.000***	–.000***	–.000***	–.000***	–.000***	–.000*	.000	.000
	(.000)	(.000)	(.000)	(.000)	(.000)	(.000)	(.000)	(.000)	(.000)	(.000)	(.000)	(.000)	(.000)	(.000)	(.000)
Male	.348***	.349***	.351***	.348***	.349***	.350***	.350***	.351***	.348***	.350***	.351***	.213***	.189*	–.203**	.014
	(.034)	(.034)	(.034)	(.034)	(.034)	(.035)	(.034)	(.034)	(.034)	(.034)	(.035)	(.047)	(.090)	(.064)	(.077)
Education	.182***	.182***	.183***	.182***	.182***	.182***	.183***	.183***	.182***	.182***	.182***	.147***	.117***	–.021	–.096***
	(.005)	(.005)	(.005)	(.005)	(.005)	(.005)	(.005)	(.005)	(.005)	(.005)	(.005)	(.011)	(.016)	(.019)	(.014)
White	.239***	.241***	.234***	.235***	.242***	.244***	.232***	.234***	.233***	.239***	.244***	.233**	.126	–.012	–.114
	(.060)	(.061)	(.060)	(.060)	(.060)	(.060)	(.060)	(.060)	(.060)	(.060)	(.060)	(.087)	(.092)	(.094)	(.111)
Debate period	.045	.025	.035	.088#	.030	.018	.077#	.039	.079#	.049	.023	.054	.007	–.089	.082
	(.038)	(.039)	(.038)	(.046)	(.039)	(.037)	(.043)	(.039)	(.046)	(.039)	(.038)	(.068)	(.122)	(.106)	(.106)
Republican	–.354***	–.353***	–.351***	–.353***	–.354***	–.352***	–.351***	–.351***	–.352***	–.352***	–.352***	–.526***	–.170#	.108	.062
	(.042)	(.042)	(.043)	(.043)	(.042)	(.043)	(.043)	(.042)	(.043)	(.042)	(.043)	(.047)	(.096)	(.099)	(.085)
Democrat	.405***	.407***	.407***	.407***	.406***	.406***	.407***	.407***	.407***	.407***	.406***	.351***	.434***	–.174**	–.260***
	(.036)	(.036)	(.036)	(.036)	(.036)	(.036)	(.036)	(.036)	(.036)	(.036)	(.036)	(.048)	(.079)	(.062)	(.070)
Days before election	–.004***	–.003**	–.003***	–.003**	–.003**	–.003**	–.003***	–.003***	–.003**	–.003**	–.003**	–.003**	.003#	–.002	–.001
	(.001)	(.001)	(.001)	(.001)	(.001)	(.001)	(.001)	(.001)	(.001)	(.001)	(.001)	(.001)	(.002)	(.002)	(.002)
Likely	.038	.033	.037	.040	.033	.044	.050	.038	.042	.030	.042	–.012	–.132	.040	.092
	(.070)	(.066)	(.064)	(.066)	(.068)	(.069)	(.067)	(.065)	(.064)	(.064)	(.069)	(.059)	(.129)	(.123)	(.130)
Leans	.046	.017	.002	.031	.022	.038	.029	.005	.023	.009	.041	–.025	–.135	–.087	.223#
	(.082)	(.077)	(.074)	(.075)	(.079)	(.078)	(.074)	(.075)	(.073)	(.073)	(.079)	(.074)	(.136)	(.155)	(.116)
Toss-up	.163**	.085	.074	.077	.095	.093	.079	.078	.063	.079	.099	.085	–.041	–.052	.093
	(.061)	(.059)	(.057)	(.058)	(.063)	(.061)	(.061)	(.058)	(.059)	(.060)	(.063)	(.059)	(.136)	(.117)	(.122)
Volume	—	.011*	.008	–.004	.012*	.010*	–.003	.003	.001	.024**	.003	.017#	.061***	–.034*	–.027*
		(.005)	(.005)	(.006)	(.005)	(.005)	(.006)	(.010)	(.007)	(.007)	(.010)	(.009)	(.016)	(.014)	(.011)
Equality	—	—	.129*	—	—	—	.143*	.098	—	—	—	—	—	—	—

			(.056)				(.059)	(.075)							
Diversity	—	—	—	.045**	—	—	.030*	—	.056**	—	—	—	—	—	—
				(.014)			(.014)		(.020)						
Dialogue	—	—	—	—	−.093	—	−.066	—	—	.107	—	.177	.575#	−.884**	.309
					(.082)		(.091)			(.120)		(.163)	(.291)	(.259)	(.259)
Negativity	—	—	—	—	—	.215***	.176**	—	—	—	.172*	—	—	—	—
						(.060)	(.059)				(.079)				
Volume*equality	—	—	—	—	—	—	—	.008	—	—	—	—	—	—	—
								(.014)							
Volume*diversity	—	—	—	—	—	—	—	—	−.001	—	—	—	—	—	—
									(.001)						
Volume*dialogue	—	—	—	—	—	—	—	—	—	−.039**	—	−.033	−.111*	.080*	.031
										(.014)		(.020)	(.044)	(.037)	(.039)
Volume*negativity	—	—	—	—	—	—	—	—	—	—	.013	—	—	—	—
											(.013)				
Intercept	.943***	.869***	.848***	.792***	.883***	.762***	.716***	.853***	.772***	.845***	.782***	1.631***	.943**	1.421***	2.636***
	(.138)	(.142)	(.142)	(.148)	(.144)	(.139)	(.146)	(.141)	(.149)	(.143)	(.142)	(.222)	(.278)	(.264)	(.264)
N	7,261	7,261	7,261	7,261	7,261	7,261	7,261	7,261	7,261	7,261	7,261	3,000	1,477	1,477	1,477
R^2	.158	.159	.159	.160	.159	.160	.161	.159	.160	.159	.160	.184	.088	.040	.046

*** $p < 0.001$; ** $p < 0.01$; * $p < 0.05$; # $p < 0.1$; two-tailed. Sources: 2004 National Annenberg Election Study; Goldstein et al. 2002; Goldstein and Rivlin 2005, 2007. Cell entries are OLS coefficients with robust standard errors in parentheses. The dependent variable in Models 1–13 is respondent's score on a 5-item campaign knowledge index, ranging from 0 to 5. The sample in Model 12 is restricted to political sophisticates (Soph.); the sample in Model 13 is restricted to political novices (Nov.). The dependent variable in Model 14 is number of "Don't know" responses offered (0–5); the dependent variable in Model 15 is number of incorrect responses offered (0–5). Samples in Models 14 and 15 are restricted to political novices.

Table A.9. Explaining Turnout in House, Senate, and State-Level Presidential Elections

	House turnout	*Senate turnout*	*State-level presidential turnout*
Average turnout last 2 midterms	—	—	.594***
			(.058)
Median age	.005*	.004	—
	(.002)	(.003)	
% White	.001*	.002***	—
	(.000)	(.000)	
% with B.A.	.003***	.005**	—
	(.001)	(.002)	
Median income	.000	.002	—
	(.001)	(.002)	
South	–.055***	–.037*	—
	(.012)	(.016)	
% Urban	–.133***	–.069	—
	(.023)	(.063)	
Density	–.000***	–.000**	—
	(.000)	(.000)	
Voting age population	—	.000	—
		(.000)	
Gubernatorial race	.021*	.017	.018#
	(.008)	(.011)	(.011)
Senate race	.007	—	–.008
	(.010)		(.009)
2004	—	—	.072***
			(.008)
Midterm	–.158***	–.151***	—
	(.008)	(.014)	
Likely	.004	.006	.008
	(.011)	(.023)	(.013)
Leans	.033*	.020	.026*
	(.013)	(.028)	(.012)
Toss-up	–.008	.047**	.052***
	(.015)	(.016)	(.011)
Likely*midterm	.022#	–.007	—
	(.013)	(.036)	
Leans*midterm	–.023	.017	—
	(.017)	(.034)	

	House turnout	*Senate turnout*	*State-level presidential turnout*
Toss-up*midterm	.052**	.008	—
	(.016)	(.023)	
Intercept	.258***	.121	.291***
	(.068)	(.150)	(.026)
N	**1,725**	**135**	**102**
Adjusted R^2	**.63**	**.74**	**.65**

*** $p < 0.001$; ** $p < 0.01$; * $p < 0.05$; # $p < 0.1$; two-tailed. Sources: Federal Election Commission; Michael McDonald. Cell entries are ordinary least squares coefficients with standard errors in parentheses.

Table A.10. Effect of Advertising on Non-Voting Forms of Participation in House Races

	Model 1	*Model 2*	*Model 3*	*Model 4*	*Model 5*	*Model 6*	*Model 7*	*Model 8*	*Model 10*	*Model 11*	*Model 12*	*Model 13*	*Model 14*
Age	–.020	.026*	.021	.021	.021#	.021	.021	.021	.021	.021	.021#	.021	.020
	(.082)	(.013)	(.013)	(.013)	(.013)	(.013)	(.013)	(.013)	(.013)	(.013)	(.013)	(.013)	(.013)
Age*age	.044	–.000#	–.000#	–.000#	–.000#	–.000#	–.000#	–.000#	–.000#	–.000#	–.000#	–.000#	–.000#
	(.121)	(.000)	(.000)	(.000)	(.000)	(.000)	(.000)	(.000)	(.000)	(.000)	(.000)	(.000)	(.000)
Education	.132***	.174***	.162***	.167***	.167***	.167***	.167***	.167***	.167***	.166***	.166***	.169***	.168***
	(.017)	(.028)	(.028)	(.028)	(.028)	(.028)	(.028)	(.028)	(.028)	(.028)	(.028)	(.028)	(.028)
Income	.117***	.083*	.061	.065	.065	.062	.065	.065	.063	.061	.065	.067	.065
	(.025)	(.042)	(.043)	(.043)	(.042)	(.043)	(.043)	(.042)	(.043)	(.043)	(.042)	(.042)	(.043)
Male	.101*	.168*	.171*	.164*	.165*	.165*	.164*	.163*	.167*	.166*	.162*	.160*	.168*
	(.049)	(.077)	(.078)	(.078)	(.078)	(.078)	(.078)	(.079)	(.078)	(.078)	(.079)	(.078)	(.078)
White	.014	.004	–.049	–.047	–.046	–.047	–.047	–.048	–.049	–.048	–.048	–.048	–.040
	(.060)	(.102)	(.103)	(.102)	(.102)	(.102)	(.102)	(.102)	(.102)	(.102)	(.102)	(.102)	(.102)
Senate race	.018	.013	–.014	–.004	.006	.025	.005	.001	.009	.024	.003	.004	.020
	(.055)	(.086)	(.086)	(.087)	(.086)	(.089)	(.086)	(.087)	(.087)	(.090)	(.087)	(.086)	(.087)
Republican	.204#	–.048	–.032	–.043	–.045	–.037	–.044	–.043	–.036	–.038	–.042	–.038	–.035
	(.108)	(.172)	(.174)	(.175)	(.175)	(.175)	(.175)	(.175)	(.174)	(.175)	(.175)	(.175)	(.174)
Democrat	.114	–.100	–.093	–.107	–.108	–.099	–.107	–.105	–.098	–.099	–.104	–.099	–.096
	(.108)	(.172)	(.173)	(.174)	(.174)	(.174)	(.174)	(.175)	(.174)	(.174)	(.174)	(.174)	(.173)
Gubernatorial race	.007	.005	.004	.031	.029	.023	.032	.034	.052	.025	.031	.040	.055
	(.081)	(.102)	(.099)	(.100)	(.100)	(.100)	(.100)	(.102)	(.101)	(.102)	(.102)	(.100)	(.101)
Days read newspaper	.043***	.047***	.047**	.046**	.046**	.047***	.046**	.046**	.046**	.047**	.046**	.045**	.046**
	(.009)	(.014)	(.014)	(.014)	(.014)	(.014)	(.014)	(.014)	(.014)	(.014)	(.014)	(.014)	(.014)
Partisanship Strength	.267***	.337***	.317***	.319***	.319***	.318***	.319***	.319***	.319***	.318***	.319***	.317***	.317***
	(.031)	(.050)	(.050)	(.050)	(.050)	(.050)	(.050)	(.050)	(.050)	(.050)	(.050)	(.050)	(.050)
Pres. competitiveness	.078***	.103***	.081*	.085**	.084**	.086**	.085**	.086**	.089**	.084*	.086**	.089**	.086**
	(.020)	(.031)	(.032)	(.032)	(.032)	(.032)	(.032)	(.033)	(.032)	(.033)	(.033)	(.032)	(.032)
2004	.345***	.396***	.348***	.295***	.292***	.304***	.294***	.290**	.288***	.300***	.285**	.296***	.297***
	(.051)	(.083)	(.084)	(.087)	(.087)	(.087)	(.087)	(.094)	(.087)	(.090)	(.094)	(.087)	(.087)
Likely	–.020	.100	.090	.035	.026	.002	.034	.034	.019	–.004	.021	.061	.043
	(.082)	(.103)	(.103)	(.105)	(.108)	(.103)	(.105)	(.106)	(.103)	(.107)	(.107)	(.107)	(.105)

Leans	.044	.008	−.010	−.176	−.204	−.255$^{\#}$	−.178	−.163	−.230	−.260	−.210	−.117	−.219
	(.121)	(.139)	(.135)	(.146)	(.162)	(.154)	(.153)	(.161)	(.151)	(.159)	(.181)	(.161)	(.150)
Toss-up	−.240*	−.179$^{\#}$	−.180$^{\#}$	−.466**	−.469**	−.517**	−.467**	−.453**	−.532**	−.519**	−.470**	−.439**	−.548***
	(.114)	(.124)	(.127)	(.158)	(.159)	(.162)	(.159)	(.173)	(.164)	(.163)	(.178)	(.162)	(.163)
Contact	—	—	.447***	.450***	.452***	.446***	.450***	.450***	.455***	.448***	.450***	.444***	.451***
			(.079)	(.079)	(.079)	(.079)	(.079)	(.079)	(.079)	(.079)	(.079)	(.079)	(.079)
Volume	—	—	—	.007*	.009	.005	.007$^{\#}$	.007$^{\#}$	.007*	.006	.009$^{\#}$	−.001	.002
				(.003)	(.007)	(.003)	(.004)	(.004)	(.003)	(.008)	(.005)	(.009)	(.006)
Volume*volume	—	—	—	—	−.0004	—	—	—	—	—	—	—	—
					(.0001)								
Equality	—	—	—	—	—	.206	—	—	—	.222	—	—	—
						(.181)				(.199)			
Dialogue	—	—	—	—	—	—	.013	—	—	—	—	−.091	—
							(.272)					(.287)	
Diversity	—	—	—	—	—	—	—	−.006	—	—	.015	—	—
								(.042)			(.058)		
Negativity	—	—	—	—	—	—	—	—	.203	—	—	—	.115
									(.172)				(.193)
Volume*equality	—	—	—	—	—	—	—	—	—	−.002	—	—	—
										(.010)			
Volume*diversity	—	—	—	—	—	—	—	—	—	—	−.001	—	—
											(.001)		
Volume*dialogue	—	—	—	—	—	—	—	—	—	—	—	.015	—
												(.014)	
Volume*negativity	—	—	—	—	—	—	—	—	—	—	—	—	.013
													(.014)
N	**2584**	**991**	**991**	**991**	**991**	**991**	**991**	**991**	**991**	**991**	**991**	**991**	**991**
Log likelihood	**−3497.24**	**−1344.14**	**−1325.93**	**−1322.80**	**−1322.73**	**−1322.00**	**−1322.80**	**−1322.78**	**−1321.99**	**−1321.97**	**−1322.61**	**−1322.61**	**−1321.52**
Pseudo-R^2	**.080**	**.098**	**.109**	**.111**	**.111**	**.112**	**.111**	**.111**	**.112**	**.112**	**.111**	**.112**	**.112**

*** $p < 0.001$; ** $p < 0.01$; * $p < 0.05$; $^{\#}$ $p < 0.1$; two tailed. Sources: NES Cumulative File; Goldstein et al. 2002; Goldstein and Rivlin 2007. Cell entries are ordered probit coefficients with standard errors in parentheses. The dependent variable is a non-voting participation index (0–5). Model 1 is included so the reader can confirm that the same relationship between competitiveness and participation in House races holds for largest possible sample and the sample for which all ad measures could be calculated.

Table A.11. Effect of Advertising on Non-Voting Forms of Participation in Senate Races

	Model 1	*Model 2*	*Model 3*	*Model 4*	*Model 5*	*Model 6*	*Model 7*	*Model 8*	*Model 10*	*Model 11*	*Model 12*	*Model 13*
Age	.016#	.009	.009	.010	.010	.010	.010	.010	.010	.010	.010	.010
	(.009)	(.009)	(.009)	(.009)	(.009)	(.009)	(.009)	(.009)	(.009)	(.009)	(.009)	(.009)
Age*age	–.000	–.000	–.000	–.000	–.000	–.000	–.000	–.000	–.000	–.000	–.000	–.000
	(.000)	(.000)	(.000)	(.000)	(.000)	(.000)	(.000)	(.000)	(.000)	(.000)	(.000)	(.000)
Education	.133***	.115***	.115***	.115***	.115***	.116***	.114***	.115***	.116***	.117***	.114***	.115***
	(.018)	(.017)	(.017)	(.018)	(.018)	(.018)	(.018)	(.018)	(.018)	(.018)	(.018)	(.017)
Income	.123***	.105***	.106***	.101**	.101**	.101***	.101***	.100**	.098**	.099**	.100**	.099**
	(.030)	(.031)	(.031)	(.031)	(.031)	(.031)	(.031)	(.031)	(.031)	(.031)	(.031)	(.031)
Male	.167**	.200***	.197***	.192***	.191***	.190***	.190***	.192***	.189***	.191***	.190***	.192***
	(.051)	(.051)	(.051)	(.052)	(.051)	(.051)	(.052)	(.052)	(.051)	(.052)	(.052)	(.052)
White	–.089	–.153*	–.150*	–.141*	–.141*	–.138*	–.144*	–.143*	–.146*	–.144*	–.142*	–.143*
	(.063)	(.064)	(.064)	(.064)	(.064)	(.064)	(.064)	(.064)	(.064)	(.064)	(.064)	(.064)
Republican	.151	.134	.133	.117	.117	.114	.114	.117	.120	.129	.114	.113
	(.117)	(.117)	(.117)	(.117)	(.117)	(.118)	(.117)	(.118)	(.118)	(.118)	(.117)	(.118)
Democrat	–.013	–.013	–.014	–.023	–.022	–.024	–.020	–.023	–.026	–.013	–.021	–.023
	(.117)	(.117)	(.118)	(.118)	(.118)	(.118)	(.117)	(.118)	(.118)	(.118)	(.117)	(.118)
Days read newspaper	.045***	.042***	.042***	.044***	.044***	.044***	.045***	.044***	.044***	.044***	.045***	.044***
	(.009)	(.009)	(.009)	(.010)	(.009)	(.010)	(.009)	(.010)	(.010)	(.010)	(.009)	(.010)
Strength of partisanship	.267***	.257***	.258***	.259***	.259***	.259***	.258***	.260***	.260***	.257***	.257***	.260***
	(.033)	(.033)	(.033)	(.033)	(.033)	(.033)	(.033)	(.033)	(.033)	(.033)	(.033)	(.033)
Gubernatorial race	–.038	–.082	–.105	–.155*	–.153*	–.155*	–.122	–.161*	–.133	–.126	–.119	–.176*
	(.078)	(.075)	(.075)	(.077)	(.078)	(.077)	(.078)	(.077)	(.083)	(.078)	(.081)	(.082)
House leans	–.078	–.107	–.143	–.120	–.122	–.121	–.105	–.125	–.142	–.109	–.106	–.127
	(.089)	(.090)	(.096)	(.096)	(.096)	(.096)	(.096)	(.096)	(.097)	(.097)	(.096)	(.095)
House likely	–.014	–.061	–.058	–.065	–.064	–.068	–.060	–.072	–.070	–.045	–.052	–.087
	(.107)	(.110)	(.110)	(.111)	(.111)	(.112)	(.111)	(.112)	(.111)	(.112)	(.111)	(.114)
House toss–up	–.180	–.188	–.190	–.213#	–.212#	–.207#	–.177	–.218#	–.227#	–.193	–.173	–.206#
	(.125)	(.125)	(.126)	(.122)	(.122)	(.123)	(.124)	(.123)	(.124)	(.124)	(.127)	(.123)
2002	–.169	–.218*	–.214#	–.234*	–.234*	–.254*	–.247*	–.236*	–.228*	–.265*	–.255*	–.242*
	(.114)	(.110)	(.110)	(.111)	(.111)	(.116)	(.111)	(.111)	(.110)	(.116)	(.111)	(.110)
Leans	–.153*	–.146*	–.119#	–.244***	–.240**	–.240**	–.142#	–.247***	–.269***	–.217**	–.131	–.248***
	(.069)	(.068)	(.069)	(.074)	(.077)	(.073)	(.086)	(.073)	(.080)	(.078)	(.094)	(.074)
Likely	.186*	.148	.220*	.004	.019	.014	.133	–.030	.006	.070	.145	–.052
	(.091)	(.092)	(.100)	(.115)	(.136)	(.115)	(.129)	(.125)	(.141)	(.121)	(.130)	(.135)

Toss-up	−.108#	−.107#	.049	−.092	−.078	−.055	.039	−.119	−.045	.049	.065	−.133
	(.061)	(.061)	(.110)	(.118)	(.138)	(.130)	(.133)	(.125)	(.141)	(.140)	(.136)	(.128)
Contact	—	.568***	.567***	.557***	.557***	.556***	.561***	.558***	.551***	.556***	.561***	.559***
		(.052)	(.052)	(.052)	(.052)	(.053)	(.053)	(.052)	(.052)	(.052)	(.053)	(.052)
Volume	—	—	−.010#	.058**	.058**	.060**	.058**	.056**	.058	.101***	.064*	.039
			(.006)	(.018)	(.018)	(.019)	(.018)	(.018)	(.036)	(.029)	(.031)	(.027)
Volume*volume	—	—	—	−.003***	−.003***	−.003***	−.002***	−.002***	−.001	−.006***	−.003*	−.002
				(.001)	(.001)	(.001)	(.001)	(.001)	(.003)	(.001)	(.001)	(.002)
Equality	—	—	—	—	−.027	—	—	—	.109	—	—	—
					(.127)				(.231)			
Diversity	—	—	—	—	—	−.008	—	—	—	−.037	—	—
						(.012)				(.039)		
Dialogue	—	—	—	—	—	—	−.404*	—	—	—	−.449	—
							(.159)				(.331)	
Negativity	—	—	—	—	—	—	—	.157	—	—	—	−.171
								(.218)				(.423)
Volume*equality	—	—	—	—	—	—	—	—	−.002	—	—	—
									(.006)			
Volume²*equality	—	—	—	—	—	—	—	—	−1.46–9	—	—	—
									(3.70–9)			
Volume*diversity	—	—	—	—	—	—	—	—	—	−.000	—	—
										(.001)		
Volume²*diversity	—	—	—	—	—	—	—	—	—	3.10–10#	—	—
										(2.09–10)		
Volume*dialogue	—	—	—	—	—	—	—	—	—	—	−.001	—
											(.008)	
Volume²*dialogue	—	—	—	—	—	—	—	—	—	—	1.12–9	—
											(1.91–9)	
Volume*negativity	—	—	—	—	—	—	—	—	—	—	—	.010
												(.012)
Volume²*negativity	—	—	—	—	—	—	—	—	—	—	—	−4.57–9
												(7.08–9)
N	**2,353**	**2,353**	**2,353**	**2,353**	**2,353**	**2,353**	**2,353**	**2,353**	**2,353**	**2,353**	**2,353**	**2,353**
Log likelihood	**−3204.13**	**−3130.72**	**−3128.78**	**−3117.61**	**−3117.58**	**−3117.36**	**−3113.99**	**−3117.28**	**−3116.23**	**−3111.79**	**−3113.57**	**−3116.81**
Pseudo R^2	**.076**	**.096**	**.096**	**.100**	**.100**	**.100**	**.101**	**.100**	**.100**	**.101**	**.101**	**.100**

*** $p < 0.001$; ** $p < 0.01$; * $p < 0.05$; # $p < 0.1$; two tailed. Sources: NES Cumulative File; Goldstein et al. 2002; Goldstein and Rivlin 2005; Goldstein and Rivlin 2007. Cell entries are ordered probit coefficients with standard errors in parentheses. The dependent variable is a non-voting participation index (0–5).

Table A.12. Effect of Advertising on Non-Voting Forms of Participation in State–Level Presidential Elections

	Model 1	*Model 2*	*Model 3*	*Model 4*	*Model 5*	*Model 6*	*Model 7*	*Model 8*	*Model 10*	*Model 11*	*Model 12*	*Model 13*
Male	.042	.045	.046	.047	.050	.048	.042	.047	.051	.049	.041	.042
	(.050)	(.050)	(.050)	(.050)	(.050)	(.051)	(.050)	(.050)	(.050)	(.051)	(.050)	(.051)
Age	.004	.005	.005	.005	.005	.005	.005	.005	.004	.005	.005	.005
	(.006)	(.006)	(.006)	(.006)	(.006)	(.006)	(.006)	(.006)	(.007)	(.006)	(.006)	(.006)
Age*age	–.000	–.000	–.000	–.000	–.000	–.000	–.000	–.000	–.000	–.000	–.000	–.000
	(.000)	(.000)	(.000)	(.000)	(.000)	(.000)	(.000)	(.000)	(.000)	(.000)	(.000)	(.000)
Education	.101***	.098***	.098***	.097***	.098***	.097***	.098***	.097***	.099***	.097***	.097***	.098***
	(.011)	(.011)	(.011)	(.011)	(.011)	(.011)	(.011)	(.011)	(.011)	(.011)	(.011)	(.011)
White	.021	.036	.036	.034	.031	.035	.037	.034	.037	.033	.029	.033
	(.111)	(.111)	(.111)	(.113)	(.114)	(.113)	(.113)	(.113)	(.115)	(.114)	(.113)	(.113)
Debate period	–.067	–.071	–.073	–.076	–.063	–.084	–.073	–.067	–.073	–.081	–.071	–.106
	(.061)	(.063)	(.064)	(.065)	(.065)	(.065)	(.067)	(.067)	(.065)	(.063)	(.065)	(.065)
Republican	.563***	.553***	.553***	.554***	.557***	.554***	.553***	.553***	.555***	.556***	.558***	.555***
	(.077)	(.077)	(.077)	(.077)	(.077)	(.077)	(.078)	(.078)	(.078)	(.078)	(.078)	(.077)
Democrat	.570***	.570***	.571***	.571***	.572***	.571***	.573***	.572***	.572***	.568***	.574***	.568***
	(.070)	(.071)	(.071)	(.070)	(.070)	(.070)	(.070)	(.070)	(.070)	(.071)	(.069)	(.070)
Days before Election	–.004	–.003	–.003	–.003	–.003	–.004	.000	–.004	–.002	–.003	.002	–.001
	(.003)	(.003)	(.003)	(.003)	(.003)	(.003)	(.003)	(.003)	(.003)	(.004)	(.003)	(.003)
Gubernatorial race	–.109	–.104	–.098	–.094	–.088	–.093	–.054	–.084	–.056	–.105	–.074	–.079
	(.124)	(.122)	(.124)	(.122)	(.121)	(.122)	(.122)	(.121)	(.126)	(.125)	(.118)	(.122)
Senate race	–.044	–.046	–.044	–.035	–.038	–.033	–.027	–.036	–.060	–.034	–.010	–.035
	(.059)	(.060)	(.061)	(.066)	(.064)	(.065)	(.068)	(.066)	(.064)	(.068)	(.071)	(.064)
House leans	.285*	.274*	.271*	.267*	.259*	.271*	.274*	.268*	.264*	.266*	.266*	.226#
	(.122)	(.114)	(.116)	(.119)	(.121)	(.122)	(.113)	(.118)	(.123)	(.115)	(.119)	(.119)
House likely	–.035	–.047	–.045	–.047	–.043	–.047	–.060	–.049	–.041	–.042	–.066	–.059
	(.077)	(.083)	(.084)	(.084)	(.082)	(.084)	(.082)	(.084)	(.080)	(.084)	(.082)	(.086)
House toss-up	.108	.112	.113	.112	.114	.108	.112	.112	.117	.109	.111	.097
	(.127)	(.127)	(.128)	(.128)	(.127)	(.127)	(.126)	(.128)	(.127)	(.128)	(.126)	(.127)
Likely	.079	.068	.064	.063	.065	.062	.042	.060	.053	.074	.050	.059
	(.124)	(.123)	(.124)	(.125)	(.126)	(.125)	(.121)	(.122)	(.133)	(.130)	(.118)	(.117)
Leans	.011	–.019	–.025	–.036	–.051	–.041	–.015	–.039	–.038	–.032	–.024	–.003
	(.083)	(.087)	(.090)	(.090)	(.088)	(.091)	(.090)	(.091)	(.090)	(.094)	(.087)	(.093)
Toss-up	.089	.055	.037	.021	.026	.020	.025	.020	.030	.023	.029	.031

	(.072)	(.075)	(.109)	(.116)	(.116)	(.116)	(.114)	(.115)	(.119)	(.119)	(.112)	(.119)
Contact	—	.238*	.237*	.238*	.243**	.239*	.237*	.239*	.245**	.240*	.239*	.237*
		(.094)	(.094)	(.094)	(.094)	(.094)	(.095)	(.095)	(.094)	(.095)	(.096)	(.096)
Volume	—	—	.002	.008	–.005	.011	.024#	.009	–.045	–.005	.060*	–.084
			(.006)	(.015)	(.019)	(.018)	(.016)	(.016)	(.040)	(.026)	(.025)	(.053)
Volume*volume	—	—	—	–.0003	.0001	–.0003	–.001	–.0003	.002	.001	–.003*	.006*
				(.000)	(.001)	(.000)	(.000)	(.000)	(.002)	(.001)	(.001)	(.003)
Equality	—	—	—	—	.178	—	—	—	–.178	—	—	—
					(.143)				(.185)			
Diversity	—	—	—	—	—	–.008	—	—	—	.075	—	—
						(.020)				(.063)		
Dialogue	—	—	—	—	—	—	–.534*	—	—	—	–.246	—
							(.211)				(.317)	
Negativity	—	—	—	—	—	—	—	–.078	—	—	—	–.217#
								(.103)				(.116)
Volume*equality	—	—	—	—	—	—	—	—	.095	—	—	—
									(.061)			
Volume²*equality	—	—	—	—	—	—	—	—	–.004	—	—	—
									(.003)			
Volume*diversity	—	—	—	—	—	—	—	—	—	–.006	—	—
										(.006)		
Volume²*diversity	—	—	—	—	—	—	—	—	—	1.97–5	—	—
										(.0002)		
Volume*dialogue	—	—	—	—	—	—	—	—	—	—	–.117#	—
											(.061)	
Volume²*dialogue	—	—	—	—	—	—	—	—	—	—	.006*	—
											(.003)	
Volume*negativity	—	—	—	—	—	—	—	—	—	—	—	.160*
												(.078)
Volume²*negativity	—	—	—	—	—	—	—	—	—	—	—	–.010*
												(.004)
N	**1,624**	**1,624**	**1,624**	**1,624**	**1,624**	**1,624**	**1,624**	**1,624**	**1,624**	**1,624**	**1,624**	**1,624**
Log likelihood	**–2276.24**	**–2271.00**	**–227.97**	**–227.84**	**–227.23**	**–227.67**	**–2267.50**	**–227.68**	**–2269.22**	**–2269.81**	**–2266.11**	**–2268.56**
Pseudo-R^2	**.037**	**.039**	**.039**	**.039**	**.039**	**.039**	**.040**	**.039**	**.040**	**.039**	**.041**	**.040**

*** $p<0.001$; ** $p<0.01$; * $p<0.05$; # $p<0.1$; two-tailed. Sources: 2004 National Annenberg Election Study; Goldstein et al. 2002; Goldstein and Rivlin 2007. Cell entries are negative binomial regression coefficients with robust standard errors in parentheses (clustered by media market). The dependent variable is a non-voting participation index (0–5).

Table A.13. Effect of Competitiveness on Non-Voting Forms of Participation in House and Senate Campaigns (Models for Figures 2, 4)

	House participation		*Senate participation*	
	Model 1 Midterm	*Model 2 Pres*	*Model 3 Midterm*	*Model 4 Pres*
Age	.034***	–.001	.032*	–.003
	(.010)	(.008)	(.013)	(.010)
Age*age	–.000**	.000	–.000#	.000
	(.000)	(.000)	(.000)	(.000)
Education	.097***	.069***	.124***	.044*
	(.019)	(.018)	(.023)	(.021)
Income	.137***	.082**	.113*	.104***
	(.040)	(.027)	(.051)	(.031)
Male	.295***	.153**	.210**	.162**
	(.057)	(.052)	(.073)	(.060)
White	–.215**	.026	–.280**	.017
	(.071)	(.064)	(.094)	(.074)
Senate race	.053	.032	—	—
	(.057)	(.059)		
Republican	–.086	.105	–.038	.110
	(.141)	(.116)	(.180)	(.137)
Democrat	–.183	.026	–.169	–.048
	(.141)	(.115)	(.183)	(.135)
Gubernatorial race	–.005	.062	–.005	.039
	(.069)	(.082)	(.096)	(.092)
Days read newspaper	.063***	.037***	.069***	.044***
	(.011)	(.010)	(.014)	(.011)
Strength of partisanship	.242***	.227***	.196***	.225***
	(.038)	(.034)	(.047)	(.039)
State presidential competitiveness	—	.062**	—	.069**
		(.021)		(.026)
2002	–.003	—	.182	—
	(.175)		(.210)	
2004	—	.402***	—	.435***
		(.054)		(.066)
House "likely"	.106	–.036	.067	–.045
	(.095)	(.087)	(.127)	(.109)
House "leans"	.065	.102	–.246	.061
	(.131)	(.114)	(.183)	(.126)
House "toss-up"	.232*	–.192	.264*	–.254
	(.093)	(.132)	(.128)	(.162)
Senate "likely"	—	—	.065	–.120
			(.128)	(.074)

	House participation		Senate participation	
	Model 1 *Midterm*	*Model 2* *Pres*	*Model 3* *Midterm*	*Model 4* *Pres*
Senate "leans"	—	—	.319**	.133
			(.107)	(.154)
Senate "toss-up"	—	—	.058	−.080
			(.088)	(.079)
N	**2,545**	**2,578**	**1,539**	**1,888**
Log likelihood	**−2188.39**	**−2819.58**	**−1323.78**	**−2054.64**
Pseudo-R^2	**.08**	**.06**	**.08**	**.06**

*** $p<0.001$; ** $p<0.01$; * $p<0.05$; # $p<0.1$; two-tailed. Source: NES Cumulative File. Cell entries are ordered probit regression coefficients with standard errors in parentheses. All models estimated using NES post-election weights.

Table A.14. Effect of State-Level Competitiveness on Non-Voting Forms of Participation in Presidential Campaigns (Models for Figures 6, 7)

	NES		*Annenberg*
	2000	*2004*	*2004*
Age	.026*	.003	−.006
	(.011)	(.013)	(.004)
Age*age	−.000	.000	.000#
	(.000)	(.000)	(.000)
Education	.158***	.123***	.080***
	(.022)	(.026)	(.008)
Income	.140***	.137***	.047***
	(.034)	(.037)	(.008)
Male	.152*	.011	.014
	(.065)	(.073)	(.030)
White	−.122	.165#	.048
	(.081)	(.087)	(.049)
Republican	.747***	.606***	.428***
	(.111)	(.137)	(.044)
Democrat	.658***	.531***	.487***
	(.109)	(.138)	(.039)
House "likely"	−.068	.302#	.058
	(.100)	(.181)	(.070)
House "leans"	−.137	.259	.013
	(.167)	(.164)	(.052)
House "toss-up"	−.347*	−.231	.021
	(.146)	(.184)	(.065)

	NES		*Annenberg*
	2000	*2004*	*2004*
Gubernatorial race	.063	–.118	–.030
	(.121)	(.118)	(.055)
Senate race	–.082	.195*	–.023
	(.075)	(.083)	(.041)
Pres "likely"	–.033	–.091	.109#
	(.137)	(.104)	(.060)
Pres "leans"	.038	.069	.132**
	(.073)	(.123)	(.050)
Pres "toss-up"	.287**	.238*	.149***
	(.087)	(.099)	(.037)
Debate period	—	—	–.021
			(.033)
Days until election	—	—	–.005***
			(.001)
N	**1,530**	**1,054**	**5,259**
Log likelihood	**–1968.22**	**–1557.15**	**–7029.15**
Pseudo R^2	**.073**	**.052**	**.033**

*** $p<0.001$; ** $p<0.01$; * $p<0.05$; # $p<0.1$; two-tailed. Sources: NES Cumulative File; 2004 National Annenberg Election Study. Cell entries are ordered probit regression coefficients with standard errors in parentheses.

NOTES

Chapter 1. Introduction

1. I am not arguing that reformers should pursue reforms to enhance electoral competitiveness purely for the sake of generating rich information environments. Most scholars believe that declining electoral competitiveness undermines democracy and should be addressed irrespective of whether doing so improves campaign information environments.

2. A 2002 telephone survey of 2,000 Californians found that 50 percent of the respondents believed the main purpose of a campaign is to educate, by informing citizens about candidates or candidates about citizens; 33 percent said the main purpose of a campaign is "to win"; and 11 percent said it was "to get citizens talking to one another about politics" (Lipsitz et al. 2005).

3. This all depends, of course, on how interested he is in the election. If he has no interest, he is likely to get a drink when the local anchorman starts talking about the campaign, change the channel when a political ad comes on, skip over the newspaper articles about the election, let the answering machine pick up the call, toss the voter pamphlet in the trash, and ignore the doorbell.

4. Specifically, the provision states that advertisements that do not include "an unobscured, full-screen view of the candidate" and a voiceover of the candidate's actual voice stating that he or she approves the ad are not eligible for reduced advertising rates.

5. It is worth noting that the competitiveness of the race is a stronger predictor of how much money a candidate spends than how much money the candidate raises. Interest groups will often give money to incumbents, regardless of how close a race is, simply because they want access to whoever wins the election. As one scholar puts it, "they waste no money on sure losers but have no qualms about giving money to sure winners, even when it is not really needed" (Jacobson 1997: 38).

6. I omit these drivers of electoral competitiveness in Figure 1.1 to focus the reader on the most important factor for the purposes of this discussion, election law.

7. Of course, the primaries in such districts may be competitive even if the general elections are not.

8. Two states do not have the majority-take-all system with respect to electoral votes. Nebraska and Maine give two electoral votes to the winner of the statewide popular vote.

The winner of the popular vote in each congressional district receives an additional electoral vote.

9. The quantitative analyses in the chapters that follow address the issue of this feedback loop, which suggests a problem of endogeneity, by using measures of competitiveness developed before the start of the general election campaign.

10. A candidate's access to funds is, of course, limited by a complex regulatory system. The point is that candidates may spend the money they raise in any way they choose.

11. Although we now know more about how campaign regulation differs across democracies, much less is known about the precise consequences of this variation for candidate strategy and the campaign information environment. This is an area that would benefit from much more scholarly attention.

Chapter 2. Democratic Theory and the Campaign Information Environment

Portions of the first half of this chapter originally appeared in *Journal of Political Philosophy* (Lipsitz 2004).

1. In this chapter, I distinguish between political competition and competitiveness or the closeness of an election. Political competition refers to the number of candidates or parties contesting an election, while competitiveness refers to the closeness of the outcome. Thus, when I talk of enhancing political competition, I mean increasing the number of candidates competing in an election. Enhancing electoral competitiveness means adopting reforms that will make the outcomes of elections closer.

2. Scholars have also argued that third party candidates, in particular, have been especially important for generating new policy ideas that their candidates typically trumpet during campaigns. For example, Rosenstone et al. argue that "The power of third parties lies in their capacity to affect the content and range of political discourse, and ultimately public policy, by raising issues and options that the two major parties have ignored" (1984: 8).

3. Schumpeter would probably disagree with this statement. After all, he argued that a certain amount of corruption or anticompetitive behavior is to be expected in elections. Military insurrections may stray beyond the limits of what is acceptable, but for the most part, "cases that are strikingly analogous to the economic phenomena we label 'unfair' or 'fraudulent' competition or restraint of competition" are tolerable. The only justification he offers for this claim is that any attempt to create more perfect competition in politics is bound to fail given the nature of those who seek political power, and is therefore an "unrealistic ideal" (Schumpeter 1947: 271).

4. The relationship between redistricting and the declining competitiveness of U.S. House elections is unclear. A number of studies suggest the former is at least partially responsible for the latter, while several studies claim there is no relationship whatsoever. See Chapter 7 for a more thorough discussion of this debate.

5. For an example, see Dahl 1989.

6. Money in campaigns affects equality of political influence in two ways: (1) it may

enable contributors to influence political decisions after the campaign (the corruption argument); and (2) it allows wealthy candidates to communicate more with voters, which frequently translates into an electoral advantage. Although the former is certainly important, here I focus on the latter because it is more relevant to campaign information environments.

7. In *Sovereign Virtue*, Dworkin stresses that this conception of equality does not require that each citizen have the same influence over the minds of other citizens. He argues it is "inevitable and desirable" that some citizens have more influence over others. What he objects to is a situation in which groups of citizens "have no or only sharply diminished opportunity to appeal for their convictions because they lack the funds to compete with rich and powerful donors" (364).

8. Dworkin tries hard to distance himself from majoritarian conceptions of democracy like Dahl's. For example, he specifically claims that majoritarians have no basis for demanding that we reduce the overall quantity of political information in order to make the influence of all candidates more equal (361). This analysis suggests that Dworkin overstates his case.

9. See Rawls 1996, esp. 223–27.

10. For one such response, see Galston 1999: 39–48.

11. Another example of such an institution is James Fishkin's "Deliberative Poll" (1995).

12. Huckfeldt and Sprague 1988 found that citizens who hold a minority view generally cannot avoid being exposed to opposing opinions.

13. See Issacharoff and Pildes 1998 and Rosenstone et al. 1984, particularly chapter 2.

14. *Greensboro News & Record*, Editorial, "Give Four-Year Terms for Balanced Districts," February 12, 2009, http://www.news-record.com/content/2009/02/11/article/editorial_give_four_year_terms_for_balanced_districts.

15. *Christian Science Monitor*, "Redrawing Voting Maps," January 12, 2005, http://www.csmonitor.com/2005/0112/p08s01-comv.html.

16. Obviously, the analysis would need to be confirmed with data from state and local elections.

17. Ansolabhere and Snyder 2002 contend that the margins in statewide races from 1942 to 2000 exhibit no clear trend. They examine Senate and gubernatorial races together, however. This may explain why they do not find the trend in declining marginals that Gary Jacobson does.

18. The Republican tide in 1994 failed to produce more competitive Senate races as well. Only 31 percent of the Senators elected won by less than 55 percent. Others have noticed the declining affect of partisan tides on competitiveness as well. See Ansolabehere and Snyder 2002.

19. Gubernatorial election data from 1978 to 2000 were provided by Thad Beyle and Jennifer M. Jensen's Gubernatorial Campaign Expenditures Database, http://www.unc.edu/~beyle/guber.html. Data for the elections from 2001 to 2010 were provided

by http://uselectionatlas.org/. Since off-year elections often involve only two or three gubernatorial races, I combined races for even-numbered years with those of the following year.

20. This number is for the 42 states with single-member districts. Competitiveness in the lower houses of the state legislatures was higher in the eight states with multimember districts, with the state median percentages hovering in the 35–45 percent range. Niemi et al. also found that electoral competitiveness steadily declined in the upper houses of state legislatures from 1992 to 2000, making a slight recovery in the 2002 elections.

Chapter 3. Electoral Competitiveness and the Campaign Information Environment

1. Quoted in Jacobson 1997: 43; Fenno 1978: 13.

2. When deciding which Senate races to target, however, interest groups and parties are in a situation similar to that for presidential candidates because they must decide how to allocate finite resources to maximize the outcome of the election for them.

3. The Wisconsin Advertising Project (WAP) has 2006 CMAG data from only five states. Some CMAG data are available for the 1996 presidential election, but they are very limited and not useful for this analysis.

4. The efforts of WAP and the datasets it has produced have revolutionized the study of political advertising. Before these data became available, researchers usually visited the University of Oklahoma Political Communication Archive or asked candidates for digitized copies of their television ads. But even after doing so, the researcher had no way of knowing where the ad was aired, if it was aired at all. The only way to gather such information was to visit individual television stations and pore through their logs. Thus, the availability of CMAG data, which include the storyboards of the ads, so we know exactly what the ad looked like and what it said as well as when and where it was aired, changed the nature of political communication research.

5. For example, the analyses in Chapters 4, 5, and 6 will include the measures of competitiveness, as well as the number of days left until the election, to soak up the effects of other elements in the campaign information environment.

6. Many things can change between one election year and the next. Incumbents can retire, new challengers of dramatically different quality can emerge, a political tide favoring a party can sweep across the nation, or a general sentiment of "throw the bums out" can seize voters, among others.

7. I omitted from this analysis all ads that were paid for by coordinated expenditures.

8. The full models for all the following analyses can be found in Tables A.1–A.3.

9. I also examined the effect of electoral competitiveness on advertising volume in open House races. Its effect is still quite significant but not as large. As competitiveness increases across the four categories, the predicted number of total ad airings is 111, 887, 2,494, and 3,705. The percentage increase between the first and second categories is 803 percent, between the second and third 281 percent, and between the last two categories 149 percent. See Model 3 in Table A.1 for the full model.

10. http://www.citizen.org/congress/article_redirect.cfm?ID=4538.

11. The difference in the predicted number of sponsors is not statistically significant.

12. The median equality ratios were .63, .67, and .66 for House, Senate, and presidential contests respectively.

13. The vertical lines in the following graphs show the upper and lower bounds of 95 percent confidence intervals. I did not include these in Figure 3.1 for clarity of presentation.

Chapter 4. Competitiveness and Campaign Knowledge in Congressional Elections

1. Recent research suggests that the effects of political advertisements decay rapidly, sometimes in as little as two to three days (Gerber et al. 2007; Hill et al. 2007; Hill et al. 2008). This means most people must be reexposed to advertisements throughout a campaign to ensure that they retain information from them. Again, this suggests that there will be a linear relationship between information volume and voter knowledge.

2. This may be why some prefer the term "issue convergence" to candidate dialogue. Irrespective of the term used, the criticism still holds.

3. Others have made this argument as well; see Jamieson et al. 2000.

4. Obviously, the NES is not ideal for studying competitiveness in House races because so few races in any given year are considered close. This problem is mitigated in this study because I am pooling the survey from three years.

5. The questions asked by the National Annenberg Election Study for congressional elections are no better. In the future, scholars will be able to use the Cooperative Congressional Election Study to examine these questions, but it was first administered in 2006. At the time of writing, CMAG advertising data were not available for 2006.

6. Two other versions of the candidate rating variable were also created and analyzed. The first coded respondents who could not rate a candidate as a "0," those who rated a candidate as a "50" on the feeling thermometer as a "1," and those who rated a candidate anywhere else on the feeling thermometer as a "2." The respondent's ratings for each candidate were then averaged to get a single measure of her ability to rate the candidates. The other measure coded those who rated a candidate as a "50" the same as those who could not rate a candidate, that is, as a "0," and those who offered any other response of the feeling thermometer as a "1." The respondent's ratings for each candidate were then added to create a scale from 0 to 2. These two measures were correlated at .90 and .62 respectively with the measure ultimately used in the analysis. An examination of the relationship between these variables and the information environment measures revealed that ad volume was the only significant predictor of a respondent's score on either measure, just as in the case of the measure ultimately discussed in the text.

7. To create more variation in the dependent variable, a measure was created that reflected the difference between the respondent's score and the converted ADA score. This measure ranged from "0" if the respondent correctly identified the candidate's ideology to "3" if the difference between the response and the ADA converted score was 3 points or higher. People who were unable to offer a response were coded "3" as well.

The relationship between competitiveness measures and this measure was similar to the relationship between competitiveness and the one discussed in the text, with knowledge increasing through moderately competitive races and then plummeting in the most competitive. The dichotomous measure is discussed since it is the one used by Coleman and Manna.

8. Obviously, it is important to examine the interaction of campaign information and individual characteristics. For example, it is important to know if certain types of campaign information widen the knowledge gap by benefiting people who are already politically knowledgeable. As the reader will see, however, the following analysis is complicated enough as is and secondary questions such as these must be left for future inquiries.

9. The regression models from which these predicted probability were derived can be found in Models 1, 2, and 3 of Table A.4.

10. Note that races with an unopposed candidate were excluded from the analysis because a respondent could not possibly rate both candidates.

11. The NES Cumulative file has two measures of political interest. The one discussed here asks, "would you say that you have been/were very much interested, somewhat interested, or not much interested in the political campaigns so far this year?" The other measure of interest asks, "Would you say you follow what's going on in government and public affairs most of the time, some of the time, only now and then, or hardly at all?" Electoral competitiveness was not significantly correlated with the responses to this measure either.

12. I am not advocating that voters in noncompetitive jurisdictions be lied to in the interest of promoting engagement and participation—only that those who live in competitive districts and states be informed or reminded of their race's status.

13. An additional model was estimated that included a quadratic term for the measure of advertising volume to allow for the possibility that there are diminishing returns to advertising. Although the direction of the quadratic term (negative) suggested that there might be diminishing returns to the volume of advertising for knowledge, a likelihood-ratio test revealed that the model including the quadratic term did not provide a significantly better fit than the one presented here. When a quadratic term was included in the models explaining the ability to correctly identify an incumbent's ideology and the ability to rate the Senate candidates, the direction of the term was positive and insignificant in both cases. Based on these analyses, I have concluded that the relationship between advertising volume and knowledge is linear in House campaigns.

14. In order to maintain the same sample across all these models, the sample was restricted to individuals living in districts where the candidates generated at least one ad airing. The reason is that some of the measures of interest, such as proportion of attack ads aired, equality ratio, and degree to which the candidates engaged in dialogue, could not be calculated if no ads were aired.

15. Despite this finding, the authors remained committed to their argument that higher spending in House elections is better for democracy. This argument about challenger deceptiveness was the one qualifier.

16. To be fair, the CMAG data were not available for the elections they examined, so collecting such data would have been arduous if not impossible.

17. In addition to the variables discussed earlier in the text, these models also control for the number of years that an incumbent has served in office. Respondents may have an easier time identifying the ideology of an incumbent who has served in office longer.

18. For the full series of models, see Table A.6.

19. These measures are all highly correlated, so I confirmed the findings in Model 11 by running six different models with each of these measures included without the others. The size and direction of the coefficients were not significantly different from those in Model 11. The only difference worth noting was that the coefficient for positive challenger ads was statistically significant at $p < .05$.

20. It is important to keep in mind that more than 85 percent of House races do not feature a single House challenger ad and less than 2 percent feature more than 500 ads.

21. Positive incumbent ads are the most prevalent form of ad, however, with at least one being aired in approximately 40 percent of House races.

22. This finding was confirmed under a number of different model specifications.

23. Although the analysis in the previous section might make one wary of using the ability to rate Senate candidates as a measure of political knowledge, we have no other options in the NES for the three years examined.

24. The full models can be found in Table A.7.

25. Models including all of the information content measures were estimated for the House knowledge measures as well, but they were not included in Tables 4.1 and 4.2 because they did not reveal any findings of note.

26. In Model 8, the equality coefficient is significant, but further testing revealed that the effect disappears when the dialogue measure is included.

27. Approximately one-third of the respondents were exposed to advertising in which there was no dialogue or issue convergence.

28. Further analysis did not find a significant triple interaction between advertising volume, dialogue, and negativity. It did find that attack advertising in the absence of dialogue harms voter knowledge, however. Furthermore, dialogue in the absence of negativity has no effect on voter knowledge. Thus, there is a highly significant positive interaction between information negativity and dialogue.

Chapter 5. Competitiveness and Campaign Knowledge in a Presidential Election

1. According to OpenSecrets.org, House and Senate candidates spent a total of $1.37 billion on their campaigns, while McCain and Obama spent $1.33 billion.

2. I also examined 5, 10, and 14 day measures. The effects of the 5 and 7 day measures were virtually identical. The 10 and 14 day measures were weaker, supporting recent studies that have found that most advertising effects dissipate within a week (Hill et al. 2008; Hill et al. 2007; Gerber et al. 2007).

3. The substantive results of the analyses do not change significantly if these cases are included. These models are available from the author upon request.

4. It also asks a number of questions to gauge the respondent's level of political knowledge more generally. This is especially useful for separating general political sophistication from knowledge gained during a campaign. There is an additional measure that asks the interviewer to grade the respondent's political knowledge. Although this measure correlates with the other knowledge measures at a fairly high level (.44 with general political knowledge and approximately .35 with the campaign knowledge measures), it is problematic in the sense that educated older males tend to be rated more highly irrespective of their actual knowledge levels.

5. The answer to the question regarding the extension of the Assault Weapons Ban was not straightforward. Kerry was in favor of the ban, but Bush's position was less clear. As president, he had stated he was in favor of the ban, but he did not press Congress to extend it, allowing it to expire on September 13, 2004. At this point, it became a campaign issue as Kerry accused Bush of "caving in" to the demands of the National Rifle Association. To capture the dynamics of this issue, I coded a respondent as having answered the question correctly if they responded "Kerry" or "both" to the question prior to expiration of the ban. After September 13, only a "Kerry" response was coded as correct.

6. The Cronbach's α for these five items is .56.

7. Unfortunately, the Annenberg survey only begins asking this series of questions in August, at which point it appears that there are already some significant differences in the knowledge levels of respondents living in different types of states. Still, given how much campaign information battleground state residents receive over the course of the general election campaign, one would expect their knowledge levels to increase at a much steeper rate over the course of the campaign.

8. I examined the way electoral competitiveness affects one other measure of campaign knowledge. In Chapter 4 I used a traditional measure of campaign knowledge in congressional races, which is the ability of respondents to rate candidates on a feeling thermometer. Using such a measure during a presidential campaign does not make much sense because there is no variation in how people respond to the measure: virtually everyone can rate presidential candidates on a feeling thermometer. Presidential elections are highly visible and voters are able to familiarize themselves with the candidates during the long primary season. The Annenberg survey does ask respondents to rate the candidates along approximately twenty different dimensions. For example, they are asked to indicate on a 10-point scale if each candidate is inspiring, trustworthy, and shares their values. They are also asked if they believe each candidate "has the right experience" and "is a strong leader." In order to construct a measure that was roughly equivalent to the candidate rating measure used in the previous chapter, I coded respondents as "1" if they could answer all the questions in this series for both candidates and as "0" if they ever responded "I don't know" to a question or simply refused to answer one. This measure is similar to the candidate rating measure in the previous chapter because it is quite possible for a person to answer all these questions without actually knowing much information about the candidates. Forty-six percent of respondents

could respond to all the questions, while 54 percent could not respond to one or more. I created a number of less stringent versions of this measure, but the one developed in this manner was the most highly correlated with interest, education and the other measures of campaign knowledge. Electoral competitiveness had absolutely no effect on this particular measure of campaign knowledge.

9. Using the National Election Studies from 2000 and 2004, I also examined how competitiveness was related to the ability of respondents to state what they like and dislike about the presidential candidates. This particular measure is often used as an indicator of how knowledgeable respondents are about the candidates. Only respondents in battleground states were able to mention significantly more likes and dislikes than voters in safe states (4 versus 3.4 respectively). Again, one is left wondering why the effect of competitiveness is not larger.

10. The Annenberg survey was not in the field on Election Day. The model controlled for standard demographic and political variables and included an interaction between the number of days before the election and the dummy variable for living in a battleground state. This interaction term was included to capture the fact that campaign interest rose at a slightly steeper rate in battleground than non-battleground states during the time period examined.

11. The Annenberg study uses a 9–point scale, which ranges from having an eighth grade education or lower to having a professional or graduate degree, to measure education. On a scale from 1 to 9, the residents of safe and modestly competitive states score a 5.5 on average, while the average for residents of moderately and highly competitive states is 5.3. A one-way anova test revealed this difference to be significant at $p < .001$.

12. Recall that Kerry's major competitors in the 2004 primary were Howard Dean and John Edwards. Dean withdrew from the race on February 18 and Edwards on March 3, immediately following his poor showing in the Super Tuesday primaries (March 2). In addition to these hypotheses, I also considered the possibility that the residents of swing states in 2004 were more partisan and read newspapers more because their states were also swing states in 2000. To test this hypothesis, I examined whether there was a significant correlation between these measures and state competitiveness in 2000. I found no such correlation.

13. "Kerry, Bush Battle over Gas Prices," *Chicago Tribune*, March 31, 2004.

14. This analysis raises a considerable amount of concern about the use of the NES post-election survey to capture campaign effects in general. More research is needed to understand the strengths and weaknesses of that survey relative to the Annenberg survey when conducting research on campaign dynamics. Of course, the NES is often the best survey available, as the author's use of it in Chapter 4 illustrates.

15. Because the analysis in this chapter uses dynamic seven-day measures of the various information environment characteristics, multicollinearity is less of a threat than it was in the previous chapter. The only variables one might worry about are the volume and diversity measures, which are correlated at .83. As I will argue in the text, it appears that diversity has a stronger effect on knowledge than volume.

16. Models 12 through 15 have different samples and explain different dependent variables, so it is inappropriate to compare their R^2 value to those of the first 11 models.

17. All the models in Table 5.1 were estimated using ordinary least squares regression. They were also calculated using ordered probit and poisson (or negative binomial where the dependent variable was sufficiently skewed) regression models and the substantive results did not change.

18. All findings reported in this chapter have a significance level of $p < .05$ or better unless otherwise noted.

19. One should beware of concluding that these effects are additive. In other words, one cannot conclude that people exposed to campaign information that is high in equality, negativity, and diversity will have significantly higher levels of knowledge than those exposed to information that is only high in one of these characteristics. This is because each characteristic in the presence of the others may not have as high an impact on knowledge as it does, *ceteris paribus*. Further analysis indicates that this is in fact the case. A model that includes an interaction between all three variables shows that each variable has a very strong effect when the others are set to zero, but this effect decreases as the others increase. This suggests that these information qualities can substitute for one another.

20. The significance at this level of advertising volume is $p < .10$. The coefficient increases even more at higher levels of advertising, but is no longer significant since there are so few cases in which advertising during a previous week achieves such elevated levels.

21. The significance of this coefficient is $p < .10$.

22. Further analysis reveals that there is a positive and significant triple interaction between equality, negativity, and information volume. The model suggests that information must be voluminous, equal, *and* negative for it to positively affect voter knowledge.

23. Dialogue was also helpful for identifying an incumbent's ideology, but its effect was not substantively large, much smaller than the beneficial effects of equality, diversity, and negativity.

24. The large positive effect that advertising volume has on political novices has been noted by others (see Freedman et al. 2004; Franz et al. 2007).

25. Recall that the dialogue score ranges from 0 to 1 where a "1" indicates a 100 percent overlap.

26. Even more remarkable is that the dialogue measure has the highest *t*-value of any variable in the model. This means that its effect on the number of "Don't know" responses offered is stronger than education, age, gender, and race, which are normally some of the strongest predictors of knowledge. See Table A.8 for the full model.

Chapter 6. Competitiveness and Political Participation

1. The relationship between partisan redistricting and declining competitiveness in elections is actually contested. See Chapter 7 for an elaboration of this debate.

2. The relationship between electoral competitiveness and turnout has been confirmed in other countries as well (see Endersby et al. 2002; Denver and Hands 1974).

3. The same study also found this to be true of gubernatorial elections.

4. Initially, I examined the effect of competitiveness on each form of participation in each election, but no obvious patterns emerged and I had no theoretical reason to believe that certain forms of participation would be more influenced by competitiveness, so I opted to use the index as my dependent variable. This also greatly simplified the chapter's analysis.

5. At http://elections.gmu.edu/Turnout.html. For a discussion of the significance of the VEP, see McDonald and Popkin 2001.

6. Only 991 respondents were included in these models because I am analyzing the effect of the advertising measures on the same group of people, and some of the measures, such as equality and negativity, can only be calculated for races in which both candidates were advertising. In Table A.10, Models 1 and 2 show the effect of House competitiveness on the largest possible sample (*N*=2578), which was not restricted by the availability of advertising measures, and the smaller one used here (*N*=991). A comparison of the two models reveals that the demobilizing effect of competitive House races in presidential election years emerges in both samples.

7. If either measure is included without the other, it is highly significant, yet these models have less explanatory power than the one here that includes both of them.

8. They appear to have started asking it again in 2008.

9. In 1998, the correlation was .01 (n.s.); in 2000 it was .04 ($p < .10$).

10. This holds true in the data examined here.

11. A log-likelihood ratio test was performed on Models 7 and 12, which include the dialogue measures, to see whether Model 12 fit the data significantly better than Model 7. It did not. The interaction does suggest, however, that at low levels of advertising it is better for candidates to talk past each other, that is, to engage in less dialogue, than to focus on the same issues. At a higher volume of advertising, more dialogue is better.

12. The difference between the two lines is statistically significant at $p < .05$ between approximately 3,000 and 8,000 ad airings, and then again between approximately 13,000 and 17,000 ad airings.

13. Although the pseudo-R^2 in Model 13 indicates that its specification does not provide a significantly better fit than Model 3, which simply contains the volume measure, the coefficients for the interaction terms suggest that at higher levels of negativity, advertising volume becomes positive and significant. This is indeed the case. When negativity is at its 80th percentile, the coefficient for the volume measure is a marginally significant .041 ($p < .10$).

14. The 2000 NES is discussed here because the House and Senate analysis included the 2000 NES as well.

15. If this model is estimated without the quadratic term, the volume measure coefficient is .008 and not significant. The fit is also poorer.

Chapter 7. Improving Electoral Competitiveness Through Reform

1. Some have suggested making the franking privilege available to challengers in congressional elections, but this would clearly be for campaign use, which is against existing regulations.

2. There are still dissenters to this line of argument. Gary Jacobson (2006) argues that elections following rounds of reapportionment in the 1980s and 1990s were more competitive than in the previous decade, but this changed after the 2000 round when competitiveness severely declined after reapportionment. Abramowitz and Saunders 2005; Abramowitz et al. 2005, 2006a, b argue that redistricting plays no role the declining competitiveness of House elections.

3. Specifically, Carson and Crespin found that this held after reapportionment in the 1990s and 2000s for U.S. House elections.

4. A handful of states such as Iowa and North Carolina have adopted principles from all three categories, while others have adopted none of them, preferring a more hands-off approach to redistricting. States can also choose to apply the criteria to the congressional redistricting process, the state legislative redistricting process, or both. The result, more often than not, is that states apply different criteria to each process.

5. It is important to distinguish between two types of gerrymanders: incumbent and partisan. Incumbent gerrymanders are designed to guarantee that incumbents will be reelected in their district. Doing this usually requires packing the minority party into as few districts as possible, creating larger victory margins in the remaining districts for the majority party. Such gerrymanders clearly undermine electoral competitiveness by padding incumbent margins. Partisan gerrymanders may actually enhance competitiveness, however. A party creating such a gerrymander will try to maximize the number of districts it controls by "cracking" the minority party and spreading it throughout as many districts as possible. By doing this, the majority party exchanges smaller victory margins for the chance of winning more districts and greater representation.

6. In House elections, research has examined how the number of population-based criteria affects margins (Forgette and Platt 2005), while the work on state legislative elections has examined how each specific type of population-based criterion affects margins (Forgette et al. 2009). The latter finds that preserving the core of prior districts helps incumbents, while a "community of interest" criterion has no significant effect on incumbent performance. The principle of respecting political subdivisions is the only population-based criterion that significantly undermines incumbent victory margins in state legislative elections. It is possible that the same is true for House elections as well, but we cannot be certain.

7. *Arizona Minority Coalition for Fair Redistricting v. Arizona Redistricting Commission* (2007).

8. In 2002, only three minor party candidates ran in races where they attracted a higher percentage of the vote than the margin by which the winner won (120–21). In

all three cases, the incumbent won anyway, again suggesting the "spoiler effect" of third party candidates is quite small.

9. For comprehensive discussion of how to do this, see Issacharoff and Pildes 1998 and Rosenstone et al. 1984, particularly chap. 2.

10. Abramowitz and Saunders 2005 specifically challenge Morris Fiorina and his colleagues' contention that Americans remain moderate and that there is little evidence of polarization.

11. See Fiorina and Abrams 2008 for a thorough review of this debate.

12. The rotation system is favored by the National Association of Secretaries of State while the lottery system is favored by Larry Sabato (2006). Sabato favors a lottery several months before the first regional primary to prevent candidates from "camping out" in one region for months ahead of time.

13. The electoral votes were allocated to each candidate by multiplying the number of electoral votes in the state by the candidate's percent of the two-party vote.

14. Although candidates allocate visits less efficiently than advertisements, competitive states or jurisdictions still receive a disproportionate share of candidate visits.

15. Such media markets would not necessarily be smaller. Since the cost of advertising in a media market is determined by the size of the population it serves, the cost-per-persuadable-voter calculation hinges almost entirely on the percentage of the population that remains undecided about their vote. A small district with a large percentage of swing voters should be just as attractive as a large district with a large percentage of swing voters because the cost of reaching each persuadable voter is similar.

16. One might also argue that the federalism argument more often provides normative cover for those who oppose election reform on partisan grounds.

17. For a modern defense of the anti-Federalist position, see Samples 2001.

18. *Timmons v. Twin Cities Area New Party*, 520 U.S. 351.

19. President Clinton had already demonstrated his half-hearted commitment to campaign finance reform. He and Speaker Newt Gingrich had agreed to form a commission to examine the issue in 1995, but the commission was never formed. Clinton later asked former vice president Walter Mondale and former U.S. Senator Nancy Kassebaum Baker to lead a campaign finance reform effort, but he never funded them (Mycoff and Pika 2009: 119).

BIBLIOGRAPHY

Abramowitz, Alan I., and Kyle Saunders. 2005. "Why Can't We All Just Get Along? The Reality of a Polarized America." *Forum: A Journal of Applied Research in Contemporary Politics* 3, 2, Article 1.

Abramowitz, Alan I., Brad Alexander, and Matthew Gunning. 2006a. "Incumbency, Redistricting, and the Decline of Competition in U.S. House Elections." *Journal of Politics* 68, 1: 75–88.

——. 2006b. "Don't Blame Redistricting for Uncompetitive Elections." *PS: Political Science and Politics* 39, 1: 87–90.

——. 2006c. "Drawing the Line on District Competition: A Rejoinder." *PS: Political Science and Politics* 39, 1: 95–98.

Abramson, Paul R., and John H. Aldrich. 1982. "The Decline of Electoral Participation in America." *American Political Science Review* 76: 502–21.

Achen, Christopher. 1982. *Interpreting and Using Regression*. Beverly Hills, Calif.: Sage.

Ackerman, Bruce, and James S. Fishkin. 2005. *Deliberation Day*. New Haven, Conn.: Yale University Press.

——. 2002. "Deliberation Day." *Journal of Political Philosophy* 10, 2: 129–52.

Althaus, Scott L., and Todd C. Trautman. 2008. "The Impact of Television Market Size on Voter Turnout in American Elections." *American Politics Research* 36, 6: 824–56.

Alvarez, R. Michael, and Jonathan Nagler. 1995. "Economics, Issues and the Perot Candidacy: Voter Choice in the 1992 Presidential Election." *Journal of Political Science* 39, 3: 714.

Ansolabehere, Stephen, John M. Hansen, Shigeo Hirano, and James M. Snyder, Jr. 2006. "The Decline of Competition in U.S. Primary Elections, 1908–2004." In *The Marketplace of Democracy*, ed. Michael P. McDonald and John Samples. Washington, D.C.: Brookings Institution Press. 74–101.

Ansolabehere, Stephen, and Shanto Iyengar. 1994. "Riding the Wave and Claiming Ownership Over Issues: The Joint Effects of Advertising and News Coverage in Campaigns." *Public Opinion Quarterly* 53: 334–57.

Ashworth, Scott, and Joshua D. Clinton. 2007. "Does Advertising Exposure Affect Turnout?" *Quarterly Journal of Political Science* 2: 27–41.

Atkin, Charles, and Gary Heald. 1976. "Effects of Political Advertising." *Public Opinion Quarterly* 40: 216–28.

Barcellona, Miriam M., and Andrew P. Grose. 1994. *Term Limits: A Political Dilemma.* San Francisco: Council of State Governments.

Barrett, Andrew W., and Jeffrey S. Peake. 2007. "When the President Comes to Town." *American Politics Research* 35, 1: 3–31.

Bartels, Larry M. 1996. "Uninformed Votes: Information Effects in Presidential Elections." *American Journal of Political Science* 40: 194–230.

——. 1985. "Resource Allocation in a Presidential Campaign." *Journal of Politics* 47: 928–36.

Bartels, Larry M., and Lynn Vavreck, eds. 2000. *Campaign Reform: Insights and Evidence.* Ann Arbor: University of Michigan Press.

Benoit, William L., Glenn J. Hansen, and R. Lance Holbert. 2004. "Presidential Campaigns and Democracy." *Mass Communication and Society* 7, 2: 177–90.

Bergan, Daniel E., Alan S. Gerber, Donald P. Green, and Costas Panagopoulos. 2005. "Grassroots Mobilization and Voter Turnout in 2004." *Public Opinion Quarterly* 69, 5: 760–77.

Borjas, George, Stephen Bronars, and Stephen Trejo. 1992. "Self-Selection and Internal Migration in the United States." *Journal of Urban Economics* 32, 2: 159–85.

Brams, Steven J., and Morton D. Davis. 1974. "The 3/2's Rule in Presidential Campaigning." *American Political Science Review* 68: 113–34.

Broder, David. 2001. "Long Road to Reform: Negotiators Forge Education Legislation." *Washington Post*, December 17, A1.

Brookings Institution. 2006. "Polarizing the House of Representatives: How Much Does Gerrymandering Matter?" October 30. http://www.brookings.edu/comm/events/20061030gerrymander.pdf.

Brunell, Thomas L. 2008. *Redistricting and Representation: Why Competitive Elections Are Bad for America.* New York: Routledge.

Bruni, Frank. 2000. "The 2000 Campaign: The Bush Strategy: Working to Color Gore as a Chameleon." *New York Times*, September 4, A14.

Buchler, Justin. 2005. "Competition, Representation, and Redistricting: The Case Against Competitive Congressional Districts" *Journal of Theoretical Politics* 17, 4: 431–63.

Buchanan, Bruce I. 2001. *Mediated Electoral Democracy: Campaigns, Incentives, and Reform.* In *Mediated Politics: Communication in the Future of Democracy*, ed. Lance Bennett and Robert M. Entman. New York: Cambridge University Press.

Budge, Ian, and Dennis J. Farlie. 1983. *Explaining and Predicting Elections: Issue Effects and Party Strategies in Twenty-Three Democracies.* London: George Allen.

Bush, George W. 2002. "Remarks on Signing the Help America Vote Act of 2002." *Weekly Compilation of Presidential Documents* 38, 44: 1886–87.

Cain, Bruce E. 1999. "Garrett's Temptation." *Virginia Law Review* 8: 1589–1603.

Cain, Bruce E., John Hanley and Thad Kousser 2006. "Term Limits: A Recipe for More Competition?" In *The Marketplace of Democracy*, ed. Michael P. McDonald and John Samples. Washington, D.C.: Brookings Institution Press. 199–221.

Cain, Bruce E., Karin MacDonald, and Michael McDonald. 2005. "From Equality to Fairness: The Path of Political Reform." In *Party Lines: Competition, Partisanship, and Congressional Redistricting*, ed. Thomas E. Mann and Bruce E. Cain. Washington D.C.: Brookings Institution Press. 6–30.

Caldeira, Gregory A., Samuel C. Patterson, and Gregory A. Markko. 1985. "The Mobilization of Voters in Congressional Elections." *Journal of Politics* 47, 2: 490–509.

Caren, Neal. 2007. "Big City, Big Turnout? Electoral Participation in American Cities." *Journal of Urban Affairs* 29, 1: 39–46.

Carson, Jamie L., and Michael H. Crespin. 2004. "The Effect of State Redistricting Methods on Electoral Competition in United States House of Representative Races." *State Politics and Policy Quarterly* 4, 4: 455–69.

Carter, Jimmy. 2004. "Florida Will Not Play Fair." *The Guardian*, September 28.

Charnock, Emily Jane, James A. McCann, and Kathryn Dunn Tenpas. 2009. "Presidential Travel from Eisenhower to George W. Bush: An 'Electoral College' Strategy." *Political Science Quarterly* 124, 2: 323–39.

Chebat, Jean-Charles, Michel Laroche, Daisy Badura, and Pierre Filiatrault. 1995. "Affect and Memory in Advertising: An Empirical Study of the Compensatory Processes." *Journal of Social Psychology* 135, 4: 425–37.

Christiano, Thomas. 1996. *The Rule of the Many: Fundamental Issues in Democratic Theory*. Boulder, Colo.: Westview Press.

Clarke, Peter, and Susan Evans. 1983. *Covering Campaigns: Journalism in Congressional Elections*. Stanford, Calif.: Stanford University Press.

Cohen, Joshua. 1998. "Democracy and Liberty." In *Deliberative Democracy*, ed. Jon Elster. Cambridge: Cambridge University Press.

Colantoni, Claude S., Terrence J. Levesque, and Peter C. Ordeshook. 1975. "Campaign Resource Allocation Under the Electoral College." *American Political Science Review*, 69, 1: 141–54.

Coleman, John J., and Paul F. Manna 2000. "Congressional Campaign Spending and the Quality of Democracy," *Journal of Politics* 62, 3: 757–89.

Converse, Philip E. 1975. "Public Opinion and Voting Behavior." In *Handbook of Political Science*, vol. 4., ed. Frederick Greenstein and Nelson Polsby. Reading, Mass.: Addison-Wesley.

——. 1972. "Change in the American Electorate." In *The Human Meaning of Social Change*, ed. Angus Campbell and Philip E. Converse, 263–38. New York: Russell Sage Foundation.

Cook, Rhodes. 2004 "Will Your Vote Be the One That Matters? Don't Count on It: Inclusion's Mostly an Illusion in the Primary System." *Washington Post*, January 25, B1.

Corrado, Anthony and Thomas E. Mann. 1997. *Campaign Finance Reform: A Sourcebook*. Washington, D.C.: Brookings Institution Press.

Cox, Gary W. 1988. "Closeness and Turnout: A Methodological Note." *Journal of Politics* 50, 3: 768–75.

Cox, Gary W., and Michael C. Munger. 1989. "Closeness, Expenditures, and Turnout in the 1982 U.S. House Elections." *American Political Science Review* 83, 1: 217–31.

Dahl, Robert A. 1989. *Democracy and Its Critics*. New Haven, Conn.: Yale University Press.

——. 1956. *A Preface to Democratic Theory*. Chicago: University of Chicago Press.

Dalton, Russell J., Paul Allen Beck, Robert Huckfeldt, and William Koetzle. 1998. "A Test of Media-Centered Agenda Setting: Newspaper Content and Public Interests in a Presidential Election." *Political Communication* 15: 463–81.

De Tocqueville, Alexis. *Democracy in America*. Garden City, N.Y.: Doubleday, 1969.

Delli Carpini, Michael X., and Scott Keeter. 1996. *What Americans Know About Politics and Why It Matters*. New Haven, Conn.: Yale University Press.

Denver, David T., and Gordon Hands. 1974. "Marginality and Turnout in British General Elections." *British Journal of Political Science* 4, 1: 17–35.

Doherty, Brendan J. 2007. "Elections: The Politics of the Permanent Campaign: Presidential Travel and the Electoral College, 1977–2004." *Political Science Quarterly* 37, 4: 749–73.

"Drop Out of the College." 2006. *New York Times*, February 14.

Dunkelman, Marc. 2008. "Gerrymandering the Vote: How a 'Dirty Dozen' States Suppress as Many as 9 Million Voters." *Democratic Leadership Council*, June 18.

Dworkin, Ronald. 2000. *Sovereign Virtue*. Cambridge, Mass: Harvard University Press, 2000.

Endersby, James W., Steven E. Galatas, and Chapman B. Rackaway. 2002. "Closeness Counts in Canada: Voter Participation in the 1993 and 1997 Federal Elections." *Journal of Politics* 64, 2: 610–31.

Fallows, James. 1996. *Breaking the News: How the Media Undermine American Democracy*. New York: Pantheon.

Farnsworth, Stephen J. and S. Robert Lichter. 2007. *The Nightly News Nightmare: Network Television's Coverage of U.S. Presidential Elections, 1988–2004*. 2nd ed. Lanham, Md.: Rowman and Littlefield.

Fenno, Richard. 1978. *Home Style: House Members in Their Districts*. Boston: HarperCollins.

Fiorina, Morris P., and Samuel J. Abrams. 2008. "Political Polarization in the American Public." *Annual Review of Political Science* 11: 563–88.

Fiorina, Morris., Samuel J. Abrams, and Jeremy C. Pope. 2005. *Culture War? The Myth of a Polarized Electorate*. New York: Pearson Longman.

Fishkin, James S. 1995. *The Voice of the People: Public Opinion and Democracy*. New Haven, Conn.: Yale University Press.

Forgette, Richard, and Glenn Platt. 2005. "Redistricting Principles and Incumbency Protection in the U.S. Congress." *Political Geography* 24: 934–51.

Forgette, Richard, Andrew Garner, and John Winkle. 2009. "Do Redistricting Principles and Practices Affect U.S. State Legislative Electoral Competition?" *State Politics and Policy Quarterly* 9, 2: 24–55.

Fowler, Erika Franklin, and Travis N. Ridout. 2009. "Local Television and Newspaper Coverage of Political Advertising." *Political Communication* 26, 2: 119–36.

Franz, Michael M., Paul B. Freedman, Kenneth M. Goldstein, and Travis N. Ridout. 2007. *Campaign Advertising and American Democracy*. Philadelphia: Temple University Press.

Freedman, Paul, Michael Franz, and Kenneth Goldstein. 2004. "Campaign Advertising and Democratic Citizenship." *American Journal of Political Science* 48, 4: 723–74.

Freedman, Paul, and Ken Goldstein. 1999. "Measuring Media Exposure and the Effects of Negative Campaign Ads." *American Journal of Political Science* 43, 3: 1189–1208.

Freeman, Samuel. 2000. "Deliberative Democracy: A Sympathetic Comment." *Philosophy and Public Affairs* 29, 4: 371–418.

Fund, John. 1991. "Term Limitation: An Idea Whose Time Has Come." In *Limiting Legislative Terms*, eds. Gerald Benjamin and Michael J. Malbin. Washington, D.C.: CQ Press.

Galston, William A. 1999. "Diversity, Toleration, and Deliberative Democracy." In *Deliberative Politics: Essays on Democracy and Disagreement*, ed. Stephen Macedo. New York: Oxford University Press, 1999.

Geer, John. 2006. *In Defense of Negativity: Attack Ads in Presidential Campaigns*. Chicago: University of Chicago Press.

——. 2000. "Assessing Attack Advertising: A Silver Lining." In *Campaign Reform: Insights and Evidence*, ed. Larry Bartels and Lynn Vavreck. Ann Arbor: University of Michigan Press. 62–78.

Gelman, Andrew, and Gary King. 1994a. "A Unified Method of Evaluating Electoral Systems and Redistricting Plans." *American Journal of Political Science* 38, 2 (May): 514–54.

——. 1994b. "Enhancing Democracy Through Legislative Redistricting." *American Political Science Review* 88, 3 (September): 541–59.

Gerber, Alan S. 1998. "Estimating the Effect of Campaign Spending on Senate Election Outcomes Using Instrumental Variables." *American Political Science Review* 92, 2: 401–11.

Gerber, Alan S., James G. Gimpel, Donald P. Green, and Daron R. Shaw. 2007. "The Influence of Television and Radio Advertising on Candidate Evaluations: Results from a Large-Scale Randomized Experiment." Manuscript.

Gerber, Alan S., and Donald P. Green. 2000. "The Effects of Canvassing, Direct Mail, and Telephone Contact on Voter Turnout: A Field Experiment." *American Political Science Review* 94, 3: 653–63.

Gerken, Heather. 2010. *The Democracy Index*. Princeton, N.J.: Princeton University Press.

Gilens, Martin, Lynn Vavreck, and Martin Cohen. 2007. "The Mass Media and the Public's Assessments of Presidential Candidates, 1952–2000." *Journal of Politics* 69, 4: 1160–75.

Gimpel, James G., Karen M. Kaufmann, and Shanna Pearson-Merkowitz. 2007. "Battleground States Versus Blackout States: The Behavioral Implications of Modern Presidential Campaigns." *Journal of Politics* 69, 3: 786–97.

Gimpel, James G., and Jason E. Schuknecht. 2001. "Interstate Migration and Electoral Politics." *Journal of Politics* 63, 1: 207–31.

Goldenberg, Edie N., and Michael W. Traugott. 1984. *Campaigning for Congress*. Washington, D.C.: CQ Press.

Goldstein, Kenneth, Michael Franz, and Travis Ridout. 2002. "Political Advertising in 2000." Combined File [dataset]. Final release. Madison: Department of Political Science at the University of Wisconsin-Madison and Brennan Center for Justice at New York University.

Goldstein, Kenneth, and Paul Freedman. 2002. "Lessons Learned: Campaign Advertising in the 2000 Elections." *Political Communication* 19: 5–28.

Goldstein, Kenneth, and Joel Rivlin. 2007. "Presidential Advertising, 2003–2004" Combined File [dataset]. Final release. Madison: University of Wisconsin Advertising Project, Department of Political Science at the University of Wisconsin-Madison.

——. 2005. "Political Advertising in 2002." Combined File [dataset]. Final release. Madison: Wisconsin Advertising Project, Department of Political Science at the University of Wisconsin-Madison.

Goux, Darshan J., and David A. Hopkins. 2008. "The Empirical Implications of Electoral College Reform." *American Politics Research* 36: 857–79.

Graber, Doris. 1989. *Mass Media and American Politics*. Washington, D.C.: CQ Press.

Green, Donald P., Alan S. Green, and David W. Nickerson. 2003. "Getting Out the Vote in Local Elections: Results from Six Door-to-Door Canvassing Experiments." *Journal of Politics* 65, 4: 1083–96.

Green, Donald P., and Jonathan S. Krasno. 1990. "Rebuttal to Jacobson's 'New Evidence for Old Arguments.'" *American Journal of Political Science* 34, 2: 363–72.

——. 1988. "Salvation for the Spendthrift Incumbent: Reestimating the Effects of Campaign Spending in House Elections." *American Journal of Political Science* 32, 4: 884–907.

Gronke, Paul. 2000. *The Electorate, the Campaign, and the Office*. Ann Arbor: University of Michigan Press.

Gutmann, Amy, and Dennis Thompson. 1996. *Democracy and Disagreement*. Cambridge, Mass.: Harvard University Press.

Hagen, Michael G., Richard Johnston, and Kathleen Hall Jamieson. 2002. "Effects of the 2000 Presidential Campaign." Paper prepared for the Midwest Political Science Association Annual Meeting, Chicago, April 25–28.

Hale, Jon F., Jeffrey C. Fox, and Rick Farmer. 1996. "Negative Advertisements in U.S. Senate Campaigns: The Influence of Campaign Context." *Social Science Quarterly* 77, 2: 329–43.

Hamilton, Alexander, James Madison, and John Jay. 1961. *The Federalist Papers*. New York: Penguin.

Hansen, Richard. 2010. "Election Administration Reform and the New Institutionalism. *California Law Review* 98, 3: 1075–1100.

——. 2005. "Beyond the Margin of Litigation: Reforming U.S. Election Administration to Avoid Electoral Meltdown." *Washington and Lee Law Review* 62: 937.

Hart, Roderick P. 2000. *Campaign Talk: Why Elections Are Good for Us*. Princeton, N.J.: Princeton University Press.

Hayes, Danny. 2010. "The Dynamics of Agenda Convergence and the Paradox of Competitiveness in Presidential Campaigns." *Political Research Quarterly* 63: 594–611.

Herrnson, Paul S. 2006. "Minor-Party Candidates in Congressional Elections." In *The Marketplace of Democracy*, ed. Michael P. McDonald and John Samples. Washington, D.C.: Brookings Institution Press. 102–24.

——. 2005. "The Evolution of Political Campaigns." In *Guide to Political Campaigns in America*, ed. Paul Herrnson. Washington, D.C.: CQ Press.

——. 2004. *Congressional Elections: Campaigning at Home and in Washington*. Washington, D.C.: CQ Press.

Hertzberg, Hendrik. 2006. "Count 'Em." *New Yorker* (March 6): 27–28

Hibbing, John R., and Elizabeth Theiss-Morse. 2002. *Stealth Democracy: Americans' Beliefs About How Government Should Work*. New York: Cambridge University Press.

Highton, Benjamin, and Raymond E. Wolfinger. 1998. "Estimating the Effects of the National Voter Registration Act of 1993." *Political Behavior* 20: 79–104.

Hill, David, and Seth C. McKee. 2003. "The Electoral College, Mobilization, and Turnout in the 2000 Presidential Election." *American Politics Research* 33, 5: 700–725.

Hill, Seth J., James Lo, Lynn Vavreck, and John Zaller. 2008. "The Duration of Advertising Effects in the 2000 Presidential Campaign." Paper prepared for the Annual Meeting of the Midwest Political Science Association, April 3–7.

——. 2007. "The Duration of Advertising Effects in Political Campaigns." Paper prepared for the Annual Meeting of the American Political Science Association, Chicago, August 29–September 3.

Hillygus, D. Sunshine. 2005. "Campaign Effects and the Dynamics of Turnout Intention in Election 2000." *Journal of Politics* 67, 1: 50–68.

Holbrook, Thomas M., and Scott D. McClurg. 2005. "The Mobilization of Core Supporters: Campaigns, Turnout, and Electoral Composition in United States Presidential Elections." *American Journal of Political Science* 49, 4: 689–703.

Huang, Taofang and Daron Shaw. 2009. "Beyond the Battlegrounds? Electoral College Strategies in the 2008 Presidential Election." *Journal of Political Marketing* 8, 4: 272–91.

Huber, Gregory A., and Kevin Arceneaux. 2007. "Identifying the Persuasive Effects of Presidential Advertising." *American Journal of Political Science* 51, 4: 957–77.

Huckfeldt, Robert, Edward G. Carmines, Jeffery J. Mondak, and Eric Zeemering. 2007. "Information, Activation, and Electoral Competition in the 2002 Congressional Elections." *Journal of Politics* 69, 3: 798–812.

Huckfeldt, Robert, and John Sprague. 1995. *Citizens, Politics, and Social Communication: Information Influence in an Election Campaign*. Cambridge: Cambridge University Press.

——. 1988. "Choice, Social Structure, and Political Information: The Informational Coercion of Minorities." *American Journal of Political Science* 32, 2: 467–82.

Ingram, Carl, and Jean Merl. 2002. "Safe Seats Mean Few Voters Get Real Choice." *Los Angeles Times*, October 27.

Issacharoff, Samuel. 2002. "Gerrymandering and Political Cartels." *Harvard Law Review* 116, 2: 593–648.

Issacharoff, Samuel, and Richard H. Pildes. 1998. "Politics as Markets: Partisan Lockups of the Democratic Process." *Stanford Law Review* 50: 643–717.

Jacobson, Gary C. 2006. "Competition in U.S. Congressional Elections." In *The Marketplace of Democracy*, ed. Michael P. McDonald and John Samples. Washington, D.C.: Brookings Instititution Press. 27–52.

——. 1997. *The Politics of Congressional Elections*. New York: Addison-Wesley.

——. 1990. "The Effects of Campaign Spending in House Elections: New Evidence for Old Arguments." *American Journal of Political Science* 34, 2: 334–62.

——. 1978. "The Effects of Campaign Spending in Congressional Elections." *American Political Science Review* 72: 769–783.

Jackson, Robert A. 2002. "Gubernatorial and Senatorial Campaign Mobilization of Voters." *Political Research Quarterly* 55, 4: 825–44.

Jackson, Robert A. 1993. "Voter Mobilization in the 1986 Midterm Election." *Journal of Politics* 55, 4: 1081–99.

Jamieson, Kathleen Hall. 1992. *Dirty Politics: Deception, Distraction and Democracy*. Cambridge: Oxford University Press.

Jamieson, Kathleen Hall, Paul Waldman, and Susan Sherr. 2000. "Eliminate the Negative?" In *Crowded Airwaves: Political Advertising in Elections*, ed. James A. Thurber, Candice J. Nelson, and David A. Dulio. Washington, D.C.: Brookings Institution Press.

Jensen, Jennifer M., and Thad Beyle. 2003. "Of Footnotes, Missing Data, and Lessons for 50-State Data Collection: The Gubernatorial Campaign Finance Project, 1977–2001." *State Politics and Policy Quarterly* 3: 203–14.

Jerit, Jennifer, Jason Barabas, and Toby Bolsen. 2006. "Citizens, Knowledge, and the Information Environment." *American Journal of Political Science* 50, 2: 266–82.

Johnston, Richard, Michael G. Hagen, and Kathleen Hall Jamieson. 2004. *The 2000 Presidential Campaign and the Foundations of Party Politics*. New York: Cambridge University Press.

Joslyn, Richard. 1984. *Mass Media and Elections*. Reading, Mass.: Addison-Wesley.

Just, Marion R., Ann N. Crigler, Dean E. Alger, Timothy E. Cook, Montague Kern, and Darrell M. West. 1996. *Crosstalk: Citizens, Candidates, and the Media in a Presidential Election*. Chicago: University of Chicago Press.

Kahn, Kim Fridkin. 1995. "Characteristics of Press Coverage in Senate and Gubernatorial Elections: Information Available to Voters." *Legislative Studies Quarterly* 20, 1: 23–35.

Kahn, Kim Fridkin, and Patrick J. Kenney. 1999. *The Spectacle of U.S. Senate Campaigns*. Princeton, N.J.: Princeton University Press.

Kaplan, Noah, David K. Park, and Travis N. Ridout. 2006. "Dialogue in American Political Campaigns? An Examination of Issue Convergence in Candidate Television Advertising." *American Journal of Political Science*, 50, 3: 724–36.

Kaplan, Noah, and Travis N. Ridout. 2007. "The Campaign Dynamics of Issue Dialogue." Paper prepared for the annual meeting of the Midwest Political Science Association, Chicago, April 12–15.

Keele, Luke, and Jennifer Wolak. 2008. "Contextual Sources of Ambivalence." *Political Psychology* 29, 5: 653–73.

Kelley, Stanley. 1966. "The Presidential Campaign." In *The National Election of 1964*, ed. Milton C. Cummings, Jr. Washington, D.C.: Brookings Institution Press.

——. 1961. "The Presidential Campaign." In *The Presidential Election in Transition, 1960–1961*, ed. Paul T. David. Washington, D.C.: Brookings Institution Press.

——. 1960. *Political Campaigning: Problems in Creating an Informed Electorate*. Washington, D.C.: Brookings Institution Press.

Kelman, Herbert C. 1961. "Processes of Opinion Change." *Public Opinion Quarterly* 25, 1: 57–78.

"Kerry, Bush Battle over Gas Prices." 2004. *Chicago Tribune*, March 31.

King, Anthony. 1997. *Running Scared: Why America's Politicians Campaign Too Hard and Govern Too Little*. New York: Simon & Schuster.

King, Gary, and Robert X. Browning. 1987. "Democratic Representation and Partisan Bias in Congressional Elections." *American Political Science Review* 81, 4: 1252–73.

Klinkner Philip A., and Ann Hapanowicz. 2005. "Red and Blue Déjà Vu: Measuring Political Polarization in the 2004 Presidential Election." *Forum* 3, 2, Article 2. http://www.bepress.com/forum/vol3/iss2/art2

Kousser, Thad, and Ray La Raja. 2002. "The Effect of Campaign Finance Laws on Electoral Competition: Evidence from the States." *Cato Institute Policy Analysis* 426, February.

Krasno, Jonathan S. 1994. *Challengers, Competition, and Reelection: Comparing Senate and House Elections*. New Haven, Conn.: Yale University Press.

Krasno, Jonathan S., and Donald P. Green. 2008. "Do Televised Presidential Ads Increase Voter Turnout? Evidence from a Natural Experiment" *Journal of Politics* 70, 1: 245–61.

Lake, Mark. 1979. "A New Campaign Resource Allocation Model." In *Applied Game Theory*, ed. Steven J. Brams, Andrew Schotter, and Gerhard Schwodiauer. Wurzburg: Physica-Verlag.

Lakoff, George, and Mark Johnson. 1980. *The Metaphors We Live By*. Chicago: University of Chicago Press.

Lau, Richard R., and David P. Redlawsk. 2008. "Older But Wiser? Effects of Age on Political Cognition." *Journal of Politics* 70, 1: 168–85.

Lau, Richard R., and Lee Sigelman. 1999. "The Effects of Negative Political Advertisements: A Meta-Analytical Assessment." *American Political Science Review* 93, 4: 851.

Lau, Richard R., Lee Sigelman, and Ivy Brown Rovner. 2007. "The Effects of Negative

Political Campaigns: A Meta-Analytic Reassessment." *Journal of Politics* 69, 4: 1176–1209.

Levitt, Steven D. 1994. "Using Repeat Challengers to Estimate the Effect of Challenger Spending on Election Outcomes in the U.S. House." *Journal of Political Economy* 102, 4: 777–98.

Levy, Dena, and Peverill Squire. 2000. "Television Markets and the Competitiveness of U.S. House Elections." *Legislative Studies Quarterly* 25, 2: 313–25.

Lipsitz, Keena. 2009. "The Consequences of Battleground and 'Spectator State' Residency for Political Participation." *Political Behavior* 31: 187–209.

——. 2004. "Democratic Theory and Political Campaigns." *Journal of Political Philosophy* 12, 2: 163–89.

Lipsitz, Keena, and Jeremy Teigen. 2010. "Orphan Counties and the Effect of Irrelevant Advertising on Turnout in Statewide Races" *Political Communication* 27, 2: 178–98.

Lipsitz, Keena, Christine Trost, Matthew Grossman, and John Sides. 2005. "What Voters Want from Campaign Communication." *Political Communication* 22: 357–54.

Lodge, Milton, and Ruth Hamill. 1986. "A Partisan Schema for Political Information Processing." *American Journal of Political Science* 80, 2: 505–19.

Long, J. Scott, and Jeremy Freese. 2005. *Regression Models for Categorical Outcomes Using Stata*. 2nd ed. College Station, Tex.: Stata Press.

Luskin, Robert C. 1990. "Explaining Political Sophistication." *Political Behavior* 12: 331–61.

Lyons, Michael, and Peter F. Galderisi. 1995. "Incumbency, Reapportionment and U.S. House Redistricting." *Political Research Quarterly* 48, 4: 857–71.

Macedo, Stephen, Yvette Alex-Assensoh, Jeffrey M. Berry, Michael Brintnall, David E. Campbell, Luis Ricardo Fraga, Archon Fung. William A. Galston, Christopher F. Karpowitz, Margaret Levi, Meira Levinson, Keena Lipsitz, Richard G. Niemi, Robert D. Putnam, Wendy M. Rahn, Rob Reich, Robert R. Rodgers, Todd Swanstrom, and Katherine Cramer Walsh. 2005. *Democracy at Risk: How Political Choices Undermine Citizen Participation, and What We Can Do About It*. Washington, D.C.: Brookings Institution Press.

Maisel, L. Sandy, Cherie Maestas, and Walter J. Stone. 2002. "The Party Role in Congressional Competition." In *The Parties Respond: Change in American Parties and Campaigns*, ed. L. Sandy Maisel. Boulder, Colo.: Westview. 121–27.

Maisel, L. Sandy, Darrell M. West, and Brett M. Clifton. 2007. *Evaluating Campaign Quality: Can the Electoral Process Be Improved?* New York: Cambridge University Press.

Mansbridge, Jane J. 1980. *Beyond Adversary Democracy*. New York: Basic Books.

Matalin, Mary, and James Carville. 1994. *All's Fair: Love, War, and Running for President*. New York: Random House.

Matsusaka, John C. 2006. "Direct Democracy and Electoral Reform." In *The Marketplace of Democracy*, ed. Michael P. McDonald and John Samples. Washington, D.C.: Brookings Institution. 151–70.

Mayer, Kenneth R., Timothy Werner, and Amanda Williams. 2006. "Do Public Financing Programs Enhance Competition?" In *The Marketplace of Democracy*, ed. Michael P. McDonald and John Samples. Washington, D.C.: Brookings Institution Press. 245–67.

Mayhew, David R. 1974. "Congressional Elections: The Case of the Vanishing Marginals." *Polity* 6, 3: 295–317.

McCarty, Nolan, Keith T. Poole, and Howard Rosenthal. 2006. "Does Gerrymandering Cause Polarization?" Manuscript.

McDonald, Michael P. 2008. "Reforming Redistricting." In *Democracy in the States: Experiments in Elections Reform*, ed. Bruce Cain, Todd Donovan, and Caroline Tolbert. Washington, D.C.: Brookings Institution Press.

——. 2006a. "Drawing the Line on District Competition." *PS: Political Science and Politics* 39, 1: 91–94.

——. 2006b. "Re-Drawing the Line on District Competition" *PS: Political Science and Politics* 39, 1: 99–102.

——. 2006c. "Redistricting and Competitive Districts." In *The Marketplace of Democracy*, ed. Michael P. McDonald and John Samples. Washington, D.C.: Brookings Institution Press. 222–44.

McDonald, Michael, and Samuel Popkin. 2001. "The Myth of the Vanishing Voter." *American Political Science Review* 95, 4: 963–74.

McIntire, Mike. 2007. "Retired Politicians Spend Unused Campaign Funds." *New York Times*, February 24. http://www.nytimes.com/2007/02/24/nyregion/24retire.html?pagewanted=all#

McKinnon, Lori Melton, and Lynda Lee Kaid. 1999. "Exposing Negative Campaigning or Enhancing Advertising Effects: An Experimental Study of Adwatch Effects on Voters' Evaluations of Candidates and their Ads." *Journal of Applied Communication Research* 27, 3: 217–36.

Monmonier, Mark. 2001. *Bushmanders and Bullwinkles: How Politicians Manipulate Electronic Maps and Census Data to Win Elections*. Chicago: University of Chicago Press.

Mutz, Diane. 2007. "How the Media Divide Us." In *Red and Blue Nation? Characteristics and Causes of America's Polarized Politics*, ed. Pietro S. Nivola and David W. Brady. Washington, D.C.: Brookings Institution Press.

——. 2006. *Hearing the Other Side: Deliberative Versus Participatory Democracy*. Cambridge: Cambridge University Press.

——. 2002. "The Consequences of Cross-Cutting Cleavages for Political Participation." *American Journal of Political Science* 46, 4: 838–55.

Mycoff, Jason D., and Joseph August Pika. 2007. *Confrontation and Compromise: Presidential and Congressional Leadership, 2001–2006*. Lanham, Md.: Rowman & Littlefield.

Niemi, Richard G., Lynda W. Powell, William D. Berry, Thomas M. Carsey, and James M. Snyder, Jr. 2006. "Competition in State Legislative Elections, 1992–2002." In *The*

Marketplace of Democracy, ed. Michael P. McDonald and John Samples. Washington, D.C.: Brookings Instititution. 53–73.

Papke, Leslie E., and Jeffrey M. Wooldridge. 1996. "Econometric Methods for Fractional Response Variables with an Application to 401(k) Plan Participation Rates." *Journal of Applied Econometrics* 11, 6: 619–32.

Patterson, Samuel C., and Gregory A. Caldeira. 1983 "Getting Out the Vote: Participation in Gubernatorial Elections." *American Political Science Review* 77, 3: 675–89.

Patterson, Thomas E. 2002. *The Vanishing Voter*. New York: Knopf.

——. 1994. *Out of Order*. New York: Vintage.

——. 1980. *The Mass Media Election*. New York: Praeger.

Petrocik, John R. 1996. "Issue Ownership in Presidential Elections, with a 1980 Case Study." *American Journal of Political Science* 40: 825–50.

——. 1980. "Contextual Sources of Voting Behavior: The Changeable American Voter." In *The Electorate Reconsidered*, ed. John C. Pierce and John L. Sullivan. Beverly Hills, Calif.: Sage.

Petracca, Mark P. 1991. *The Poison of Professional Politics*. Policy Analysis 151. Washington, D.C.: Cato Institute.

Petrocik, John R., William L. Benoit, and Glenn J. Hansen. 2003. "Issue Ownership and Presidential Campaigning, 1952–2000." *Political Science Quarterly* 118: 599–626.

Petty, Richard E., John T. Cacioppo, and David Schumann. 1983. "Central and Peripheral Routes to Advertising Effectiveness: The Moderating Role of Involvement." *Journal of Consumer Research* 10: 135–46.

Pew Research Center for People and the Press. 2006. "Lack of Competition in Elections Fails to Stir Voters." http://people-press.org/reports/pdf/294.pdf.

Pitney, John. 2000. *The Art of Political Warfare*. Norman: University of Oklahoma Press.

Plasser, Fritz, and Gunda Plasser. 2002. *Global Political Campaigning: A Worldwide Analysis of Campaign Professionals and Their Practices*. Westport, Conn.: Praeger.

Powell, Bingham G. 2000. *Elections as Instruments of Democracy: Majoritarian and Proportional Visions*. New Haven, Conn.: Yale University Press.

Powell, Bingham G., and Guy D. Whitten. 1993. "A Cross-National Analysis of Retrospective Voting: Integrating Economic and Political Factors." *American Journal Political Science* 36: 391–414.

Price, Vincent, Joseph N. Cappella, and Lilach Nir. 2002. "Does Disagreement Contribute to More Deliberative Opinion?" *Political Communication* 19, 1: 95–112.

Primo, David, Jeffrey Milyo, and Tim Groseclose. 2006. "State Campaign Finance Reform, Competitiveness, and Party Advantage in Gubernatorial Elections" in *The Marketplace of Democracy*, ed. Michael P. McDonald and John Samples. Washington, D.C.: Brookings Institution Press. 268–85.

Prior, Markus. 2001. "Weighted Content Analysis of Political Advertisements." *Political Communication* 18: 335–45.

Rae, Douglas. 1967. *The Political Consequences of Electoral Rules*. New Haven, Conn.: Yale University Press.

Rawls, John. 1996. *Political Liberalism*. New York: Columbia University Press.

Ridout, Travis N., and Rob Mellen. 2007. "Does the Media Agenda Reflect the Candidates' Agenda?" *International Journal of Press/Politics* 12, 2: 44–62.

Ridout, Travis N., Dhavan V. Shah, Kenneth M. Goldstein, and Michael M. Franz. 2004. "Evaluating Measures of Campaign Advertising Exposure on Political Learning." *Political Behavior* 26, 3: 201–25.

Ridout, Travis N., and Glen R. Smith. 2008. "Free Advertising: How the Media Amplify Campaign Messages." *Political Research Quarterly* 61, 4: 598–608.

Rollins, Ed. 1997. *Bare Knuckles and Back Rooms*. New York: Random House.

Romer, Daniel, Kate Kenski, Paul Waldman, Christopher Adasiewicz. 2004. *Capturing Campaign Dynamics: The National Annenberg Election Survey*. New York: Oxford University Press.

Rosenstone, Steven J., Roy L. Behr, and Edward H. Lazarus. 1984. *Third Parties in America: Citizen Response to Major Party Failure*. Princeton, N.J.: Princeton University Press.

Rosenstone, Steven J., and John Mark Hansen. 2003. *Mobilization, Participation, and Democracy in America*. New York: Macmillan.

Sabato, Larry. 2006. "Politics: American's Missing Constitutional Link." *Virginia Quarterly Review* 82, 3: 149–61.

Samples, John. 2001. *Election Reform, Federalism, and the Obligations of Voters*. Policy Analysis (The Cato Institute) 417. Washington, D.C.: Cato Institute.

Schumpeter, Joseph. 1947. *Capitalism, Socialism and Democracy*. New York: Harper & Brothers.

Shapiro, Ian. 2003a. *The Moral Foundations of Politics*. New Haven, Conn.: Yale University Press.

——. 2003b. *The State of Democratic Theory*. Princeton, N.J.: Princeton University Press.

Shaw, Daron. 2006. *Race to 270: The Electoral College and the Campaign Strategies of 2000 and 2004*. Chicago: University of Chicago Press.

——. 2004. "Erratum for 'The Methods Behind the Madness: Presidential Electoral College Strategies, 1988–1996,' *Journal of Politics* 61:4 (November 1999): 893–913." *Journal of Politics* 66, 2: 611–15.

——. 1999. "The Methods Behind the Madness: Presidential Electoral College Strategies, 1988–1996." *Journal of Politics* 61: 893–913.

Shepsle, Kenneth A. 1972. "The Strategy of Ambiguity: Uncertainty and Electoral Competition." *American Political Science Review* 66, 2: 555–68.

Sides, John. 2006. "The Origins of Campaign Agendas." *British Journal of Political Science*, 36, 3: 407–36.

Sigelman, Lee, and Emmett H. Buell, Jr. 2004. "Avoidance or Engagement? Issue Convergence in U.S. Presidential Campaigns, 1960–2000." *American Journal of Political Science* 48, 4: 650–661.

Simon, Adam F. 2002. *The Winning Message: Candidate Behavior, Campaign Discourse, and Democracy*. Cambridge: Cambridge University Press.

Spiliotes, Constantine J., and Lynn Vavreck. 2002. "Campaign Advertising: Partisan Convergence or Divergence." *Journal of Politics* 64, 1: 249–61.

Stevens, Daniel. 2009. "Elements of Negativity: Volume and Proportion in Exposure to Negative Advertising," *Political Behavior* 31, 3: 429–54.

Sunstein, Cass. 1994. "Political Equality and Unintended Consequences." *Columbia Law Review* 94: 1390–1414.

Surowiecki, James. 2000. "The Financial Page How to Bust the Baseball Trust." *New Yorker* (May 15): 43

Tamas, Bernard Ivan. 2006. "Why Congress Banned Multimember Districts in 1842." *New Political Science* 28: 1–23.

Teixeira, Ruy A. 1992. *The Disappearing American Voter*. Washington, D.C.: Brookings Institution Press.

——. 1987. *Why Americans Don't Vote: Turnout Decline in the United States 1960–1984*. New York: Greenwood Press.

Thompson, Dennis. 2002. *Just Elections*. Chicago: University of Chicago Press.

Thurber, James. 2001. *The Battle for Congress: Candidates, Consultants and Voters*. Washington, D.C.: Brookings Institution Press.

Thurber, James, and Candice Nelson. 2000. *Campaign Warriors: Political Consultants in Elections*. Washington, D.C.: Brookings Institution Press.

Tufte, Edward R. 1973. "The Relationship Between Seats and Votes in Two-Party Systems." *American Political Science Review* 67, 2: 540–55.

Vavreck, Lynn. 2009. *The Message Matters: The Economy and Presidential Campaigns*. Princeton, N.J.: Princeton University Press.

——. 2001. "The Reasoning Voter Meets the Strategic Candidate." *American Politics Research* 29, 5: 507.

Verba, Sidney, Kay Lehman Schlozman, and Henry E. Brady. 1995. *Voice and Equality: Civic Voluntarism in American Politics*. Cambridge, Mass.: Harvard University Press.

Walzer, Michael. 1977. *Just and Unjust Wars: A Moral Argument with Historical Illustrations*. New York: Basic Books.

Weber, Ronald E., Harvey J. Tucker, and Paul Brace. 1991. "Vanishing Marginals in State Legislative Elections." *Legislative Studies Quarterly* 16, 1: 29–47.

West, Darrell M. 2005. *Air Wars: Television Advertising in Election Campaigns 1952–2004*. Washington, D.C.: CQ Press.

——. 2000. "How Issue Ads Have Reshaped American Politics." In *Crowded Airwaves: Campaign Advertising in Elections*, ed. James A. Thurber, Candice J. Nelson, and David A. Dulio. Washington, D.C.: Brookings Institution Press. 149–69.

Westlye, Mark C. 1991. *Senate Elections and Campaign Intensity*. Baltimore: Johns Hopkins University Press.

——. 1983. "Competitiveness of Senate Seats and Voting Behavior in Senate Elections." *American Journal of Political Science* 27, 2: 253–83.

Wichowsky, Amber. 2008. "Let's Get Serious: Ads, Issues, Knowledge and Engagement in Congressional Elections." Paper prepared for annual meeting of the Midwest Political Science Association, Chicago, April 3–6.

Wolak, Jennifer. 2006. "The Consequences of Presidential Battleground Strategies for Citizen Engagement." *Political Research Quarterly* 59, 3: 353–61.

Wolfinger, Raymond, and R. B. Arseneau. 1978. "Partisan Changes in the South, 1952–1976." In *Political Parties: Development and Decay*, ed. Louis Sandy Maisel and Joseph Cooper. Beverly Hills, Calif.: Sage. 179–210.

Wolfinger, Raymond, and Michael G. Hagen. 1985. "Republican Prospects: Southern Comfort." *Public Opinion* 8: 8–13.

Zaller, John. 1992. *The Nature and Origins of Mass Opinion.* New York: Cambridge University Press.

Zhao, Xinshu, and Glen L. Bleske. 1995. "Measurement Effects in Comparing Voter Learning from Television News and Campaign Advertisements." *Journalism and Mass Communication Quarterly* 72: 72–83.

Zhao, Xinshu, and Steven H. Chaffee. 1995. "Campaign Advertisements Versus Television News as Sources of Political Issue Information." *Public Opinion Quarterly* 59: 41–64.

Zukin, Cliff, and Robin Snyder. 1984. "Passive Learning: When the Media Environment is the Message." *Public Opinion Quarterly* 48, 3: 629–38.

INDEX

ACKNOWLEDGMENTS

This book was very long in the making. As a result, I am indebted to a somewhat alarming number of people. I owe my interest in campaign effects to Bruce Cain, who got me involved with a project funded by the Pew Charitable Trusts to study ethics (or rather, the lack thereof) in campaigns. Bruce has also been a long-time supporter and offered encouragement at some of the hardest points in the writing process. On earlier drafts, Laura Stoker served as a ruthlessly constructive editor. She also served as role model both as a woman in the profession and as someone who has succeeded at combining normative questions and political behavior. Samuel Scheffler pushed me to clarify and develop the book's theoretical framework early on. Finally, this book would have never been written without Eric Schickler's patient and unrelenting support. I owe him a tremendous amount of gratitude.

After getting married in 2003, I followed my spouse to Princeton, New Jersey. Larry Bartels was kind enough to give me office space and I was invited to join the "Breakfast Club," which included Josh Clinton, Shigeo Hirano, David Lewis, Adam Meirowitz, and Josh Tucker. Marty Gilens, Stephen Macedo, Nolan McCarty, Chris Karpowitz, Stanley Kelley, and Tali Mendelberg also provided useful feedback on my project at various points. Despite the intellectual vitality of the Princeton community, moving to a new place is never easy. Daniela Bleichmar, Olivier Doré, Brian Hatt, Ryan Jusko, Karen Long Jusko, Maite Garcia Lechner, Grace Lyall, Jay Lyall, Ceci Martinez-Gallardo, Graeme Robertson, Alison Rose, Jessica Trounstine, and Andrew Youdin made the transition much easier and our time in Princeton more enjoyable.

The contents of this book also reflect the comments of numerous conference discussants and fellow panelists, including Scott Althaus, Chuck Beitz, John Hibbing, Jane Mansbridge, Rick Pildes, Art Sanders, and Dennis Thompson. I am also indebted to Robert Goodin, who solicited part of my theory chapter for the *Journal of Political Philosophy*. David Menefee-Libey,

John Seery, and Rick Worthington commented on Chapter 5 in its early stages. Closer to home, my Queens College colleague, John Bowman, provided helpful comments on Chapter 7. I also had the good fortune of participating in the City University of New York's Faculty Fellowship Publication Program, where I received feedback from other CUNY social scientists, including Christopher Burton, Jeanette Espinoza-Sanchez, Steve Lang, Katherine Opello, Saadia Toor, Xiaodan Zhang, and Sharon Zukin. Throughout this process, the project received funding from a variety of sources, including the National Science Foundation, the Pew Charitable Trusts, and the Professional Staff Congress of the City University of New York.

I must also thank my editor at Penn Press, Peter Agree, as well as Rick Valelly for giving my book a home in their promising new series. Rick also provided helpful guidance during the revision process. In addition, I owe a big thanks to Julia Rose Roberts and Alison Anderson for shepherding my book through the production process. Carol Ehrlich provided excellent copyediting. Finally, I am especially indebted to Markus Prior and Travis Ridout, who read the entire manuscript and offered extensive comments that made this book much better than it might have been.

Writing a book is never easy, but it is easier when one is surrounded by friends and family who offer unwavering support. Bill Baren, Michelle Benger Merrill, John Borland, Ben Bowyer, Matthew Dallek, Saar Demeuse, Dwight Dyer, Rosa Brion Caiño, John Cioffi, Sandy Cruger, Sebastian Etchemendy, Carlos Frias, Julie George, Ben Goldfrank, Ivette Goldfrank, Shanda Hunt, Bronwyn Leebaw, Naomi Levy, Corii Liau, Josh Lurie-Terrell, Anders Lustgarten, Aimee Male, David Merrill, Augusto Moreno, Serban Nacu, Caitlin Price, Mike Rowe, Anna Schmidt, Michael Signer, Anais Sonder, Tobias Schulze-Cleven, Christine Schick, Nadav Shelef, John Sides, Jeremy Teigen, and Chris Tucker have been such friends. Kerry, Paula, and Sherwin Lipsitz endured more than their fair share of whining, remaining steadfast in their conviction that I would finish even when I was not so sure. In addition to my own family, I am also fortunate to have incredible in-laws. Grigore Pop-Elecheş, Renate Pop-Elecheş, Kiki Pop-Elecheş, Cristina Văţulescu, and Veronica Văţulescu-Elecheş provided warm encouragement and child care at crucial moments in the writing process. In addition, Grigore and Renate provided a home away from home in Romania where I spent many summers writing. Rica and Lia Elecheş-Lipsitz both made their appearance during the writing of this book and taught me that it is possible to combine a career and motherhood and that the latter can energize the former.

In the end, I owe my biggest debt of gratitude to Grigo Pop-Eleches, without whom this book would never have been dragged into existence. He played a variety of roles throughout the process, including editor, statistics adviser, devil's advocate, therapist, and cheerleader. It is to him that this book is dedicated.